# BELLS

## THEIR HISTORY, LEGENDS MAKING, AND USES

*By*

### SATIS N. COLEMAN

*The Lincoln School of Teachers College,*
*Columbia University*

*With a Foreword by*

### OTIS W. CALDWELL

*The Lincoln School of Teachers College,*
*Columbia University*

## GREENWOOD PRESS, PUBLISHERS
### WESTPORT, CONNECTICUT

## ACKNOWLEDGMENTS

For much of the material in this book the author is indebted to Mr. William Gorham Rice, author of several works on the carillon, and to Mr. H. B. Walters, whose book on *The Church Bells of England* afforded a text of great value.

Acknowledgment is also due for courtesies shown by the following publishers: Houghton Mifflin Company (by permisssion of and by arrangement with) for poems by Henry W. Longfellow and two selections from Longfellow's Diary; Dodd, Mead & Company; the Grolier Society; by the *Asia* and *Mentor* magazines, and for a large number of photographs from the Crosby-Brown Collection of Musical Instruments furnished by the Metropolitan Museum of New York.

For courtesies extended by Mrs. Marjorie Barstow Greenbie, Mrs. Eloise Roorbach, Mrs. De Witt Hutchings, Mr. Frank A. Miller, Mr. Frederick Rocke, Mr. John D. Rockefeller, Mr. Adolph Weinman, and many others, thanks are due.

To the bell makers—Gillett & Johnston of Croydon, England; John Taylor & Co. Bell Foundry of Loughborough, England; Meneely Bell Company of Troy, New York; Bevin Bros. of East Hampton, Connecticut—all of whom have contributed to the making of this book, the author is most grateful.

The author is especially indebted to the children of the Lincoln School, whose interest in bells gave stimulus to the research which has resulted in this book.

Originally published in 1928
by Rand McNally & Company, Chicago & New York

Reprinted from an original copy in the collections
of the Brooklyn Public Library

First Greenwood Reprinting 1971

Library of Congress Catalogue Card Number 70-109722

SBN 8371-4212-1

Printed in the United States of America

# THE CONTENTS

v

# A FOREWORD

An abundance of good reading material adds much to the value of music in education. But the reading material must be vital; it must really mean something to the reader. This idea is accepted, indeed is basic in the educational practices regarding history, science, and literature; and those subjects have an abundance of books which are fairly well graded to the different levels of advancement. Music, like other fine arts, of necessity has been largely a "doing" subject, and because of that fact it has become much less of a "reading" subject than seems best. It has its wonderful literature, although inadequate perhaps as a full record of its cultural development. Certainly more needs to be done toward the development of reading on music subjects for both school and home. It is hoped that this book about bells will prove interesting to adults as well as to pupils in schools.

*Bells* is the outcome of studies made especially for the benefit of a group of pupils in the Lincoln School who were learning to play Swiss bells in their Creative Music periods. These pupils had already explored the field of other percussion instruments; they had made drums, Pan pipes, and marimbas, and had played on them not only original tunes but folk songs and classic themes. Bells seemed also to challenge them to exploration. They wanted to make bells: to know who invented bells, how many kinds there are, how tuned, what they are used for, what countries have the best bells. These and other questions caused the author and the children who were guided by her to begin a genuine search for facts about bells.

At first there seemed to be little material available. Mr. William Rice's books about carillons, and Mary Tabor's small bell anthology were useful American books on the subject. The Old World offered several interesting volumes, many of them gray with age and hidden away as if the world were to forget the old legends and superstitions and the many interesting facts about the bell, which has been a common messenger to all mankind.

None of the printed material as found, however, was quite suitable for the needs. But many a musty old magazine of forgotten days yielded a rich contribution to the subject. From many divisions of the New York Public Library, from the Congressional Library at Washington, and from foreign countries, materials were gathered. This material was organized into the thirty-six divisions shown by the chapter headings. Then began the preparation of short accounts of famous bells, or of the folk lore or religious stories associated with certain bells and their uses. Most of this material was mimeographed for the children whose interest had initiated the search. Adults who were interested in music also used and enjoyed the stories. The pupils made bells — wooden bells, clay bells, glass bells — and wrote stories and poems about bells. The search for authentic source materials was long and extended to far countries, and continued as the writing proceeded. Collections were made of drawings and photographs and separate descriptions of bells from all over the world, with the hope that the various types might be adequately represented. Effort has been made to include the world's famous bells, and to present, as fully as one volume may, the kinds of bells and the uses which people have made of them.

This book is designed for the instruction and growing pleasure of those students and citizens who may be led to catch a bit of the inexpressible glow of satisfaction which music has given to sensitive humans throughout the ages. In all countries one may see the busy streets slow down and a measure of appreciation become evident when any of the famous bells begin to ring. The aim of this book is to carry to all a little of this widespread feeling for the music of bells. The language is universal and is interpreted through training in sensing of emotional values, not by learning technical language forms. It is hoped that *Bells* may make a contribution to America's growing acceptance of music as an essential to the best life of her people.

OTIS W. CALDWELL
*Director of the Lincoln School*

# BELLS

## CHAPTER I

## INTRODUCTORY

In the Middle Ages there lived in a European monastery a friar whose life was one of cheerful devotion to his church.  Every day—a dozen times a day—he moved at the summons of a sweet-toned bell that hung in a tower within the monastery. It was a large bronze bell which had been cast more than a hundred years before, on those very grounds, and a Latin inscription ran around the bell which Lorenz had one day climbed the tower to read: *Cantabo laudes tuas Domini*[1] (*"I will sing thy praises, Lord"*); and many times after that he said to himself, "How well the bell carries out its own plan!"

There were other bells, but this one seemed to speak most intimately to Lorenz.  The first thing the friar heard, every morning in the year, was:

"Arise, Lorenz!  To prayers, Lorenz!"

and as he listened further, he always thought he heard it sing the motto which it carried on its shoulders:

*"Cantabo laudes tuas Domini!"*

[1] The Latin of medieval times is not the perfect Latin of Cicero. Wherever medieval inscriptions are quoted in this book, divergences are retained as found.

After it had signaled to him many times during the day, its last ring seemed to say:

"To rest, Lorenz, and sleep in peace!"

The bell was to Lorenz a dear companion that roused him, inspired, cheered, encouraged, and soothed him; and he loved its clear and vibrant voice.

Then there came the time[1] when the monastery was destroyed, and all the bells were taken away. The friars grieved over the loss of their home, their treasures and sacred relics; but Lorenz missed nothing so much as his bell. Morning after morning he awoke, unbidden, to miss anew the cheerful call to prayers; and night after night he found it hard to go to sleep without the bell's vibrant blessing.

After many weeks of loneliness, his restless spirit could bear it no longer. So he took his staff, and started out to find his lost companion. The bell had been carried away by two husky men who fastened it to a pole, and placed the pole on their shoulders; but whether they carried it away to have it melted down for bullets, or to send it into another country, he had no means of finding out.

In those days the way was long from one village to another, and the paths were rough. But Lorenz little minded that, if he could only find some one who could tell him where the bell had been taken. For weeks he traveled on foot from village to village,

[1] The Reformation.

and listened to the bells. "No, that one is too harsh," or "That sound is not my bell," he would say to himself, as he heard the different bells of every town in that part of the country. Perhaps, after all, it was melted, and made into something else!

One evening, after walking almost all day, he came within sight of the lights of a village. The sun had gone down long before. If he could reach the village before time for the curfew, he thought, perhaps he could rest there for the night, and perhaps some one would give him food, for he was hungry. So he hastened his steps. But it was too late! The ringing of the curfew began, and he knew that no stranger might enter the village after that. But listen! His keen ear had learned to catch every tone quality in the ringing of a bell. This curfew bell was signaling the people of the village to put out their fires and go to bed, but to Lorenz it was singing:

> "*Cantabo laudes tuas Domini!*
> To rest, Lorenz, and sleep in peace!"

He had remembered its tone and recognized it. What did he care if he must sleep on the cold ground that night, and without food?

He slept, and dreamed that he was in his old place at the monastery, and in the gray of the morning his beloved bell was calling, "Arise, Lorenz! *Cantabo laudes tuas Domini!*"

When he opened his eyes and saw the fields around him, and felt the damp earth beneath him, he remembered; and hastened into the village.  The bell was fastened in the belfry of the village church.  It was indeed his lost companion.

Here Lorenz would be content to live and die. His happiness required nothing more than the bell's cheery greeting to remind him of its nearness during the day, and send him to peaceful rest at night.  So the friar gave himself up to be a common laborer among the humble peasants of this village, that he might end his days within the sound of the bell's voice.

In years to come, little did the peasants of the village know how sweet in the ears of the old man who had worked among them for so long was the sound of the Gabriel bell, still saying:

> "Arise, Lorenz!  To prayers, Lorenz!
> *Cantabo laudes tuas Domini!*"

or how eagerly the tired old friar listened every evening for the curfew bell to ring its benediction:

> "To rest, Lorenz!  Good night,
> And sleep in peace!"

The strange, wild music of quivering metal! How fitting that this magic token from the bosom of the earth should have been, always, the people's messenger and reminder, in all parts of the world, to rouse them or summon them or frighten them, and also to cheer, console, and inspire them!

Bells are ever with us, and ring for all the great changes that come to us, from the cradle to the grave. Nations rejoice with bell ringing, and the same bells give voice to a nation's sorrow in times of national calamity. Who did not hear the bells ringing for joy on November the 11th, 1918? The hearts of nations were so full of joy and thanksgiving for the message of peace which came on that day, that there was no adequate expression except to ring the bells. How joyfully the ringers hurried to their ropes, until all the bells in the world must have been ringing at once! For this is one way in which all nations alike may express their rejoicing. A hundred and fifty years ago bells joyfully announced the independence of our nation. The writer well remembers the tolling of the bells in London when King Edward VII died; and there are probably many people still living who heard the tolling bells express a nation's sorrow over the death of our great Lincoln.

"Bells have rung in historical events, enriched literature, colored romances, inspired architecture, struck terror to the superstitious, or given consolation. They have rejoiced with the rejoicing, mourned with the grieving, chanted with the praying of all nations. They have opened markets, announced guests, roused for danger, summoned to war, welcomed the victor. They have pealed merrily for rustic weddings, joyfully announced the birth of royal heirs, and tolled with muffled tone

the passing soul along his way. They have tinkled
from the ankles of pagan dancing girls, and from
the sacrificial robes of Levitical high priests. They
have sorrowfully mourned 'The King is dead!' then
loyally shouted 'Long live the King!' "[1]

A traveler asleep in the broad expanse of the great
desert may be suddenly awakened by what he
believes to be the ringing of the church bells of his
native village, hundreds of miles away. A weary
sailor in a tumbling ship on the vast mid-ocean
thinks he hears the Angelus ringing from the steeple
of the little church at home, and falls asleep. Napoleon rides over the battlefield, gazing stern and
unmoved on the dead and dying that cover the
ground about him by thousands. "The evening bells
of the neighboring town begin to ring. Napoleon
pauses to listen; he is no longer the Conqueror of
Austerlitz, but an innocent, happy boy in Brienne.
He dismounts from his horse, seats himself on the
stump of an old tree, and weeps!"

The simple sound of bells always stirred the
inmost depths of the soul of this great conqueror of
Europe.

"How often," it has been written of Napoleon, "has
the booming of the village bell broken off the most
interesting conversations! He would stop lest the
moving of our feet might cause the loss of a single
beat of the tones which charmed him. Their influence, indeed, was so powerful that his voice trembled

[1]Eloise Roorback, "Bells of History and Romance," in *The Craftsman*, December, 1912.

with emotion while he said, 'That recalls to me the first years I passed at Brienne.' "[1]

Even the stern, iron-hearted William the Conqueror was often made to feel and weep by the sound of bells. They seemed to him to ring "with a thousand tongues, and every tongue had its own quick saying unto his ears; and if they spoke of saints in heaven; if they gave out mutterings about sin and hell;—softly, too, did they whisper of saint's love and heaven's forgiveness, and hearten him, while yet time was, to crave mercy of Jesus, and help from Mary."[2]

To a tired old grandmother, sitting in the chimney corner, the ringing of a bell conjures up her wedding day, the festive decorations and the gay clothes, the rejoicing of all the merry party, and again she walks slowly down the aisle, radiant and happy.

To another it is a school bell ringing on an early morning sixty years ago; the children hurry up the lane, and the whiff of a warm lunch basket—alas! it is only the sigh of an old man!

To Mathias, the burgomaster of the play,[3] the sweet, musical jangle of sleigh bells brings the wildest terror, because it recalls to him the night he betrayed his trust, and murdered the rich traveler for gold.

To a poor beggar sleeping on the street, the church bells ring Christmas time again in his mother's

[1]De Bourrienne.      [2]*Miscellanea Critica.*      [3]*The Bells.*

home, and the happy voices of those he once loved call him out of his lethargy to be a man again.

The witchery—the mastering magic—of bells! Where will one find a talisman more powerful?

Is it any wonder that the feelings of people are so bound up with their sounds? When the vast still air between earth and heaven is suddenly made alive and quivering by the sound of the magic metal, is it any wonder that there are then set free, phantoms, spirits, memories, that run riot with the imaginations of men?

## CHAPTER II

## BELLS OF PRIMITIVE PEOPLES

In the early ages of the human race, when primitive man first evoked a vibrant sound from a stone, it must have seemed to him the voice of his God speaking the mysterious language of Mother Earth. For was not stone a part of the sacred underworld? Was not the tree also attached to Mother Earth in a mysterious way, and would not the peculiar sound of hard wood, when struck, seem to have some hidden power attached to it?

The strangeness of these sounds led primitive man to invest them with a sacred character. To his thinking, everything which he could not understand was something to be worshiped, and the sound of stricken metal and hollow wood must have conveyed to him much that was supernatural. His gods spoke to him in the crash of thunder, and in all other vibrant and mysterious sounds.

It was probably a great revelation to him when he realized that he too could make mysterious sounds by using those things which the gods had given him for special communication with them. And the first bell—whatever may have been its shape or tone—was probably fashioned as a means by which man could make his gods hear him. What

9

thrills of hope and fear those crude sounds must
have stirred within him!

Ever since those early ages, the sound of stone,
of hollow, resonant wood, and of all the metals
that come out of the earth, have made a strange
appeal to the mind and emotions of man. He has
fashioned these materials into various forms; bells,
of some kind, have been known all over the world—
civilized and uncivilized—and practically all primitive peoples have used them. Rude tribes living in
the remotest islands in the midst of the sea have
been found to possess bells; and no matter how
civilized and cultured people become, they are still
moved in some way by their sound.

The first sound-producing instrument which primitive man invented was probably a rattle. Maybe
it was a handful of pebbles in a hard sea shell, shaken
to call the attention of his gods to the dances he
gave for their benefit. Or he may have used first
a natural rattle (a nutshell or a dried gourd with
the seeds rattling on the inside), and later fashioned
his first instruments in imitation of these.

The bell, as we know it, was gradually developed
from these simple rattles. Many tropical nuts and
fruits (the coconut, for instance) offer possibilities
for natural bells, and primitive peoples still use
them as such, and also as models for bells of their
own make.

The first bells fashioned by primitive man were
probably made of wood, unless the ancient "click

stone"[1] may be called a bell.[2]  Wooden bells of various shapes have been made by primitive peoples. Figure 1—a bell from Africa—was cut from a single block of wood.  A common type is made of two pieces of wood, hollowed out and fastened together, with a clapper, or several clappers, hanging between them.  Large bells made in this way are

[1]This was a resonant stone suspended by a thong and struck with a stick or with another stone.

[2]The question naturally arises, What is a bell?  Webster's Dictionary implies that a bell must be made of metal.  But that definition does not take into consideration the wooden and horn and clay bells of primitive peoples, nor the wooden temple bells of the Chinese which they called *chung*, the same word they used for their metal bells long before European bells or dictionaries in the English language were thought of.  So if the usage of thousands of years is to be counted, we must give to bells a broader definition.  There are several instruments which seem so closely related to the bell that, in order to distinguish among them, they also must be defined and the typical characteristics of each class of instruments given.

*Rattle.*  A closed cavity in some hard substance, containing one or more loose bits of hard substance which, when shaken, strike the inside of the cavity and make a noise.

*Jingle.*  Bits of hard substances so fastened that they strike against each other or against another hard substance when shaken.  (Often called a rattle.)

*Drum.*  A hollow substance with one or two coverings of skin or cloth or some kind of membrane which vibrates when struck.  (Kettledrums have one membrane; barrel drums have two.)

*Bell.*  A sonorous substance with an open cavity which emits a musical tone when struck either on the inside or outside of the cavity.  (A musical tone is a sound of definite pitch.)

*Gong.*  A slab or plate of sonorous substance which, when struck, emits a resonant tone.

*Cymbals.*  Two plates of metal which, when clashed together, make a resonant tone.

*Castanets.*  Two pieces of wood or bone which, when knocked together in the hand, make a clicking sound.

*Triangle.*  A bar of metal bent into triangular shape, open at one angle.

*Tambourine.*  A shallow circle of wood covered with a membrane on one side, and with bits of metal fastened to the rim.  (Sometimes classed with drums.)

The ancient "click stone" mentioned above would be more properly called a gong.  The gong is older than the metal bell, and may be considered its direct ancestor.  When the gong took on a hollow, cuplike form it became a bell.  When the rattle employed an open cavity it, too, became a bell.  And when the bell (whether it was made

very sonorous when hard wood is used, and wonderful effects can be obtained with them. In some parts of Asia and Africa the natives fasten bells of

this kind on the necks of elephants, so they may be found easily, and also that the sound of the bell may keep away snakes and other dangerous enemies.

In the New Hebrides Islands the natives have a most remarkable kind of bell, made from the entire trunk of a large tree! These instruments are often called "drums" because of their deep, drum-like tones, but their shape is more that of a bell; they have no membranes covering the openings, and are more correctly called "bells." One of these great wooden bells stands in the Metropolitan Museum of New York. It is about six and one-

Metropolitan Museum
FIG. 1.   *A wooden bell from Liberia, Africa*

of wood, metal, or clay) acquired a skin fastened over its cavity it became a drum.

Thus we see the close relationship of the bell, the rattle, the gong, and the drum.

Some writers claim that our word "bell" is derived from the Anglo-Saxon word *bellan*, which means to roar; others think it comes from the Latin word *pelvis*, which means basin-shaped. In either case, the definition given above is consistent.

FIG. 2.  *A "bell grove" in the New Hebrides*

half feet high and sixteen inches in diameter—a tree
trunk hollowed out and rounded at the top, with the
base left solid.   A long opening appears in the side,
and through this narrow opening, only two or three
inches wide, all the inside wood is cut out.   It is
struck on the outside with a hard, wooden mallet,
and its deep boom stirs the imagination of all who
hear it.

Figure 2 represents a "grove" of these tree bells
in the New Hebrides Islands.   They are used in

the religious ceremonies of the natives. Occasionally, in one of the islands, these bells are beaten at midnight as a signal that one of the natives must be killed as an offering to their gods. Imagine the

Merl La Voy

FIG. 3.   *A native beating on a Lali at Gizo, in the Solomon Islands*

terror in the village until the name of the victim is announced!

The natives of the Fiji and Tonga Islands in the South Seas make a very interesting kind of wooden bell called *Lali* (see Fig. 3). A traveler[1] some fifty years ago described it thus: "Imagine the trunk of a tree, three or four feet long, and hollowed out in the form of a trough. It is placed upon the ground,

[1] Reported by Ellacombe, in *Church Bells of Devon*, 1872.

upon some elastic body, generally on a coil of rope, and to protect from the rain, covered by a sort of roof. When the natives want to give the signal for Divine Service, they strike the mouth of the bell with a mallet, which produces a sort of stifled roar. I should have thought that it could only be heard at a short distance, but my mistake was great. There are *Lalis* the sound of which may be heard for a distance of twelve miles when the air is calm, and yet when you are near one, the sound is not sufficiently loud to startle you in the least; but as you recede it becomes clearer, more mild and musical. When you go to a village to hear its *Lali*, do not judge from the distinctness of the sound which strikes your ear that you are approaching the place, for you may be mistaken. The *Lali* is, therefore, the favorite instrument at Tonga, and deservedly so. Each *Lali* is named in the same manner as we give names to our bells. On feast days the Tongonian artists ring or sound on the *Lali*, peals that are not wanting in harmony. They rival each other in ability and skill, and are doubtless no less proud of their performances than our bell ringers in France."

A similar instrument is used by the natives of Brazil, and on the South American continent as well as in Africa it has long been used to send signals from one village to another. The *Lali* and some kinds of drum serve the natives as very useful forms of telegraph.

Figure 4 shows a large wooden bell of strange shape, from Africa. The lump on the side is evidently the place where it is to be struck in order to bring out the best tone. Bells of this kind are used to call the people together for feasts and religious meetings, in the same manner that our modern bells call the people together.

The Chinese have used various forms of wooden

Metropolitan Museum

FIG. 4.  *A wooden bell from Africa*

bells for centuries. The fig-shaped temple bells made of teak and other hard woods are very resonant, as are also the long treelike wooden bells which are used in the monasteries. The weird chanting of the priests, and the monotonous beating on these wooden bells at intervals throughout the night, are striking features of the environment to Western travelers who may be trying to sleep in the vicinity.

The bamboo which grows in southern Asia and in the islands of the Pacific is very easily made into bells.  The bamboo tubes are hollow, very hard and resonant, and a joint of bamboo requires only a clapper or a mallet in order to become a bell.  If it is struck on the outside with a mallet, the sound may be heard at a great distance. Often a Malay, traveling at night, carries one of these bamboo bells,

Miller collection

FIG. 5. *A stone gong*

which he strikes when he is uncertain as to the way, and the people in the nearest village reply. Bells of this kind are used by guards on some of the Pacific islands.  Each sentinel is obliged to strike his bell every hour through the night, the next watcher taking up the signal, and so on around the island.

Probably the first *ringing* sound produced by a primitive man (as we think of the word "ringing") was made when he suspended a piece of sonorous stone by a thong or cord of some kind, and struck it with a stick or with another stone.  These stone gongs (see Fig. 5) doubtless led primitive peoples to experiment with the sound of various metals. The first experiences with metal must have revealed to the savage its superior resonance over wood and stone, and stimulated him to shape it into forms that would ring.  Little bells were made of metal in the exact shape of nuts, with bits of metal or pebbles on the inside to make the jingling sound.

Thus when gong material and rattle design were united, the first metal bells came into existence.

Bells of this form are very common among savages of all countries, and they are put to all kinds of uses. They are made of gold, silver, copper, tin, and every other kind of metal which can be worked into a nut shape. We use this type of bell in sleigh bells and other bells of the "jingling" kind. Figure 6 shows a ceremonial rattle from Africa, made of many small metal bells.

Metropolitan Museum
Fig. 6.  *African ceremonial rattle*

When this point had been reached in the working of metal, the field was then open to the imagination of the blacksmith (for it is he who makes bells among primitive peoples). Bells of various shapes and sizes have resulted, all the way from small, concave pieces of iron up to our own idea of what a bell should be.

Primitive people have made various uses of bells. Among certain tribes of central Africa a rude iron bell is the scepter of royalty. The same kind of sound which, with us, locates the cows or sheep, in Africa announces the coming of the king, who uses this bell only when he goes on visits of state or business of importance. Figure 7 shows an iron double bell which is carried before princes in the Congo region.

Other tribes carry clumsy iron "magic bells," which are always a sign of the priest. With these bells the priests go in procession from the villages, and firmly believe they will find treasure on their return.

Metropolitan Museum

FIG. 7. *African double bell*

The "medicine man" wears an iron bell suspended by an iron chain. In some places in Africa the medicine man brings a small bell in his hand, and rings it from time to time. He begins his treatment by singing to the patient, who sits before him on the ground. He sings "Dabre-dabre" several times in very solemn tones, and the patient answers "Eh."[1]

Some savages wear small bells on their garments. For instance, the natives of New Guinea make bells out of shells and fasten into each bell a pig's tooth for a clapper, and these are used by the natives to decorate their scanty attire. The dress of the Naga

[1]Richard Wallaschek, in *Primitive Music*, London, 1893.

women of north Burma, which is only a short petti-
coat, is ornamented with bells, beads, and shells.
On the west coast of Africa the grown girls of Benin
city wear an apron consisting entirely of small
brass bells.

The Maoris in New Zealand use a bell called
*Pahu* for purposes of war.

The hill tribes in southern India have a small
cowbell which they worship as a god. It is the one
which is worn by the bell-buffalo of each sacred
herd. When this bell-buffalo dies her eldest daughter
inherits her rank, just as modern kings and queens
inherit their crowns and kingdoms. The holy bell
is then worn by the new bell-buffalo for three days
and nights in order that she may be thoroughly
consecrated. It is then removed and never worn
again in that cow's lifetime, but is lodged in the
priest's house where all may worship it. However, no
one except the priest may touch it or even look at it.[1]

In some parts of Africa the natives have mimic
representations of the gorilla, during which an iron
bell is rung and a hoarse rattle mingles with the
other sounds.

The Bahama negro dances to the accompaniment
of ringing bells, while various individuals in the
crowd keep time by stamping their feet and slapping
their hands against their legs.

When the first Spanish explorers came to America
they found that the Indians in Mexico used small

[1]See Chapter XXIX, "The Bells of India," pp. 332-40.

bells tied to their rattles. A wand decorated with bells and rattles of deer hoofs is still used in celebrations of the Zuñi Indians.

Some of the Indians in Peru dance in the street to the music of a pipe and tabor, while the time is marked by the ringing of small bells tied to the legs. The Morris dancers of Old England also had this custom.

The Indians of Ecuador worshiped idols shaped like lions and tigers; and when a chief was ill the natives rang bells and beat drums before these idols in order that the gods might be appeased and restore the health of their leader.

In East India the Pegu unite twenty bells into one instrument, which is beaten with sticks, and, as one traveler writes, "they make no bad music." The Javanese bells on Banda Island, to the number of twelve, from a distance sounded to one traveler "like a string orchestra."

Some of the African tribes who think that loudness is the greatest thing to be desired in music, beat their drums with immense energy, and at the same time they bang with sticks upon a row of brass kettles which hang on poles and form a kind of bell series.

The ancient shepherds tied bells to their sheep, and thought that by the sound of them the sheep grew fat.

## CHAPTER III

## BELLS OF ANCIENT CIVILIZATIONS

### CHINA

The most ancient civilizations of which we have any record seem to have made use of metal bells. Their invention cannot be claimed by any one nation, but China is, perhaps, the oldest known country where the bell appears in history. Bells are said to have been known in China for more than forty-six centuries. But since the bells of China have also a place among those of modern peoples, the discussion of the ancient as well as of the modern bells will be given in Chapter XXV.

### ASSYRIA

It is certain that the ancient Assyrians made use of bells. They are seen on the headstalls of horses

Ellacombe

FIG. 8.  *Ancient Assyrian bells*

in Assyrian monuments, and were probably used to announce the coming of the horses. Sir Austen

Henry Layard, in his excavations at Nimrud, found about eighty bronze bells that had been buried in a copper caldron.    Drawings of four of these bells (now in the British Museum) are shown in figure 8.

Ellacombe

FIG. 9.    *Egyptian bell*
*of 200 B.C.*

FIG. 10.    *Ancient Egyptian*
*hand bells*

They are so corroded that it is not possible to tell how these bells sounded in the ancient Assyrian days.

## EGYPT

Bells have been found in Egyptian mummy cases. Those found in the tombs are of bronze, and some of them resemble the bells of the Assyrians.    Imitations of bells may be seen in the ancient Egyptian necklaces made of gold and silver, and also carved of precious stones as pendants to gold necklaces.

Figure 9 shows an Egyptian bell which was probably made about 200 B.C.    Historians tell us that the Egyptians hung bells on the necks of horses, oxen, and sheep; also that small bells were sometimes hung at their doors, and were used in the houses to awaken the family in the morning. (See Fig. 10 for drawings of Egyptian hand bells found in ancient tombs.)

The *sistrum* (see Fig. 11) is a metal instrument, more properly called a jingle than a bell, which is always associated with Egyptian music. It is first

found in the ancient worship of Isis in Egypt, where it was called *seshesh*, and was used by the priestesses and "holy women," who were sometimes of highest rank. The *sistrum* consists of a metal hoop with a handle. Through the hoop are passed several rods of metal, and little bells, or sometimes jingling plates of metal, are suspended from the rods. The tinkling sounds of the *sistrum* were considered indispensable in the religious ceremonies of the Egyptians. What is more remarkable,

Metropolitan Museum

FIG. 11. *Sistrum of the ancient Egyptians*

the *sistrum* is still in use, being employed by the priests of a Christian sect in Abyssinia. The Copts, in upper Egypt, who are likewise Christians, shake a tinkling instrument of metal, called *mara-outh*, in their religious ceremonies, avowedly for the purpose of keeping off the Evil One. The *sistrum* seems to have a close relation to the sacred ceremonial bells.

## JUDEA

From several references in the Bible we know that the early Hebrews were familiar with bells, and used them. In Exodus xxviii, 34, the directions are given for the robe of the ephod: "A golden bell and a pomegranate, a golden bell and a pomegranate, upon the skirts of the robe round about." In Exodus xxxix, 25, the robe has been finished: "And they made bells of pure gold, and put the bells between the pomegranates upon the skirts of the robe round about, between the pomegranates; a bell and a pomegranate, a bell and a pomegranate, upon the skirts of the robe round about, to minister in; as Jehovah commanded Moses." The tinkling sound of these golden bells upon his robe announced the coming of the High Priest for the sacred ministrations.

In Zachariah xiv, 20, "In that day shall there be upon the bells of the horses "HOLY UNTO JEHOVAH," which implies a custom of having bells upon the horses,—probably fastened on the bridle, or upon the forehead of the horses, as they were used in Assyria, and as we find them at the present time in many countries.

Josephus says that the ancients regarded bells as signifying thunder. In many cases they looked upon them as signals of victory and dominion. He also says that the golden roof of Solomon's temple had bells fixed on it to keep birds from alighting thereon.

### ANCIENT GREECE AND ROME

Euripides says that the head gear of Greek war horses was adorned with small bells for the purpose of terrifying the foe and spurring the warriors to the fray. The Greek foot soldier carried bells attached to his shield or hidden in its hollow interior, probably for the same purpose.

Bells were hung upon Porsena's stately tomb and upon the car which carried the body of Alexander the Great. Numerous bells have been found inside tombs, and were probably buried with the dead because of their supposed power to protect bodies from evil spirits.

Augustus caused a bell to be hung before the temple of Jupiter, and probably before other temples also. Bells were used in the religious rites of the priest of Cybele in Athens; and at the moment of the death of an Athenian, brass kettles and bells were rung in order to scare away the furies. In Sparta, when a king died women went through the streets striking a bell, and this, says Herodotus, was the signal that from each household a man and a woman should put on mourning.

Bells preceded funeral processions, were hung on triumphal cars, and summoned guests, as in later days, to feasts. Pliny, who died about 79 A.D., says that in the market place at Athens the fish sales were announced by the ringing of small bells. Figure 12 represents an ancient Greek bell that has been preserved since the 4th century B.C.

A silver bell was the prize run for at races, and the familiar expression "bearing away the bell" has its origin in this custom. The silver cup which is given in modern times as a prize in races and games of skill is only the ancient bell inverted and used as a drinking vessel.

British Museum

FIG. 12. *Greek bell of the 4th century B.C.*

Bells were hung on the necks of malefactors on their way to execution, "lest innocent persons," says the historian, "should be defiled by touching them," and probably also to draw the gaze of the people upon the criminal to increase his punishment and the value of his example to the public.

It is said that from this Greek custom the Romans derived their habit of hanging a bell upon the chariot of the emperor that he, in the height of his prosperity and power, "might be admonished against pride and be mindful of human misery."

Both the Greeks and the Romans hung bells about the necks of horses, dogs, and sheep. In one place in Rome Bacchus is represented as riding upon an ass to whose neck a bell is attached, and Pan also is pictured in similar manner. There are many representations of elephants wearing bells, either for superstitious or protective reasons.

The Romans "belled" their flocks in order that wild beasts might be scared away by the sound. In the rural laws of Justinian it is enacted that "if anyone take away the bell from an ox or sheep, let him, being convicted, be scourged as a thief, and if the animal be lost thereby, let him pay the loss."

Several historians mention the custom of testing the spirit of horses by seeing whether they were frightened by the sound of bells. The custom of training horses to these sounds gave rise to the habit of speaking of an untrained person as "one not used to the noise of the bell."

In Rome the bathing hour was announced by a bell, as were other times of the day, there being no clocks. The wealthier Romans used them in domestic life to assemble their families.

In the garrison the Roman sentry wore a set of bells on his breastplate, so that the centurion might know from the sound that the sentry was faithful to his duty. The centurion's bell was used in the camp in two ways. "In one custom, a watchman, or patrol, made the rounds of the camp, ringing a bell, and the sentries replied to him by shouting, or in some other way. If they did not reply, he suspected that they were asleep, and investigated the matter. The second custom was for a bell to be sent around the circuit of the camp, each patrol-man carrying it over his beat and delivering it to the next patrol until it made the rounds and came back to the commander. If any patrolman, through sleepiness or from absence from his beat, failed to appear to take the bell from his neighbor, the bell was sent back again in the same fashion to the commander, who at once inquired into the reason for the patrolman's failure to appear."[1]

Bells played a very important part in the later warfare of both Greece and Rome. The ambitious young soldier proved his mettle by performing the trying duties of a patrolman, pacing the ramparts and rousing the guards with the hand bell which was passed from patrol to patrol. This practice once nearly caused the loss of a fortress; for, as Thucydides tells us in his *History of the Peloponnesian War*, during the siege of Potidaea, in Macedonia, the Lacedemonian general, hearing by the sound of the bell that the sentry had passed a certain spot, raised his scaling ladders there, and was driven back only with great difficulty.

A still more remarkable instance of the use of bells for military purposes is related by Plutarch in his life of Brutus, which may be thus translated:

"As a river ran close to the town (Xanthus, in Lycia), several attempted to escape by swimming and diving; but they were prevented by nets let down for that purpose which had little bells at the top to give notice when anyone was taken."

---

[1] A. S. Pease, in "Notes on Uses of Bells among the Greeks and Romans," in *Harvard Studies in Classical Philology*.

"The Roman infant played with bells as his toy, and the same sound preceded him to the funeral pile."[1]

The Romans also employed bells of various tones arranged in some order for the playing of tunes.

FIG. 13.  *Roman crotal (rattle) bells found in Ireland*

Among the Etruscan antiquities an instrument has been discovered which is constructed of a number of bronze vessels placed in a row on a metal rod. Likewise, numerous bells, varying in size and tone, have been found in Etruscan tombs.

Figure 13 shows three types of bells found in Ireland, which were probably brought there by the Romans.  They may have been used in the ancient war dances, or by the Roman pagan priests.

The use of bells continued in Rome, and increased as Christian usage brought them more and more into play.  The Greeks, however, were compelled to

[1]Benjamin Lomax, in *Bells and Bell Ringers*, London, 1879.

The Turks forbade the ringing of bells lest the sound should disturb the repose of souls which, they supposed, wander in the air; they also regarded bells as the symbols of unfaithfulness. It is quite possible that the Turks prohibited the use of bells for reasons that were as much political as religious, as the ringing of bells might serve as a signal in case of rebellion. So the lack of bells in the churches of the Greeks was not from principle, but from compulsion.

FIG. 14
*Ancient Roman hand bell*

After the edict forbidding the use of bells, the newly conquered Christians substituted for them metal or wooden plates to be struck with a hammer. Such plates are seen today in some Greek churches. The voice of the muezzin often calls the Turkish people to prayers, and the clapping of hands is the signal used for calling attendants.

FIG. 15
*Roman bell of the 1st century*

In spite of their objections to the use of bells, the Mohammedans look forward to hearing bells in Paradise, shaking on the "golden shafted trees of Eden." In "Paradise and the Peri," Thomas Moore refers to this hope:

And she already hears the trees
　　Of Eden with their crystal bells
Ringing in that ambrosial breeze
　　That from the Throne of Alla swells.

FIG. 16. *Ancient bronze bells of Central America*

The ancient civilizations of North and South America seem to have employed metal bells for various purposes. Unlike the Chinese, the Incas of Peru and the ancient civilizations of Central America and Mexico have not left records which give the use of their bells; but some very fine specimens have been found. Small gold bells have been excavated in Panama, and may be seen in the Museum of the American Indian in New York. In the same museum is a large collection of bronze bells which were found in a cave in the valley of the Chamelecon River in Central America. (Fig. 16 gives drawings of three of these bells.)

Figure 17 (p. 33) illustrates a copper bell which was found in a tomb of ancient Peru. It was doubtless used in the religious services of the Incas, ages ago.

Figure 18 shows a cluster of *yotl* bells (now in the British Museum) from the ancient civilization of Mexico.   Such *yotl* are found in the picture writings

FIG. 17.   *Ancient copper bell from Peru*

FIG. 18.   *Ancient yotl bells from Mexico*

that show the various objects which the Aztecs used to pay as tribute to their sovereigns.   The Aztecs and Incas also made bells of clay.

## CHAPTER IV

## THE FIRST CHRISTIAN CHURCH BELLS

No church bells called the first Christians of Europe together for their services, for they could meet only by stealth. Very soon after the death of Christ the Christian church was organized in Italy. The Romans in authority soon became so bitterly opposed to this religion that they sought to kill all Christians, and for a time the only way the followers of the new faith could come together was to meet in secret caves under the ground. Even today one may go through the dark tunnels into these caves or "catacombs," and see the walls black with the smoke of the torches which the early Christians used, nearly two thousand years ago, to light these caves when they held their meetings.

When more and more of the Romans became Christians, and finally the Emperor Constantine himself adopted the faith, there was no longer need for secrecy, for Christians were allowed to meet openly, in buildings above the ground. This was in the early 4th century.

For a long time the Romans had used bells to remind the citizens that the public baths were ready, so it seemed natural that bells should now be used to summon them to church. At first they probably used the same hand bells that had announced the bathing hour; and probably the bell ringers ran about the streets in the same way, ringing the bell on every street to let the people know it was time to come together for worship, just as the "town crier" in our own country, before the days of the newspaper, distributed information and called the people to meetings. Sometimes, probably, they used trumpets also for this purpose, as was the custom in Egypt and the countries of the East.

About the year 400, in the city of Campania, Italy, the bishop of Nola (whose name was Paulinus) conceived the idea of having one large bell fastened on top of the meetinghouse so that all the people might hear it, instead of having a bell ringer go about the streets. One writer says that Paulinus suspended above the roof of the church a large brass kettle, which was struck with a hammer to notify the people when prayers were supposed to begin. The records are so meager that no one knows exactly how it happened. Some writers claim that Pope Sabinianus was the first to use church bells, in the year 604, and that he had them rung at different hours of the day so the people could keep up with the times which had been set for them to pray. Paulinus, however, is the one whom the modern Italians honor. The feast of St. Paulinus is celebrated on July 25th of every year, and in many cities of Italy small clay bells, costing not more than a penny, are sold in great numbers to the poor people on that day.

FIG. 19. *French church bell of the 7th century*

FIG. 20. *German bell of the 7th century*

We do know, however, that when Clotaire, the king of the Franks, besieged the city of Sens in Burgundy in 610, his army was frightened away by the ringing of the bells in St. Stephen's Church there; so it seems that church bells were not very common at that time, especially with the French. (Figs. 19 and 20.)

About 680, says Bede, an English historian of the 7th century, church bells were introduced from Italy into England. Bells were carried by the missionaries into the British Isles, and those good saints, Patrick and Cuthbert, always announced their coming by the sound of the bell, just as the town criers did many centuries later. Bells came with Christianity into Great Britain, and they have been very closely identified with church service ever since, — more than any other musical instrument. (Fig. 21 shows an old English church bell of the earliest type.)

It must have been in the 8th century that Turketul, abbot of Croyland, hung the first peal of bells in an English belfry.  He first presented to the abbey a large bell called "Guthlac," and afterwards added six others named Pega, Bega, Betteline, Bartholomew, Tatwin, and Turketul.  Gifts of bells to the churches and monasteries became very common about this time.

FIG. 21.   *Old English church bell*

It is recorded that "a certain English nobleman named Litholf, who resided in a woodland part of the neighborhood, gave two large bells to the tower of St. Albans.  Having a good stock of sheep and goats, he sold many of them and bought a bell, of which, when he heard the new sound suspended in the tower, he jocosely said, 'Hark, how sweetly my goats and my sheep bleat!'  His wife procured another from the same place, and the two together produced most sweet harmony, which when the lady heard, she said, 'I do not think this union is wanting in Divine favor, which united me to my husband in the bond of matrimony and mutual affection.'"

During the century that followed, a great many bells were made for the churches of England and France and other European countries.  They increased in size, and were given special places in the

religious services.   (Fig. 22 shows a bell of the 9th
century.)   The Saxon king Egbert gave orders that

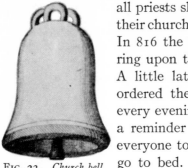

all priests should ring the bells of
their churches at appointed hours.
In 816 the bells were ordered to
ring upon the death of a bishop.
A little later, Alfred the Great
ordered the church bell to ring
every evening at eight o'clock as
a reminder that it was time for
everyone to put out the fire and

FIG. 22.   *Church bell*   go to bed.   This was known as
*of the 9th century*   the "Curfew bell" (see p. 103).

As time went on, more bell-ringing orders were
given, until the bell came to be one of the most
important parts of the church.

For a long time the bells were made in the monasteries, and it was the priest's office to ring them.

In a life of Charlemagne it is stated that in the
Abbey of St. Gall a bell maker named Tancho made
a bell the tone of which Charlemagne liked very
much.   Tancho said to him, "My Lord Emperor,
command a great quantity of copper to be brought
to me which I will purify by fire; and let me have
silver instead of tin,[1] about a hundred pounds, and
I will cast for you such a bell that the others in
comparison with it shall be mute."   Charlemagne
ordered the required amount of copper and silver
to be sent to the bell maker.   Now Tancho, being

[1]Copper and tin were the metals used by the first bell founders.

a great knave, put all the silver aside for his own use, thinking no one would know the difference, and made the bell of copper and tin. When the bell was finished the emperor ordered it to be hung and the clapper attached. The writer relates that "that was soon done, and then the warden of the church, the attendants, and even the boys of the place, tried, one after the other, to make the bell sound. But all was in vain; and so at last the knavish maker of the bell came up, seized the rope and pulled at the bell. When lo! and behold! Down from on high came the brazen mass; fell on the very head of the cheating bell founder; killed him on the spot; and passed through his carcass, and crashed to the ground. . . . When the aforementioned weight of silver was found, Charlemagne ordered it to be distributed among the poorest servants of the palace."

In the 10th century it was decreed that any Saxon churl (peasant) might become a thane (a freeman of higher rank; nobleman) if he were rich enough to own about five hundred acres of land, and had on his estate a church with a bell tower. Of course this encouraged the building of churches and the making of church bells, and they became a necessary adjunct to every church building. A canon of the Church of England especially directs that "parishes must furnish bells and bell ropes." More and more the bell came to hold a place of honor and distinction. A peal of bells was the fitting present for a king to bestow upon the people of a deserving town; to deprive a town of its bells was the worst of punishments. Henry V took away the bell from the city of Calais and gave it to the city of Monmouth. According to Scott, the town of Dunkeld became so corrupt that it sold its bell for whisky, and drank the proceeds.

O what a toun, what a terrible toun,
What a terrible toun was the toun of Dunkel;
They've hangit the minister, drooned the precentor,
Dung down the steeple, and drucken the bell.

# CHAPTER V

## THE SACRED BELLS OF IRELAND

When St. Patrick came from Gaul to Ireland about the year 440 he brought with him a group of skilled workmen and a number of bishops. Among the workmen were metal smiths, bell makers, and braziers. He founded monasteries, placed the bishops to preside over them, and set the smiths to making bells for the monasteries. He especially designated that "the smiths should make bells, and the braziers should make the patens, and the ministers the altar chalices."

The bells which these smiths made were not cast, as our modern church bells are, but were made of thin plates of beaten metal, bent into a four-sided shape, riveted along the sides, and with a handle at the top. The best ones were dipped in a solution of molten bronze which filled up all openings and coated the bell, making it more solid and resonant.

These early bells show indications that they were rung by being struck like a gong with a hammer or a small mallet, and that the clapper was added at a later period. When the clapper was once tried it proved more convenient, as it left one hand free to the ringer, and it is possible that clappers were then added to most of the old bells. However, some of the larger bells suspended in church towers in various European cities, until quite recent times, were rung by being struck like a gong.

The bells used by the early teachers of Christianity were held in such veneration that they were looked upon as sacred, and preserved with the greatest care, together with the Bibles and walking staffs of the saints. The Irish have always greatly revered their sacred relics, and preserved them so carefully that many of these bells have been handed down for over a thousand years. There are said to be fifty or sixty of them now in existence. It was the custom to place the sacred bells or other relics in the guardianship of some special family selected for that purpose, and a generous grant of land was allowed to go with the trust for the support of the family. In case of invasion, or danger from fire, the first care of the relic keeper was to see that the sacred object was safe. The sacred bells of St. Patrick, and many other relics and manuscripts, have been preserved in this way. Had it not been for this custom of the Irish we should probably know very little today of the first Christian bells.

There are several bells still preserved as having once belonged to St. Patrick. One of them is broken, and is called "The Broken Bell of Brigid." It is said that St. Patrick had this bell in his hands when he had his last encounter with the demons of the North. When he found that the violent ringing of the bell was not sufficient to rout the enemy, he

flung the bell with all his might into the thickest of
their ranks, and frightened the enemy so that they
fled terrified into the sea, and did not molest the
island again, as the story goes,
for seven years, seven months,
and seven days!

The "Black Bell" of St. Patrick
(see Fig. 23) is considered by
many to be the oldest bell in Ireland. It certainly shows signs of
wear and tear. Formerly it belonged to a family in Headford,
and the people of that locality
believed that this bell was a
present from an angel to St.
Patrick, and was originally of
pure silver. Its present black

Ellacombe

FIG. 23. *The "Black
Bell" of St. Patrick*

and corroded condition is caused, they say, by its
contact with the demons when the saint was expel-
ling them from the country. For a long time this
bell was brought every year, on Garland Sunday,
to a little oratory on Croagh Patrick, and while
here the pious pilgrim for a penny was allowed to
kiss it. If he had been suffering with rheumatic
pains, for twopence he might put it three times
around his body. But finally times got so bad that
the keeper of the bell sold it to help pay his passage to America.

Another bell of St. Patrick became the heirloom
of the Abbey of Armagh, and was used in 946 by

the abbot to measure the tribute paid to him by a northern tribe. The bell-full of silver was given to him for his "peace" as St. Patrick's successor. The most famous one of St. Patrick's bells is the

FIG. 24. *"Bell of St. Patrick's Will"*

one known as the "Bell of St. Patrick's Will" (see Fig. 24). It is made of two plates of sheet iron bent over to meet, riveted, and then dipped in bronze; it is six inches high, five inches broad, and four inches deep. The clapper is apparently of a later date than the rest of the bell. This bell was mentioned in the annals of Ulster as early as 552, and it is believed to have been buried in St. Patrick's grave and taken from his tomb about that time. It possessed great magic power, according to the people of former days, and the breach of an oath upon it in 1044 was said to have been avenged by a raid in which a large number of prisoners and twelve hundred cows were carried away. Its sound is supposed, even yet, to scare away evil spirits, and all reptiles except the deaf adder.

In the eleventh century this bell was considered worthy to be enshrined. It seems that from the 6th century onward there were found, in the principal churches of Ireland, costly shrines made for the preservation of their most sacred relics: the bells, the books, and the croziers of the early teachers of Christianity. So at some time between 1091 and 1105, the king of Ireland (Donnel O'Loughlin) had made, at his expense, a jeweled shrine worthy of the noble origin of the Bell of St. Patrick's Will. This shrine is covered with gold and silver filigree set with jewels in green, blue, dull red, and crystal (see Fig. 25).

The family of O'Mellan were the hereditary keepers of this bell and shrine until 1441. At this time, it is recorded in the annals, on account of some misdemeanor on O'Mellan's part the care of the bell was given to another family; it was later purchased by the Royal Irish Academy, and is in the Dublin Museum. This bell and its shrine are among the most famous objects in the country.

All of the bells of this period are shaped like our ordinary cowbells, though when they were to be used for church bells they were made much larger, even twelve or thirteen inches high.

*The Art Workers' Quarterly*

FIG. 25.  *Jeweled shrine of "Bell of St. Patrick's Will"*

None have been found in Ireland more than thirteen inches high.  As a church bell, this type belongs especially to Ireland, for the English soon departed from this form.

FIG. 26. *"Bronze Bell of Cumascach"*

By the end of the ninth century bells were cast in bronze in the same form as the old iron ones, which, however, did not go out of use.  One of the early bronze bells of Ireland has been preserved, the "Bronze Bell of Cumascach," shown in figure 26.  This bell is cast of bronze, without rivets; its handle and clapper are of iron; it is nearly a foot high and eight inches across the base.  We know by its inscription, which means "a prayer for Cumascach, son of Ailill," that it must have been made about the year 900.  (See p. 52.)

It is recorded that "pilgrims in the remote ages of the Celtic church carried these bells with them, especially when visiting heathen lands, and left them behind as memorials of their Christianity." The Welsh, as well as the Irish, hold their bells in the highest veneration, and in former days took great pride in making them.  Some of the church bells which date back to the seventh and eighth centuries are remarkable for beauty and workmanship, as are also the shrines that have been made for their better preservation.

# CHAPTER VI

## CELTIC BELL LORE

Just as the people in other parts of the world have always given a religious meaning to the sound of metal, most of the early Christians came to think of the sound of bells as symbolic of the voice of God. Many of them believed that bells could perform miracles and cures, and that they even had the power of going from one place to another without human help. This belief continued in some degree for hundreds of years, and bell superstitions have not yet altogether disappeared.

Early historians tell us of certain portable bells which all the people of Ireland, Scotland, and Wales looked upon as having miraculous power. They were even more afraid of swearing falsely by these bells than by the Bible itself. Even now one hears of the "bell oath" among the peasants of southern Ireland, and the "Golden Bell of St. Senan" is still famous. This golden bell, kept in safety by the Munster family for generations, has been very useful. In cases of theft and the like, where the truth cannot be found out by ordinary means, the loan of this bell will be demanded, and the suspected persons required to put their hands upon it and swear their innocence. No one who is not truly innocent will dare do this, for fear of being exposed and punished by the bell.

Once, writes Mr. Fielding, during the last century, a man who had stolen some linen was sent by his parish priest to fetch the bell for the oath. In an agony of guilt and terror he flung the bell over a high cliff into the sea, only to find, when he came to the priest's house, that the bell, mysteriously rescued, had arrived there before him, and was calmly awaiting the confession which he was now obliged to make.

The bell of St. Oudoceus, a 5th-century bishop, was supposed to have the power to heal the sick. Its legend, according to one of the old writers, is as follows: "St. Oudoceus, being thirsty after undergoing labor, and more accustomed to drink water than any other liquor, came to a fountain in the vale of Llandaff, not far from the church, that he might drink, where he found women washing butter, after the manner of the country; and sending to them his messenger and disciples, they requested that they would accommodate them with a vessel that their pastor might drink therefrom; who, ironically, as mischievous girls, said, 'We have no other cups besides that which we hold in our hands, namely, the butter'; and the man of blessed memory taking it, formed a cup in the shape of a *small bell*, and he raised his hand so that he might drink therefrom, and he drank. And it remained in that form, that is, a golden one, so that it appeared to those who beheld it, to consist altogether of purest gold; which, by Divine power, is from this day reverently preserved in the church of Llandaff, in memory of the holy man, and it is said that by touching it, health is given to the diseased."

Many suffering pilgrims came to the church where it was preserved, in the hope of being healed. It had lost its clapper—being such an old bell—and made an excellent cup from which to drink; and no matter what one drank from this bell, it was supposed to have wonderful healing power, even though it were only pure water.

In a small village in Wales there is preserved a bell which is said to have belonged to St. David, and it is endowed with great virtues. Once a man was confined in a castle near Warthremon, and his wife secretly sent this bell to him, in order that it might enable him to be set free. The keepers of the castle not only refused to let him go, but kept the bell and hung it on the wall. On that same night, so the story goes, by "Divine vengeance the whole town, with the exception of the wall on which the bell hung, was consumed by fire."

The Scottish people also preserved their sacred bells with superstitious reverence. There is said to be a very ancient bell in the chapel of St. Fillans, in Scotland, an oblong bell about a foot high, which was very highly respected in the olden days, and this bell had remarkable curative powers. It was usually kept on a gravestone in the churchyard, and used to cure mad people. The sufferer was first dipped in the saint's pool, and had various rites performed over him; then he had to remain in the chapel all night, bound with ropes. Next morning this bell was very solemnly set upon his head in order to complete the cure, and the patient's wits returned. It was believed that if this bell were stolen it would extricate itself out of the thief's hands, and return home, ringing all the way. For some years past it has been locked up to prevent its being used for superstitious purposes.

The power to return home of its own accord was also attributed to a bell in Leinster. A chieftain of Wicklow got possession of it, and he was obliged to tie it with a strong cord to prevent its escaping to its home, at St. Fillans' church in Meath.

The ability to prevent its being lifted was one of the miraculous powers of another bell of St. Fillans. It seems that some one who lived in a neighboring parish at one time stole this bell and ran away. In the course of his flight he sat down to rest on the top of a hill, where he might draw his breath, and laid the bell on a stone beside him. When he started to continue his journey, however, the bell would not leave the rock. Try as hard as he might, he could not move it. He was terribly frightened, and in the face of this magic he decided that the only thing to do was to go back and confess his theft. Fully resolved to restore the treasure if he could but get it loose from the rock, he made one more effort. The bell now came up quite easily, and was light enough while the thief carried it back to its home. This bell of St. Fillans was made after the fashion of most of the Celtic relics—iron riveted together and coated with bronze.

There is a story about the sacred bell which is treasured in Kenan's Convent. St. Kenan was an Irish disciple of the Welsh abbott, St. Gildas. One night when St. Kenan was staying in St. Gildas' abbey, he dreamed that he heard a voice bidding him to depart and found a house of monks of his own, in an unnamed land to which a bell should guide him. The monks of St. Gildas had no bell which they were willing to give away, so the abbott himself made one out of a piece of old iron, and blessed it, and gave it to the parting guest. For a long, long time, as they traveled, the bell was silent, and St. Kenan and his companions knew that

FIG. 27. *The "Black Bell of Drumragh"*

they must travel on until the bell should ring of its own accord, and thus let them know where to stop. Finally, in a Cornish valley, it sounded the long-hoped-for signal, and the party stopped here by the River Fal, and built Kenan's Convent, where the bell has been preserved and honored ever since.

The "Black Bell of Drumragh" (see Fig. 27) is still in the possession of its hereditary keepers, the M'Enhill family. When a member of the keeper's family died, the oldest man in the family carried this bell before the coffin and rang it at intervals until the church was reached. It seems that this bell is especially thought of as a funeral bell, and this is the story of how it came into the M'Enhill family, as related by Mr. Milligan:[1]

"Many centuries ago, before roads or bridges were made to the old Drumragh graveyard, two funerals were entering at the same time, one, a person called M'Enhill, and the other, Campbell. When the M'Enhill funeral was passing a certain spot, a bell began to ring in the ground; but when the other funeral passed that same spot, it ceased. After this, when any member of the M'Enhill family was being buried, and passed over this spot, the bell rang; but it never rang when anyone else passed over, so the M'Enhills dug down and discovered the bell, and it has been in their family ever since."

The "Bell of Cumascach" (see Fig. 26) was also called the Blessed Bell of Armagh, and was supposed to have miraculous power to heal the sick. The Henning family were the hereditary keepers of the bell. It was an ancient custom to place it near any of that family who were dangerously ill. Mr. Bell, who was an eyewitness to one of the uses of this bell, writes: "I visited Mrs. Henning, the widow of Paul Henning, on her deathbed. She lay in a large, badly lighted apartment crowded with people. The bell, which had remained several days

[1] In *Ancient Ecclesiastical Bells in Ulster*, 1902.

near her head, seemed to be regarded by those who
were present with much interest. The vapor of
the heated chamber was so condensed on the cold
metal of the bell, that occa-
sionally small streams trickled
down its sides. This 'heavy
sweating' of the bell, as it was
termed, was regarded by
everyone with peculiar horror,
and deemed a certain prog-
nostication of the death of
the sick woman, who departed
this life a few hours after I
left the room. The agonized
bell, I was told, had on many
previous occasions given similar tokens as proofs of its
sympathy of the approaching death of its guard-
ians."

Ellacombe

FIG. 28. *St. Patrick's
"Bell of Blood"*

This bell was often borrowed from its keeper that
it might be rung at funerals, and it was also used
in administering the oath, in order to find out guilty
persons. It was considered the most binding oath
that could be taken, and many miraculous judg-
ments were visited on those who violated oaths
taken on this bell.

St. Patrick is supposed to have given fifty consecrated bells to the churches of Connaught. The
"Bell of Blood" (see Fig. 28) is believed to be one
of those bells. It was, like other sacred bells, used

in administering oaths and in recovering lost property, and was hired out on the following terms: "The borrower, before it was committed to him, paid down a certain fee in silver: then he took an oath on the bell, that he would safely return it within a certain time, and that while in his possession, it should never touch the ground, or pass out of human hands. In consequence it was customary for the person who borrowed it, when he required to be disengaged, to place it in the hands of a second person, and so on; and when night came, the family used to sit up, or the neighbors to be collected as at a wake, so that when one was tired holding it, another might relieve him, and thus fulfill, until the period of its loan had expired, the terms of the oath, that it was never to pass out of the hands of man."[1]

It is said that Breslin, the keeper of the "Bell of Conall Cael," so far lost his reverence for the bell that he sold it for three young cows. The cows died the next day, and Breslin never prospered afterwards.

The legend of a bell which once hung in the bell house of Aughagower, in the county of Mayo, is still preserved among the people of that vicinity. They say it was once buried for concealment in a bog near by, and that "of a quiet evening its sound, like silver, could be heard across the waste."

The Clog-Oir was a bell that was famous for its ability to recover stolen property. The common

[1]Rev. H. T. Ellacombe, in *Church Bells of Devon*, Exeter, 1872.

people believed that if anyone was wicked enough to swear falsely upon it, the muscles of his mouth would contract at one side until the opening reached his ear. The truth of this was never tested, however, because no one was ever known to swear falsely upon it, though it was very frequently in use.

It is said that the last time it was used for this purpose was about the year 1834. "A farmer had his house broken into, and was robbed of twenty pounds. He applied for the bell, as he suspected the robbery to have been committed by persons in his neighborhood. It was brought with much ceremony to his house; and after mass on the following Sunday was the time appointed for the whole parish to assemble, and 'clear themselves from suspicion upon the bell.' On Saturday night preceding this ordeal, the farmer was frightened by a heavy crash at the window, which was broken in. He feared his days were numbered; but after waiting some time in great terror, all became quiet. On lighting a candle to see what had occurred, he found, to his great astonishment, that his twenty pounds— even the identical notes, tied with the same string— had been thrust in through the broken pane, and were on the floor! Of course there was no occasion for using the bell on the following day. Thereafter, the keepers of the bell refused all applications made for its use, because of religious scruples on the subject, chiefly caused by the above incident."

We do not hear so much of the "bell oath" in English bell lore. The sacred bells of the English were kept high upon the churches, where they could not easily be reached or carried about. And perhaps because they were kept so high up in the air, the English people of the Middle Ages thought their church bells had miraculous power over storms and evil spirits of the air.[1] These larger bells of the English served the entire community at once, while the smaller, portable bells of the Irish served individuals in a more personal way.

Some of these legends seem childish, even to children of modern times; but it would be difficult to say how much their bells meant to these people in the hard lives they were forced to lead.

The fact that bells came to them with Christianity, and were so soon invested with a deep religious meaning, together with the naturally weird qualities of bell sounds, must have done much to foster that rich Irish imagination which is still contributing so greatly to the literature of the world.

[1]This phase will be discussed in the chapter on "The Baptism of Bells," p. 84.

## CHAPTER VII

## BELL MAKING

The earliest Christian bells were made of pieces of metal riveted together into a four-sided shape. Figure 29 shows a very common pattern by which the sheet iron was cut. It was bent along the dotted lines, and when the sides were riveted, the result was a shape somewhat similar to our modern cowbells. Figure 30 shows three ways of fastening the clapper into place. In figure 32 is seen the row of rivets along the side of one of these ancient bells.

Sometimes copper and perhaps other metals were beaten into the desired form, and riveted. Figure 31 shows a rounded form with rivets in the side.

So long as these methods of bell making were followed, the bells, even church bells, were not very large. But when someone thought of melting metal and molding it into shape (as the ancient Chinese had done, centuries before), bells of much greater size and finer quality could be made. Thus there opened up a new and interesting field for European bell makers, and since then practically all church bells have been cast. This means that the melted metal is poured or cast into a mold to make it the desired shape, and left in the mold until it becomes cool and hard.

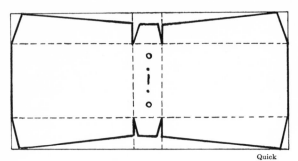

Quick

FIG. 29.  *Pattern for making bells of sheet iron*

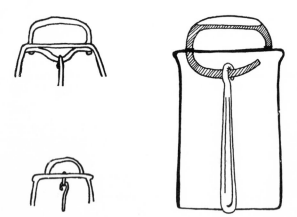

FIG. 30.  *Early methods of attaching handle and clapper to bell*

The place where bells are cast is called a "foundry," and the art of casting them, the "art of bell founding."

The development of this art not only enabled the founders to make bells of enormous size and weight, but it gave them an opportunity to mix metals by melting them together, until they learned by experiment what mixtures of metal would give the best tone. "Bell metal" is a mixture of copper and tin, with four or five times as much copper as tin; and sometimes a little zinc and lead are also added. The bells in the time of the reign of Henry III had twice as much copper as tin; in the Assyrian bronze bells shown on page 22, ten times as much copper as tin was used. But experience has proved that about four or five times as much copper as tin is the best combination to produce a good ringing

FIG. 31. *Seventh-century bell, with rounded form and rivets*

FIG. 32. *Early church bell, with rivets in side*

tone; ·and this mixture is made to vary according to the kind of tone desired. If too much tin is used, the metal will be too brittle, and will crack.

Although there are many stories of silver and gold being added to bell metal "to sweeten the tone," the value of such additions is only a myth. Bells have been made of silver, but they are not very resonant. Steel also has been used for the casting of bells, but it is not very satisfactory. Bells have been cast of glass, with a considerable thickness of the material, and these give a very fine sound, but they are too brittle to be practicable.

Since the bells of early Christianity were so closely associated with the church, and were looked upon as being sacred, it was natural that the first bell foundries should be set up in the religious houses. In some instances the bells were actually cast in the church. The casting was done with elaborate ceremonials, the priests, abbots, and often the bishops being the master founders. One of the ceremonies was that of blessing the furnace in which the metal was melted, probably to insure that the metals would mix well and produce a good ringing tone. The brethren stood around the furnace, arranged in processional order, and chanted the Psalm containing these verses:

"Praise Him with trumpet sound; praise Him with psaltery and harp.
Praise Him with timbrel and dance: praise Him with stringed instruments and pipe.

Praise Him with loud cymbals; praise Him with high
sounding cymbals.
Let everything that hath breath praise Jehovah."

Then followed certain prayers, after which the
molten metal was blessed, and God was asked to
infuse into it His grace and overshadow it with
His power, for the honor of the saint to whom
the bell was to be dedicated, and whose name it
was to bear.[1]

The early bell founders were proud of their work,
and some of them became very famous. They
stamped on the bells either their names or symbols
which stood for them. Usually the date was added,
and often a sentence or verse which ascribed a per-
sonality to the bell.

In the north aisle of the nave of York Cathedral
is a stained-glass window, called the "bell founder's
window," which shows something of the bell-making
process in those early days. This window was given
to the cathedral by the bell founder Richard Tunnoc,
who died in 1330. It is impossible to show the
wonderful colors of the glass, but the outlines are
shown in figure 33 (p. 63). The design on the left
represents the method of forming the core, or inner
mold, for the bell. One man turns a handle like a
grindstone, while another, with a long, crooked
tool, shapes the clay after the manner of the potter
at his wheel. There are two bells on the floor.

[1] John R. Fryar, in "The Functions of Church Bells in Old England,"
in *American Ecclesiastical Review*, Philadelphia, 1910.

The figures on the right are working with a furnace fanned by a bellows, and are evidently running the molten metal. A boy stands on the bellows, and, steadying himself by the rod above, jumps up and down on the bellows, to force the draft into the furnace and thus keep the metal heated. The entire window is ornamented with bells.

The practice of bell founding gradually passed into the hands of workers who cast the bells outside of the monasteries. In England some of the early founders traveled about the country and set up temporary foundries to cast bells wherever they were wanted, for the transportation of a large bell was a difficult matter in those days.[1] The art gradually spread over England, Belgium, and Holland, and little by little the principles of shape and metal mixture for the most beautiful and best toned bells were gradually worked out.

The early art of bell founding left a reminder in the names of families who took their surnames from their occupations. In reading through early English documents one finds the names "Robert Belgetter, 1333; Thomas Belgetter; Daniel Bellfounder, 1443," which doubtless applied to men in the bell-founding profession.[2]

A cast bell is nothing more than a layer of metal which has been run into a space between two molds:

[1] Traveling bell founders were known as late as the 19th century, when railroads made this unnecessary.

[2] It is probable that the modern surname "Bell" resulted, in some cases, from a shortening of those professional names.

FIG. 33. *A part of the "bell founder's window," in York Cathedral*

Fig. 34. *Making the "core"*

an inner mold called the core, and an outer mold called the cope.

This is one of the early methods of bell founding: A block of wood was first cut the exact shape and size to fill up the inside of the bell that was desired. This was the core. The core was then covered with wax, and the layer of wax was just as thick as the bell was to be. This was the wax model. Outside the model came the cope, made of clay, or hard earth, which would hold its shape when dry. When the earth was quite dry, wax was heated until it melted, and the melted wax was allowed to run out. The cavity, which was the shape of the wax model, was then filled with molten metal from the furnace, and allowed to cool. If a design of letters or ornament on the outside of the bell was desired, the design was made of strips of wax laid upon the wax model before the earthen cope was put on, and the same design appeared on the metal bell.

A modern bell maker would think this method very old-fashioned, indeed; but in the early days of bell founding it was considered very wonderful.

A later method made it possible to produce better and even larger bells, and the following is the method by which most of the large bells now hanging in Europe were made.

Instead of the core being made of a block of wood, as in the previous method, a framework of bricks was built, hollow inside, so a fire could be made under it (see Fig. 34). Covering this brick framework came a layer of clay which could be shaped to the desired form for the inside of the bell. This entire core was made to revolve on a spindle, in the same way a lump of clay revolves on a potter's wheel, and a crook, shaped something like the cut on the right and attached to the spindle, scraped off the surface of the clay, leaving it smooth and the exact shape desired for the inside. (See clay core in Fig. 34.)

When the core was dry it was smeared with grease; then upon this greased core the "false bell" or model was made of plastic clay. Another crook— a larger one—was fastened into the top of the spindle, which, as it whirled around, made the outside of the clay bell smooth. Many metal bells show lines running around the bell. These lines were caused by the revolving crook which shaped the clay model.

The inscriptions and ornaments were then molded in wax upon the clay bell. When the model was

FIG. 35. *Modern perforated molding case*

quite dry it was smeared with grease, to keep the next layer from sticking to it. Then fine clay was covered over this very carefully, to fill up the tiny holes in the design. Then came coarse clay, until the solid cope was formed.

A fire was made under the core, and everything baked hard. The layers of grease and the wax inscriptions were steamed out, leaving a little space between the model and the clay forms above and beneath it. This made the model loose enough to come out easily, leaving its exact shape in the now hollow space between the core and the cope. The molten metal was then poured into the cavity.

Figure 35 shows the form of a modern perforated molding case made by the Meneely Bell Company, in Troy, New York. They describe its use in the quotation on the following page.

"Porous loam and other substances compose the material which is put upon the cases in varying thickness, to which the necessary form and finish are given by the use of sweep patterns, shaped in such a manner as to secure, by their revolution about a common center, surfaces corresponding to the outer and inner portions of the intended bell. As bell metal shrinks in cooling, the inner case, before the loam is placed upon it, is wrapped about with straw rope, the charring of which, by the heat of the metal in pouring, gives room for the necessary contraction, and prevents the straining of the metal.

"The molds are closed upon each other in a manner securing exact regularity of thickness in the space within. The metal is poured in at the head. The gases generated in the metal, and which, if allowed to remain in the molds, would produce an explosion, or at least cause a porous casting, find vent in the perforations.

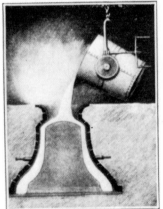

*Children's Magazine*

FIG. 36. *Section of bell mold. Pouring metal into the mold*

"These cases, also, to the advantage of the bell, allow it to cool, after casting, in such a manner as to secure precise uniformity throughout."

The actual casting of a bell, or the pouring of the metal, takes only a few minutes, but the preparation for it often requires many weeks of careful labor. In the casting of a small bell the bell metal may be poured as is shown in figure 36, but large bells are cast in deep pits. Turn to pages 171 and 175 for pictures of the casting and recasting of one of England's famous bells, "Big Ben."

If the mold is damp, or not of the proper temperature, or if the metal is poured before it is hot enough, or if gases collect and cannot escape, the bell may be porous and easily cracked. In the case of a very large bell, it may require a week or more for it to cool before it can be removed from the pit. A bell weighing a ton would be too hot to touch for two or three days, but one weighing only five hundred pounds could be dug out of the pit the following day. When a bell cracks it may be broken up and melted and cast again. Hundreds of old bells now hanging in the bell towers have been cast more than once, and many of them several times.

When an old bell is recast it is customary to take a "rubbing" of the inscription and reproduce it on the new bell.

The typical church bell has a clapper of metal which swings from the upper inside of the bell. The clapper must be made with its weight properly adjusted to the size of the bell. If it is too light, it will not draw the proper tone of the bell; if too heavy, it will in time crack or otherwise injure the bell.

The different parts of a bell are shown in figure 37, and are distinguished as follows: the bottom edge is called the "mouth" of the bell; just above this is the thick rim, or "sound bow," where the clapper strikes; above that is the concave "waist"; above that is the "shoulder," where the inscription is

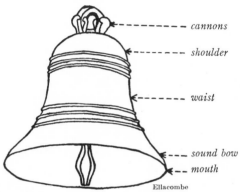

cannons

shoulder

waist

sound bow
mouth

Ellacombe

FIG. 37. *An ancient bell, showing names of parts*

usually placed. The part above the angle of the shoulder is known as the "crown," and to the highest part of the crown the loops or "cannons" are fixed. The bell is suspended by means of the cannons.[1]

At first each church had only one bell. Later, other bells were added to distinguish between the different services, and each bell had a different tone from the others. In some churches three different bells sounded the first three notes of the scale; and where five bells were needed, they were tuned, as

[1]Many modern bells, however, are suspended by other means.

nearly as was possible, to the first five notes of the major scale.

Then began the art of tuning bells. This involved problems, for, as one can imagine, it was no simple matter to cast a bell and have it come out of the mold with exactly the desired tone when it was struck.

Bell makers very early discovered that of two bells which appeared to be of the same size on the outside, the thicker one had the higher tone. Also that the larger the bell, the lower the tone, if the thickness was the same. So they made large bells for low tones, and smaller ones for high tones.

They found that a bell which sounded number 2 of the scale weighed about one-eighth less than number 1; and that number 3 weighed about one-eighth less than number 2. So by weighing the amount of metal to go into each bell, they could regulate the tones. When they used wax models they weighed the wax, and made cores of different sizes to correspond.

The making of a good bell, however, is not so simple as it may seem. As the art of bell founding developed, it was found that a bell of given weight must also have a certain diameter and thickness in order to produce the best tone. For example, a bell which weighs two thousand pounds, according to one authority[1] should be four feet in diameter at the mouth, and three and one-half inches thick

[1]A. A. Johnston, "Clocks, Carillons and Bells," in *Journal of the Society of Arts*, London, 1901.

at the sound bow; while a hundred-pound bell should be eighteen inches in diameter, and one and one-fourth inches thick. The heavier the bell, the thicker it must be; the lighter, the thinner. It should be thickest at the sound bow where it is struck, and taper upward to one-third of that thickness. If a bell were of uniform thickness throughout it would sound dull, without the desired tone quality or resonance. Figure 38 shows a cross section of the metal's thickness in a well-shaped bell.

When a bell comes out of the mold, if it does

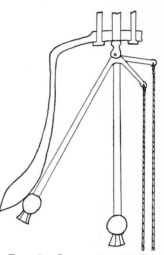

Fig. 38. *Cross section of bell to show thickness of metal*

not have exactly the required tone its pitch can be changed a little by using a file or whetstone. If the tone is too low, it can be raised a little by grinding off the lower edge of the bell; if too high, it can be made a little thinner with a file, and the tone lowered. If a bell comes out of a mold exactly in tune, it is said to have a "maiden peal."

William G. Rice[1] expresses the tuning of bells thus: "In broad terms the pitch, or note, of bells

[1] In *Carillons of Belgium and Holland,* 1914.

is determined by diameter. Their timbre, or quality of sound, is affected by their general shape, the thickness of their various parts, together with the alloy of which they are made. Their volume, or possible loudness of tone, depends chiefly upon their size and weight. The pitch can be lowered by

John Taylor & Co.

FIG. 39.    *Tuning a bell*

lengthening the bottom diameter, and raised by shortening such diameter. Small changes of diameter may be made by filing or turning off the inside at the bottom swell, thus lengthening the diameter or by cutting off a slight portion of the rim, thus shortening the diameter."

Bell makers have a revolving cutter which pares off very thin slices of the metal at the required place. A modern method of tuning bells is shown in figure 39.

A peculiarity of bells is that they give off more than one sound when struck, and what we hear is really a combination of sounds. So in order to sound well, bells must not only be in tune with each other, but each bell must be in tune with itself. A perfect bell rings its main note when struck by the clapper at the bottom or sound bow; when struck

at a point one-eighth of a bell's height above this,
the sound should be a third above the main tone;
three-quarters of the way up, the tone should be a
fifth above the main tone, and at the shoulder the
tone should be an octave above. Thus the bell,
when properly struck, gives a perfect chord. There
is also what is called the "hum tone," which is an
octave below the main tone.

The making of a good bell is a gratifying invest-
ment of time, and it gives good value for the money
it costs. There are very few articles which are as
good as new after being used for several centuries.
But even if the bell becomes cracked, it is still worth
two-thirds of its original value, for the chief cost is
the metal in it, and that can be broken up, melted
again, and recast.

When one considers all the problems involved in
producing a bell of good tone quality "in tune with
itself," regardless of any special pitch, and when
to these problems are added the complications and
cross-complications which are involved in making
a series of bells to definite pitches in tune with each
other, one cannot fail to realize that bell making
is indeed a great and intricate art.

# CHAPTER VIII

## INSCRIPTIONS

As soon as bell makers learned to cast bells instead of hammering them into shape or riveting pieces of iron together, possibilities for decoration opened, for it was not a difficult matter to cast letters and ornamental designs on the bells. This was done by making these designs on the wax or clay models which gave the exact shape of the future bell, and when the model was removed and the molten metal poured into the cavity, it took the exact form of the model—shape, letters, and all. It was most natural that the maker of such an important thing as a bell should wish to inscribe something upon it.

At first the inscriptions were in Latin, because the first bell foundries were in the monasteries (or closely connected with them) and were managed by the priests or monks, who were very learned in Latin. The church services at that time were in Latin, too. Some of the bells with Latin inscriptions, and dates of many centuries ago, have been preserved in the old churches.

The people of the Middle Ages not only thought their church bells had miraculous power, and gave them Christian names, but they also personified them by letting the inscriptions read as if the bells were speaking. For instance, the Latin inscription on an old Belgian bell reads, when translated, "I was cast in the year of our Lord 1523."

Most of the oldest bells which have been preserved bear only the names of the saints to whom they are dedicated.   Later a few praise expressions were added, and by the late sixteenth century such inscriptions appeared as *Jubilate Deo Salvatori nostro*, and *Cantabo laudes tuas Domini.*

Sometimes the inscription also states some of the uses of the bell.   One inscription on an old English bell reads: *Laudo Deum verum, plebem voco, conjugo clerum; defunctos ploro, pestem fugo, festa decoro; funera plango, fulgura frango, Sabbata pango; excito lentos, dissipo ventos, paco cruentos.*   When translated it means: "I praise the true God, I summon the people, I assemble the clergy; I mourn the dead, I put the plague to flight, I grace the feast; I wail at the funeral, I abate the lightning, I proclaim the Sabbath; I arouse the lazy, I scatter the winds, I soften the cruel."

An old storm bell in Durham bears a Latin inscription meaning, "Do thou, Peter, when rung, calm the angry waves," suggesting something of the power which was attributed to church bells in those days.

One of the bells in St. Mary's Church in Oxford has a long inscription in musical notation.   Around the crown are the words:

+ BE . YT . KNOWNE . TO . ALL . THAT . DOTH . ME . SEE . THAT . NEWCOMBE . OF . LEISCESTER . MADE . ME .        1612 .

Lower down on the bell are two lines of music, one line going all the way around the bell, the other line only part of the way. The notes are of lozenge form, and are placed on a staff of five lines. The music is in madrigal style, and is neither chime music nor psalm tune. This inscription has long baffled the efforts of those who have tried to interpret it.

A German bell of the Middle Ages bears the Latin legend which means: "I am the voice of life: I call you: Come and pray."

It seems that by the early seventeenth century bell makers began to use their own language for inscriptions. There is a bell in Lincoln, England, dated 1604, with these words: "I sweetly toiling men do call to taste on meats that feed the soule."

From that time on, many inscriptions were in English. Most of them were short, such as "God save the Church." One which dates as far back as 1595 advises: "Embrace true museck."

An old bell in Shropshire says: "Iesvs bee ovr speede 1618."[1]

Notice the spelling of this one: "My Sound the Meane Yet doth aspire To sound men's Harts and raise them Hire, 1622."

The inscription on this one in the York Minster is almost like that of the Lincoln bell:

> Sweetly tolling Men do call
> To taste on food that feeds the soul. 1627.

[1]Many bells from different places, and of different dates, have this inscription.

Another: "God Save the King 1639." There are numberless bells to be found throughout England with this inscription.

Here is a mixture of English and Latin, and a rime as well:

> God send us all the bliss of heaven
> Anno Dni. 1627.

A "passing bell" reads:

> + all men that hear my mornfvll soonde
> Repent before yov ly in ground.   York 1645.

Cardinal Wolsey brought a bell from Touray which was recast in 1670 with this inscription:

> By Wolsey's gift I measure time for all;
> To mirth, to grief, to church, I serve to call.

A bell at Coventry, dated 1675, reads:

> I ring at 6 to let men know
> When too and from thair worke to goe.

Another one of the seventeenth century:

> I ring to sermon with a lusty bome
> That all may come and none may stop at home.

Here is a favorite legend, which may be found on many old bells:

> I to the church the living call
> And to the grave do summon all.

As time passed, it seems that the bell founders fell more generally into the custom of putting their own names on the bells, just as most instrument makers do now.   Here is one which rimes with the date:

⊗ Matthew ⊗ Bagley ⊗ Made ⊗ me
16 93.
(Each ⊗ represents the picture of a coin.)

At first the inscriptions were designed by the priests, but later, when the bell maker or the church warden who ordered the bell also decided on the inscription, some of them became ridiculous and undignified, such as these:

> John Eyer gave twenty pound
> To meck mee a losty sound.

> At prayer times my voice I'll raise
> And sound to my subscribers' praise.

> Samuel Knight made this ring
> In Binstead steeple for to ding.   1695.

A bell dated 1718 bears this inscription: "Prosperity to those who love bells," and one of 1720: "When you me ring, I'll sweetly sing."   This bell was evidently one of a set of chimes:

> When you us ring
> We'll sweetly sing 1737.   (Shropshire)

A pleasing short one reads: "Peace and good neighborhood—1716."

> 1770—In tuneful peals your joys I'll tell
> Your griefs I'll publish in a knell.

1772 — Although I am both light and small
        I will be heard above you all.
1773 — I mean to make it understood
        That though I'm little, yet I'm good.

The maker of this one must have been sure of its sound before it was cast: "If you have a judicious ear you'll own my voice sweet and clear. London 1777."

In the church of St. Michael's, Coventry, a bell proclaims: "Music is medicine to the mind."

An ancient fire bell in Sherborne Abbey, which has announced fires for many centuries, has this quaint inscription:

> Lord, quench this furious flame;
> Arise; run; help; put out the same.

Many people gave bells to the churches, either in gratitude for having been guided home by them, or for other reasons. In some cases they wished to have their own names cast into the bell. On a bell in Alderton which was donated to the church by Mary Neale, are these words:

> I'm given here to make a peal,
> And sound the praise of Mary Neale.

No one knows, however, whether this was done at Mary's order or as a compliment to her.

The inscription on a bell in Glasgow Cathedral, which was recast in 1790, gives its own history: "In the year of Grace 1583, Marcus Knox, a merchant in Glasgow, zealous for the interest of the

Reformed Religion, caused me to be fabricated in Holland, for the use of his fellow citizens of Glasgow, and placed me with solemnity in the tower of their Cathedral. My function was announced by the impress on my bosom: ME AUDITO, VENIAS, DOCTRINAM SANCTAM UT DISCAS, and I was taught to proclaim the hours of unheeded time. One hundred and ninety-five years had I sounded these awful warnings, when I was broken by the hands of inconsiderate and unskilful men. In the year 1790, I was cast into the furnace, refounded at London, and returned to my sacred vocation. Reader! thou also shalt know a resurrection; may it be to eternal life! Thomas Mears *fecit*, London, 1790."

Every bell maker had his own professional mark. Some of these are shown in figure 40. Not only the inscriptions and trade-marks, but the ornamentation on many of the old bells is very interesting. The best bell founders took great pride in their work, and some of the ancient bells have ornamentation that is exceedingly beautiful. Handsome capitals of various forms were used, also vine and fleur-de-lis borders, and royal arms and emblems. The crosses, word stops, and lettering frequently gave evidence of a high artistic taste, as may be seen in the drawings on page 82 (Fig. 41).

A study of the inscriptions on old European bells gives an interesting insight into the lives and thoughts of the people of the olden times. These words and decorations are written in metal which,

Ellacombe

Ellacombe

FIG. 40. *Trade-marks and figures on early English bells*

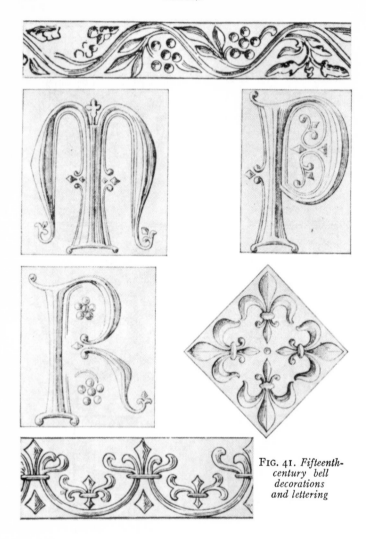

FIG. 41. *Fifteenth-century bell decorations and lettering*

unless melted by fire, will continue to bear their records for the information of those who live a thousand years from now. They should be preserved with every care, —

> Those bells "that tell a thousand tales,
>   Sweet tales of olden times,
>   And ring a thousand memories."

## CHAPTER IX

## THE BAPTISM OF BELLS

One of the strangest things in the history of bells is the custom of baptizing and christening them, after the manner of baptizing human beings. And yet it is not so strange, either, when we think of how bells were honored and cherished. The birth of a new bell really was a thing of great importance. Even yet, new church bells are often hung with some kind of celebration; and there are few persons who can listen for the first ringing of a new bell, and hear it without a feeling of awe and wonder and reverence,—the voice that has never been heard in the world before!

The people of nearly all countries have ascribed to bells, at some time, either human or divine attributes. Long ago it was a common belief that bells shivered and quaked at disasters, or when crimes were committed. In this connection the Celtic bell lore[1] will be recalled. The sound of the consecrated bells in the church of St. Stephen, in the early seventh century, drove away the army of Clotaire, as the walls of Jericho had fallen down at the sound of trumpets. When St. Hilda died, bells were heard to ring seven miles away, and there are several stories of how bells in distant

[1]See chap. VI, p. 47.

churches tolled of their own accord upon the death of certain bishops. It is therefore not so surprising that the Europeans of the Middle Ages should wish to baptize their bells with religious ceremonies, and that they believed them to possess miraculous powers after these ceremonies.

The service of baptism was held in order that the bells might have power to "act as preservatives against thunder and lightning, and hail and wind, and storms of every kind, and that they may drive away evil spirits." In those days it was a very common belief that the air was filled with evil spirits which could be frightened away by certain sounds. Nearly all primitive people have believed in evil spirits, because it was such an easy way to explain things which they did not understand; and it is not surprising that even civilized people held for a long time to a belief which gave them an excuse to put the blame of such things as bad tempers and illness upon something other than themselves. Some of the evil spirit superstitions were cherished by the Greeks.[1]

In the minds of many the ringing sound of metal had, naturally, a power over these evil spirits, and when a bell was baptized and consecrated it immediately became their most dreaded enemy. An old English writer has given us an idea of how evil spirits were supposed to dislike the sound of bells: "It is said, the evil spirytes that ben in the region

[1]See p. 26.

of the ayre, doubte moche when they here the bells
rongen; and this is the cause why the bells ringen
when it thondreth, and whan grote tempeste and
to rages of wether happen, to the end that the
fiends and wyched spirytes should ben abashed
and flee and cease of the movynge of tempests."

In the year 789 Charlemagne forbade the baptism
of bells; but it was a custom so revered by the people
that it was later revived, and baptized bells were
sacred to the people and for hundreds of years following were believed to have miraculous power.

In medieval days, when the new bell was finished
the date for its baptism was set, some important
person in the community was chosen as the god-
father or godmother of the bell, and usually a white
christening robe was made for it, as for an infant.
The form of the ceremony which took place is somewhat as follows:

The new bell is brought into the church and
hung at a height convenient for the priest to reach.
On a table near by are placed the sacred vessels
containing oil, salt, and incense; also water and
napkins. Linen cloths are placed underneath the
bell to receive the water used in washing it. The
church dignitaries in their formal robes stand near
the bell, and the choir is ready. First, psalms are
sung; the officiating priest or bishop (as the case
may be) blesses the water and salt, and the bell is
washed and wiped with a napkin (see Fig. 42).
This bathing with the salt water is to make the bell

FIG. 42. *Bell baptism in the Middle Ages: washing the bell*

demon proof. More psalms are recited; then the
priest dips his right thumb into the vessel of sacred
oil and makes the sign of the cross on the bell with
his thumb, at the same time saying a prayer. This
oil is wiped off and the choir sings the 28th Psalm.
During this psalm the priest repeats some Latin
words: *Sancti ficetur et consecretur, Domine, signum
istud in nomine Patris et Filii et Spiritus Sancti*,
etc. (which means that he is consecrating the bell
in the name of the Father, Son, and Holy Spirit),
calling the name of the bell and of the saint to

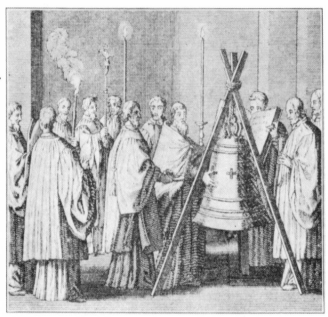

FIG. 43.   *Bell baptism in the Middle Ages: blessing the bell*

whom it is dedicated.  While reciting these Latin
words the priest anoints the bell eleven times
with more oil.  Then, after a prayer invoking blessings on the bell, it is solemnly "censed" (incense
burned under it), and the choir sings Psalm 76.
Then there is another prayer, more chanting, and
the priest in grave silence makes the sign of the
cross on the bell, covers it with a white garment,
and the ceremony is over.  Figures 42, 43, and 44,
taken from a very old book, show the three stages
in a bell-blessing ceremony of the Middle Ages.

Fig. 44. *Bell baptism in the Middle Ages: censing the bell*

Nothing in those days could exceed the pomp
and solemnity of a bell-christening service. Great
sums of money were expended, even in poor villages,
and costly feasts were given. In the accounts of
the church wardens of St. Laurence, Reading, we
find the following memorandum, dated 1499:
"Payed for halowing of the bell named Harry vj s.
viij d. And over that, Sir William Symes, Richard
Clech, and Mistress Smyth being godfaders and
godmoder at the consecracyon of the same bell,
and beryng all other costs of the suffragan."

Indulgences were sometimes granted at the consecration of a bell. In 1490 the bishop of Ely granted "40 days' indulgence to all who would say 5 Paternosters and 5 Aves at the sound of the Great bell, and 5 Aves at the sound of the small one."[1]

One of the prayers in the medieval ceremony of bell blessing is as follows: "Grant that wheresoever this holy bell, thus washed, baptized and blessed, shall sound, all deceits of Satan, all danger of whirlwind, thunder and lightning, and tempests may be driven away . . . . and the fiery darts of the devil made to fly backward at the sound thereof."

In Longfellow's *Golden Legend* we have an account of storm fiends being commanded by their master to destroy the Strasburg Cathedral bells. They fail, and the storm fiends attribute their failure to the fact that the bells have been baptized[2]:

> All thy thunders here are harmless!
> For these bells have been anointed
> And baptized with holy water.
> They defy our utmost power.

Consecrated bells were also supposed to have the power, merely by their ringing, to put out fire as well as to abate storms and protect the community from lightning and pestilence. Many a bell of the Middle Ages bore the Latin inscription *Frango fulgura!* which means "I break the lightning." The records of Old St. Paul's Church in

[1] H. B. Walters, in *The Church Bells of England*, Oxford, 1912.
[2] See poem on p. 421.

London show that the sacristan was bidden to "ringe the hallowed belle in great tempests and lightnings." In many places the ringers hurried to the church belfry as soon as threatening clouds appeared, so that the storm might be broken up before it became severe.

During the last century a traveler in the Tyrolese Alps wrote: "Bell ringing as the companion of thunderstorms is a permanent institution here. The man in charge of the chapel is on the lookout for thunderstorms, begins the bell ringing and continues to ring until the storm passes."[1] It is recorded that as late as 1852 the bishop of Malta gave orders for the church bells to be rung for an hour to allay a gale of wind; and it is said that even at the present day in France it is not uncommon for church bells to be rung to ward off the effects of lightning.

The Swiss have a curious tradition that all the baptized bells in Switzerland take a trip to Rome every year during Passion Week, and get back in time to be rung on Easter morning. In other countries, too, this story is cherished, and in some villages the return of the bells on Easter morning is celebrated with great festivity and merrymaking.

The uneducated man in Lithuania believes that a newly made church bell emits no sound until it has been consecrated and baptized. The Lithuanians also have the poetical belief that the souls

[1]Rev. H. T. Ellacombe, in *Church Bells of Devon.*

of the deceased are floated into heaven on the sounds of baptized bells.[1]

Many bells have had pet names by which the common people called them, such as Great Tom (Oxford), Big Ben (London), Old Kate (Lincoln), but in the early days of England every church bell

FIG. 45. *Baptism of four bells for Notre Dame Cathedral (Paris, 1856)*

was supposed to be christened with a religious name. There is an account, however, of the great bell of the Lateran Church (Rome) being named in the year 968 by the pope, John XIII, only for himself, John. Comparatively few of the great number of baptized bells in medieval days are still hanging in their ancient belfries, and on some of these it is difficult to trace the characters which spell their names.

[1] Carl Engel, in *Musical Myths and Facts.*

*Illustrated London News,* Nov. 9, 1878

FIG. 46. *Blessing of the bells of St. Paul's Cathedral*

The ceremonies of bell baptism were discontinued in Protestant countries after the Reformation. It was impossible, however, for the people to be

FIG. 47.   *Dedication of the great bell for Cologne Cathedral,*
*November, 1924*

indifferent to the arrival in their midst of a new
bell or of a peal of bells.   The day was observed as
a holiday, with great merrymaking.   Sometimes
the donor of a peal of bells gave orders that the

largest bell was to be set upside down on the ground
and filled with punch, of which the entire village
was permitted to partake; and the occasion was
often one of revelry and indecorous excess.

In Catholic countries, however, the baptism of
church bells has been continued to the present day.
The bells thus consecrated become spiritual things,
and cannot be rung without the consent of the
church authorities. Figure 45 (p. 92) pictures a
baptism ceremony in Paris in 1856.

Although Protestant bells are no longer baptized,
they still undergo some form of dedication. In
England it is customary for new bells to be dedicated by the bishop of the diocese. Figure 46 (p. 93)
shows the blessing of one of England's best known
chimes, those of St. Paul's Cathedral in London, in
1878. At present in nearly all Christian countries
church bells are dedicated with reverent ceremonies
and suitable hymns; not, however, for any supernatural power which the bells may derive from it, but
for the effect which such dignified ceremonial has on
the attitude of the people. Figure 47 is a photograph of the dedication of the great bell for Cologne
Cathedral in November, 1924.

## CHAPTER X

## DIFFERENT USES OF CHURCH BELLS

The important part which the church bell played in the lives of the people of Old England is perhaps best shown by the number of ways in which church bells were used. A quaint old writer thus briefly states their uses:

> To call the fold to church in time,
> We chime.
> When joy and mirth are on the wing,
> We ring.
> When we lament a departed soul,
> We toll.

Church bells not only called the people to the various services of the church, but also rang for different parts of the service, reminded the people of the different days in the church year and the anniversaries that were to be remembered, announced the hours of the day, and told of the important things that happened in the community.[1]

[1] A rich parish took pride in having separate bells, distinct in tone, for the different uses. These bells were put in different places about the church and were called by different Latin names, according to their uses. Here are some of the names given to distinguish the different bells:

The *campana* was the big bell that hung in the steeple and called the people to church. It was called *campana* from the name of the city in Italy where lived the bishop who first used a big church bell. The *squilla* was a small bell in the choir, rung at various parts of the service as a guide to the singers, and also to announce the different parts of the service to the congregation. Later this bell was called the

The big tower bell served many purposes, and rang so often during the day that it must have been bewildering to one who did not follow the meaning of all the signals. In many places it rang early in the morning to waken the people of the parish. This was called the *Gabriel bell*.

All the church services during the day were announced by the church bell. The *Sermon bell* indicated that there would be a sermon; the *Pardon bell* was tolled just before and after the service, at which time the worshipers prayed for pardon of their sins; the *Pudding bell* was rung immediately after the service was over, and was supposed to give notice to the cook to prepare the dinner.

The *Sacring* or *Holy bell* (the same as the *Sanctus bell*) was rung to call attention to the more solemn parts of the mass. It is still used in Catholic churches. At a very important point in the service called the "elevation of the Host" it is rung and everyone in the church kneels at the signal. Formerly this little sacring bell was sometimes hung in a small turret outside the church, where it still may

*sanctus* bell, or holy bell, and it is still known by that name. *Dupla* was the name of the clock bell that told the hours of the day. (This was used as early as the days of Edward the Confessor.) The *cymbalium* was the bell in the cloister to give signals to the monks. *Nola* was another bell named for the man who first used church bells, for he was bishop of Nola. The *nola* seems to have been hung in the refectory, or monks' dining hall, and was probably the ancestor of our modern dinner bell. The *corrigiunculum* was rung when some one had to receive the punishment of flagellation, or whipping.

Parishes which could afford two big bells used one of them as the *campana*, or regular church bell, and the other one, called the *signum*, was rung at least eight times a day for various announcements to the people of the parish.

be seen in some of the old churches. Often it was
hung inside the church. Sometimes the sacring
bell developed into a whole chime of bells. At

From James, *In and Out of the Old Missions of California*

FIG. 48.   *A wheel of sacring bells*

one place in England it was remembered that "in
the tyme of the old law, eighteen little bells hung in
the middle of the church which the pulling of one
bell made them all ring, which was done at the
elevation of the Host." Wheels of sacring bells
are said to be very common in Spain. Figure 48
shows one brought from Spain to America, which
was used in a California mission.

In some places the bells rang to announce that
someone was being baptized. There are still parishes where it has been usual, from time unknown,
to ring the *Christening peal*.

The Angelus is a Roman Catholic devotion in
memory of the visit of the angel who told Mary

she was to be the mother of Jesus.  *Angelus* is the
Latin word for angel.   The text of the Latin verses
is recited three times a day in the Catholic church.
A bell called the *Angelus bell* is rung at the same
time, and all who hear it are supposed to stop their
work and repeat these verses in devotion to Mary.
The hours for this devotion are (since Louis XI
so ordered in 1472) 6:00 A.M., noon, and 6:00 P.M.

Gramstorff Bros., Inc., Malden, Mass.

FIG. 49.   "*The Angelus,*" *from the painting by Millet*

The signal is three strokes, thrice repeated, followed
by nine in succession.

This was the "bidding to the people, to the sick
in bed, and to the healthy, to those at home, and
to those abroad, that they should, as the sound
floated through the villages—the maiden in her
cottage and the laborer in the field—reverently
kneel and recite the allotted prayers, beginning
*Angelus Domini nuntiavit Marie;*[1] hence it was
called the *Angelus bell*. It was also called the
"Ave bell," and sometimes the name "Gabriel
bell" was applied to all three services. In Millet's
famous picture of the Angelus (see Fig. 49, p. 99)
a man and a woman working in the fields in France
have just heard the Angelus bell from the little
church in the distant village. Being good Catholics,
with bowed heads they are repeating the Latin
verses. This picture vividly illustrates the power of
bells in the daily lives of these people. The custom
is a beautiful one, and it seems a pity that other
churches have not some similar signal for a moment
of daily reverence.

In some parts of England the bells rang a muffled
peal on Holy Innocents Day, in memory of the
massacre of the early Christian martyrs. It was
called the *Holy Innocents bell*.

The believers in evil spirits thought that these
beings wandered around in the air waiting for an
ill person to die so they could pounce on his soul
while it was passing from the body to its resting
place. If, however, the baptized bells rang while

[1]Rev. H. T. Ellacombe, in *Church Bells of Devon.*

the person was dying, the evil spirits were frightened away and the soul could pass on in peace. The ringing of the bell at this time was called the *Passing bell*. This was much like the custom in ancient Greece of beating on brazen kettles while a person was dying, to scare away the furies.

The belief in this power of bells to help the departing soul led many people to give large sums of money for the support of bells. This was also one of the factors which encouraged the making of bells of monstrous size; for if bell tones could frighten away evil spirits, how much more effectual they would be if the bell were large and its tone far-reaching! It was ordered that all within hearing of the passing bell should pray for the soul of the dying.

The *Death knell* was rung when the person was really dead, and this custom lasted much longer than the custom of ringing the passing bell. The practice of tolling church bells at deaths and during funeral services is still very common even in this country, as a way of showing respect to the person who has died. It was the custom for the death knell to indicate, by a certain number of rings, whether it was a man, woman, or child who had died. The most common signal was three rings for a child, two times three for a woman, and three times three for a man, but the rule was not the same in all places.

Often a large bell was rung for adults and a small one for children: three strokes for a male, two for a female, then it was tolled for one hour.  Sometimes the age of the person who had died was also rung at the end of the death knell.

There is a story that a wicked squire died, and no death knell was rung because his spirit came and sat upon the bell so that all the ringers together could not toll it!

In most cathedrals a "muffled peal" is rung when a church dignitary dies.  This is produced by wrapping one side of the clapper in a thick pad so as to form an echo to the clear stroke of the other half, and this is considered the most magnificent effect which can be produced by bells.[1]

In a Wiltshire village in England it is still the custom to have the church bell ring out a joyous wedding peal, instead of the doleful tolling of the muffled knell, at the burial of a young maiden.

At one time in England it was the custom to ring the bells throughout the night on Hallowe'en, or "All-hallow-tide" as it was called, "for all Christian souls."  It proved to be very annoying.  Henry VIII wrote a letter to Archbishop Cranmer "against superstitious practices wherein the vigil and ringing of bells all the night on All-hallows-day at night are directed to be abolished, and the said vigil to have no watching or ringing."  The people must have been slow to give up this custom, which they evidently liked, for we read that later Queen Elizabeth ordered "that the superstitious ringing of bells at

[1] Mary J. Taber, in *Bells, an Anthology*, Boston, 1912.

All-hallow-tide, and on All-souls day, with the two nights next, before and after, be prohibited."

The *Curfew bell* for hundreds of years was a most important time teller, and is well known both in history and literature. The ringing of this bell dates as far back as the ninth century, when Alfred the Great ordered the inhabitants of Oxford to put out their fires every night at eight o'clock when the bell at Carfax rang. About two hundred years after this William the Conqueror enforced, all over England, this same custom which Alfred had started at Oxford, though some writers give William the credit of being the originator of the custom.

In those olden days the houses were heated by open fires. As matches had not been invented, it was difficult to start a new fire; so it became the custom to cover the red-hot coals with ashes in the evening before going to bed, and these coals would keep "alive" until morning. The new fire for the day could then be started merely by raking away the ashes and putting kindling wood on the coals. Finally it was found that if all the burning wood was pushed close against the back of the fireplace and carefully covered up with a kind of metal cap which kept out most of the air, the fire would be preserved as well as when the red coals were covered with ashes. The metal cap which was made for this purpose was called a fire cover, or in the French *couvre-feu*, which finally came to be pronounced "curfew." Figure 50 is a drawing

of an old decorated copper curfew. The one pictured here is about ten inches high and sixteen
inches wide.

If fires were allowed to burn late at night there
was great danger of the houses burning, for at that
time most of the houses were built of wood and
covered with thatch (or straw) which became dry
and burned very easily. But if all fires were put
out early there was less danger of houses burning

FIG. 50.   *A copper curfew*

at night. As the eight o'clock bell was the signal
to cover the fire with the curfew, it was naturally
called the curfew bell.

William the Conqueror found the curfew custom
also very helpful in checking nightly meetings where
his enemies might form plots against him; also in
helping to prevent surprise attacks from an enemy.

In London, about the fourteenth century, it was
unlawful for any armed person to wander about
the city after the curfew rang, and at Tamworth a
law was passed in 1390 which provided that "no
man, woman or servant should go out after the
ringing of the curfew, from one place to another,

unless they carried a light in their hands, under pain of imprisonment."

The curfew law was more or less enforced for many centuries, but it has gradually died out except in a few places. The custom was brought to America by the Pilgrim Fathers, and there are said to be a few towns in the New England States where it is still in use, the people being unwilling to give up this custom of their old homeland. In Charleston, South Carolina, as late as 1851, two bells rang every night, at eight and ten o'clock in summer and at seven and nine during the winter. The first bell was the signal for the young children to go to bed; at the second bell, the "watch" for the night was set, and after that no servant might step outside his master's house without a special permit.

At Oxford, England, the big bell in Christ Church, called "Great Tom," is given one hundred and one strokes every night at nine o'clock, which is probably a survival of Alfred's law of more than a thousand years ago.[1]

A regulation somewhat like the curfew law was made for a short time during the late World War. London and other cities had no street lights at night, lest they prove helpful to the enemy in their air raids.

Many poets have written about the curfew bell. A very famous poem, Gray's "Elegy in a Country Churchyard," begins

"The curfew tolls the knell of parting day,"

[1]See p. 103.

which suggests to the mind a definite picture, even before anything more is said. Thirty or forty years ago almost every school child heard recited a poem which related a tragic story of a woman whose lover was to be unjustly killed when the curfew rang. The refrain of "Curfew shall not ring tonight" became a familiar expression.

The *Pancake bell* is associated with the curfew bell, for on Shrove Tuesday the curfew bell was the signal which stopped the eating of pancakes. Shrove Tuesday (the Tuesday which comes forty days before Easter Sunday) was the day for eating pancakes; in much the same way we eat turkey and pumpkin pie on Thanksgiving, or hot-cross buns on Good Friday. On Shrove Tuesday the church bell rang at four o'clock in the morning as a signal for the people to prepare for the feast of Lent. "As a part of this preparation, they collected all the suet, lard and drippings in the house, and made it into pancakes, for this was the last day they might eat butter for forty days," and they wished to take full advantage of it. In some places the bell rang at midday as a signal to put the pancakes on the fire.

Shakespeare refers to "a pancake for Shrove Tuesday," and in *Poor Robin's Almanac* for 1684 we find the rime:

> Hark, I hear the Pancake Bell,
> And fritters make a gallant smell.

Sometimes this signal was called the "Fritters bell."
Another familiar rime will be recalled from an old
Mother Goose song:

> Pancakes and fritters
> Say the bells of St. Peters.

The apprentices were invited to join the family
in eating the pancakes for supper. When the curfew rang at eight o'clock (on this day it was called
the pancake bell), not another pancake could be
eaten for forty days. It is said that this custom
was observed so closely that in many places not
a pancake was left in town after eight o'clock.

The church bells were very useful in directing
people home on dark winter evenings in the days
when the lands were not inclosed, the forests were
dark, and the moors were wild and pathless.

Lomax[1] wrote: "In an English village a bride
had stolen forth upon her wedding day to hide in
the furze. Becoming frightened, she left the place
of concealment, and taking the wrong path, lost
herself on the common. Darkness came on with
heavy snow, and visions of robbers made the night
more dreadful to the bewildered girl. But hark!
Through the darkness comes the sound—never so
sweet as now—of the old church bell ringing for
curfew. Guided homeward by the welcome tone,
she fell on her knees in gratitude which lasted to
her dying hour; for her first act was to present a
chime of bells to the church that had so befriended

[1]Benjamin Lomax, in *Bells and Bell Ringers.*

her, her last to bequeath a sum of money to keep up the good old custom forever."

In various parts of the country there are records of people who lost their way and only found it, or were saved from danger or drowning, by hearing the evening bell. In gratitude many of them gave large sums of money to be used in paying the sexton to ring the bells at times when their sounds might be of service to some belated traveler, to give him the time of the night and some guidance in the right direction.

The evening bell is still rung in some parishes during the winter months when darkness comes so early and travelers are likely to lose their way. A bell at Kirton-in-Lindsay is still rung at seven o'clock in winter "on Tuesday to guide travelers from Gainsborough Market, on Thursday from Brigg Market, and on Saturday from Kirton market."

The *Fire bell* has been in use for ages. In these days the fire alarm is often a gong, and sometimes a shrieking whistle, but formerly the church bell was used to give notice of a fire. At Strasburg a large bell of eight tons' weight, known as the "Holy Ghost bell," is rung only when two fires are seen in the town at once.

A *Storm bell* warned travelers in the plains of storms approaching from the mountains; a *Gate bell* gave the signal for opening and closing the city gates.

Before clocks and watches came into general use, the workers in the fields were summoned to their labors by a bell which was rung at five o'clock each morning and seven in the evening, the latter indicating that the labors of the day were to cease. The bell which called laborers to their work was called the *Harvest bell* or the *Seeding bell*, according to the kind of labor to be done.

The ringing of the *Gleaning bell* is almost an obsolete custom. It was rung at nine o'clock in the morning and in the evening at five to mark the time when the gleaners could go over the fields to get what the harvesters had left. Women were often to be seen standing in the fields before nine o'clock, patiently waiting to hear the first stroke of the bell.

There seemed to be no stated time when workmen were supposed to quit work, and this had to be regulated by each community. Formerly the curfew bell rang at eight o'clock in all English towns. In 1469 an order was given by the London Council for the bells of Bow Church to be rung every night at nine o'clock, allowing the shops and taverns to remain open for an hour later than formerly. This was the signal for all tradesmen to shut their shops and let their apprentices go home. Of course the apprentices of London were offended if there was any delay in the ringing of the Bow bells, and there is an old print that represents them as saying to the clerk who is supposed to ring the bells:

> "Clerk of the Bow bells
>     With thy yellow locks,
>     For thy late ringing,
>     Thy head shall have knocks."

And the clerk is recorded as replying:

> "Children of Cheap
>     Hold you all still;
>     For you shall have Bow bells
>     Ring at your will."

When other cities were given the privilege of keeping their shops open until nine o'clock, the ringing of the bell at that hour was called the *Bow bell* from the name of the bell used when this privilege was first granted. It was the Bow bells that, according to the story (see p. 260), Dick Whittington heard when he was a boy just reaching London. When he became a great merchant he gave a large sum of money to insure that the "tenor bell" of Bow Church should be rung every morning at six o'clock and every evening promptly at eight for the benefit of the working boys. The records and the payments to the sexton show that this was kept up as late as the beginning of the nineteenth century.[1]

It was a general custom in bygone days to ring the church bell on market day, first as a signal for the selling to begin, and afterwards as a signal for it to stop. There were laws against "forestalling," or buying before the bell rang, and heavy penalties

[1] The term "Cockney" refers to the people born within the sound of Bow bells.

were imposed upon those who were too impatient and those who persisted too long. It was unlawful, says one writer, even to handle a goose before the bell said, "You may bargain!" The *Fair bell* was rung at the beginning and end of a fair.

In some places in England, according to one writer, the church bells rang to announce the arrival of the London coach. The coach often brought fresh fish for those housewives who had ordered it, and the church bells rang that they might hasten to the coach to secure the fish while it was fresh.

The *Oven bell* gave notice when the lord of the manor's oven was ready for his tenants to use in baking their bread.

In some country districts a church bell is still rung at the dinner hour.

In times of great national danger church bells were used as signals from parish to parish to warn the people or to call them together when other means of quick communication were unknown. Macaulay, in his lay of "The Armada: a Fragment,"[1] tells how

> Right sharp and quick the bells all night rang out
>    from Bristol town,
> And ere the day three hundred horse had met on
>    Clifton Down.

The ordinary way of ringing a series of bells was to begin with the highest note and ring a descending

[1]See also "Brides of Enderby," by Jean Ingelow.

scale.   When such a series of bells was used to give
an   alarm   they   were   rung   backward, — that   is,
beginning   with   the   lowest   note   and   ringing   an
ascending   scale.   Bells   tolled   backward   was   the
signal first used as an alarm of fire, and afterwards
for any uprising of the people.

The *Tocsin* or *Alarm bell* has, in days gone by,
sounded   for   dreadful   doings.   Church   bells   have
rung for uprisings, revolts, and even for horrid human
massacres, as for example, "the Sicilian Vespers,"
which occurred in the year 1282, when eight thousand
French   settlers   in   the   island   of   Sicily   were   massacred.   The signal for the massacre was the ringing
of   the   church   bells   for   Vespers,   or   evening   prayer.

Another   famous   instance   is   the   "massacre   of
St. Bartholemew."   In   the   early   morning   hours   of
St.   Bartholemew's   Day,   August   24,   1572,   King
Charles IX of France (under the influence of his
wicked   mother,   Catherine   de   Medici)   fired   a   pistol
as   the   signal   for   tolling   the   bells   backward,   and
a   hundred   thousand   men,   women,   and   children
were massacred as the bells rang.

During   the   French   Revolution   the   backward
ringing of the bells was the call of the people for
some   united   attack   against   the   royalists.   Indeed,
many   bloody   deeds   and   many   national   crimes   in
the past have been heralded by church bells.

In   cases   of   rebellion,   also,   the   bells   are   rung
backward, or sometimes muffled.   Recall the lines
in Scott's "Bonnie Dundee," quoted on page 113.

Dundee he is mounted, he rides up the street,
The bells are rung backward, the drums they are beat.

We often see the term "bell, book and candle" in the literature of the earlier days. This was the name given to an ancient form of excommunication practiced in the Catholic church which originated in the eighth century. The formula of excommunication is read, the bell is rung, the book is closed, the candle is extinguished, and the person is no longer connected with the church or under its guardianship.

There is perhaps no use of church bells which is so widely known in Christian countries as the ringing of bells to herald the advent of the holy day, and no other season of the year is so closely associated with bells as Christmas. The custom of ringing a joyous peal of bells on Christmas morning has been for ages a beloved feature of the Christmas celebration, and we may be thankful that at least this one of the older ways has lived on. Among people of all languages and of all climates,—not only those who live where Christmas comes in winter, but also where Christmas comes in the warm summer time,—in every part of the globe where there are Christians, the church bells ring on Christmas morning.

In many places, however, the bells ring on Christmas Eve at sunset, for according to the old church usage the real beginning of Christmas was at sunset on the day we call Christmas Eve.

Numberless Christmas songs glorify the bell, and for weeks before Christmas, children everywhere sing about the merry bells heralding the glad tidings of the birth of Christ. All churches that have bells tuned to the different notes of the scale, send the old familiar Christmas hymns floating out on the air, either on Christmas morning or on the evening before. Perhaps the hymn most often heard from the belfry at that season is "O Come, All Ye Faithful."

What Christmas chimes meant to the people of Old England is shown very clearly in the books of Charles Dickens. For us, the Christmas bell has come to have a symbolic meaning. Bells are printed on Christmas cards, on all kinds of Christmas literature, paper bells are sold for decoration, and enormous bell forms hang in the stores along with the other festive decorations of holly and mistletoe; they are also used in home decorations, and tiny bells hang as symbolic ornaments on Christmas trees.

There was an old belief in England that when Christ was born the devil died, and for an hour before midnight on Christmas Eve the church bell was rung, just as it would have been rung for some dying person, and this was called "the Old Lad's passing bell" ("Old Lad" being a nickname for Satan), the tolling changing to a joyful peal exactly at midnight. Later the tolling was called the "devil's death knell." In some places of England this bell is still rung at midnight on Christmas Eve.

On December 31, at midnight, for centuries the Old Year has died to the tolling of bells, and the New Year heralded with joyful ringing. This custom has also remained with us, and wherever there are church bells they are rung for the coming of the New Year. Tennyson's "Ring Out, Wild Bells,"[1] commemorates this custom in beautiful poetic lines.

Perhaps the earliest wedding bells were pieces of metal clashed together in the market place of some ancient peoples, when all the marriageable girls of the village were placed on view, and the young men assembled to choose their wives. Centuries afterward, when church bells announced so many other important occasions, it was most fitting that they should ring to announce to the public that a new union had taken place in the church.

One seldom hears the sound of wedding bells now, especially in the noisy cities. The wedding march played on the church organ has almost usurped the place of the more poetic marriage bells. But the symbol remains with us in decoration and story.

[1]See page 412.

# CHAPTER XI

## BELL HANGING

We are accustomed to bells which are hung in a belfry or tower of some kind. But the early churches had no such towers. Many of the first Christian church bells were fastened in tall trees that stood near the church. Even today, in some villages of Russia and other countries, the bell hangs on the branches of a tall tree in the churchyard. In Iceland the bell is usually placed in the "lych gate," a covered entrance to the graveyard. The tree belfry was once very common in Scotland and Ireland.

Sometimes a tall frame for the bell was made in the churchyard; and in other cases the bell was swung in a frame on the roof of the church, like the bell in Figure 51. Soon the idea of protecting the bell from the weather led to the building of a frame with a cover over it — the early form of the bell tower. Two kinds of bell tower were developed, — one added to the roof of the church, and the other built entirely separate from the church.[1]

In Servia the church bells are often hung in a framework of timber built near the west end of the church, while the bell towers of Russia and Italy are frequently separated from the main building.

[1] See pictures of bell towers in the chapter on "Bells and Architecture," pp. 359-76.

In some of the islands of Greece, also, the belfry is apart from the church, and the reason given for this is that in case of earthquake the bells are likely to fall, and if they were placed in the church tower they would destroy the roof of the church, and might cause the destruction of the whole building.

It has often been observed that the vibrations of a large bell ringing in a tower can be felt in the masonry near it, and serious accidents have been caused by such vibrations. In 1810 the spire of a church in England fell while the bells were being rung for morning service, and twenty-three people were killed. In most church towers the bells are hung in a framework which, as far as possible, is kept clear of the walls.

York Museum

FIG. 51. *Early Christian church bell in standing frame*

The vibrations in the air around ringing bells have been observed even in the case of small hand bells. This the Swiss muleteers have noticed, and are said to tie up their little bells at certain places on the road, lest the vibration from them should shake the delicately poised snow on the mountain side and bring down an avalanche.

The hanging of bells depends in large measure on the way they are to be rung, whether by hand, by a lever, by machinery, or by swinging against the clappers.

There are four ways of ringing a bell: (1) striking by a clapper on the inside while the bell swings to and fro; (2) striking by a clapper on the inside, by some mechanical means, while the bell is stationary; (3) striking on the outside by hand while the bell is stationary; (4) striking on the outside with a hammer controlled by mechanical means.

FIG. 52. *"Liberty Bell," showing cannons bolted to wooden stock*

Until quite recent times some of the larger bells suspended in church towers in various European countries were rung by being struck like a gong, by hand, while in parts of Ireland gongs were used as church bells as late as the seventeenth century.

The bells in most of the old churches swung to and fro in their belfries, pulled over by ropes that hung down far below them. A bell that swings must have some means whereby it is turned on an axis, and its movements regulated by a rope. Until recently, this was managed by fastening the bell, with the bolts run through its "cannons," very securely to a short, solid beam of wood called the "stock," so that when this beam turned over, the bell turned with it (see Fig. 52). This stock turns over by means of pivots called "gudgeons," which rest in brass sockets set into the timbers of the bell frame. As the stock and bell turn over, the gudgeons turn in these brass sockets, usually called the "brasses." The brasses must be perfectly level, and must also be kept well oiled and free from grit or dirt of any kind. One end of the stock is fastened to the spoke of a wheel, and one of the gudgeons forms the axis of the wheel. A rope fastened to another spoke passes around the grooved rim of the wheel, and falls through the floor of the bell chamber (Fig. 53). In Figure 54 (p. 120) is shown an ornate stock of the eighteenth century.

A pull of the rope turns the wheel, revolves the stock upon the pivots of the axle, and lifts the mouth of the bell. The clapper rests against its lower side. When the rope is loosened and allowed to coil around the wheel again, the bell swings downward and the clapper strikes it on the other side. An upright bar called the "stay"

FIG. 53. *Showing method of hanging a church bell, with stock, stay, slider, wheel, pulley, and rope*

strikes the "slider" underneath the bell, keeping the bell from turning completely over.

Before wheels were used, an upright post was fixed
in the stock, and a rope tied to the top of the post.
When the rope was pulled, the bell turned over.

FIG. 54.  *An ornate stock of the eighteenth century*

The next development was to attach the rope to a
half-wheel, with a deep groove in the rim to hold
the rope.   Later a three-quarter wheel gave better
service, while now a complete wheel is used as a
guider for the rope.

In the case of very heavy bells, two wheels are
necessary for steady swinging.   Figure 55 shows a
bell which was made to be rung with four ropes,
two ropes attached to each wheel.   This bell, which
hangs in the Montreal Cathedral, weighs over
fifteen thousand pounds.

It is a common impression that a bell may be rung by pulling a rope which is tied above the ball of the clapper. But this does not produce a good tone and is dangerous to the bell. "Clappering," as this practice is called, has been the cause of the breaking of many church bells, and must be severely condemned. A ringing bell is very sensitive. Lomax, an English writer on bells, says that "a touch, a scratch, may break the largest bell. A finger

FIG. 55. *Large bell in Montreal, hung with two wheels*

pressed upon the surface, a thread tied around the barrel during its vibration, will break the bell as surely as a sledge hammer."

A group of bells, with their supporting beams, stocks and gudgeons, wheels, stays, and ropes, looks very complicated; and indeed there is much to be kept in order. Even in the case of bells rung by machinery, much careful adjustment is required, and the wires which connect the striking hammers with the mechanism which operates them must be kept in perfect order, and very carefully regulated.

John Taylor & Co.
FIG. 56.   *Modern bell bolted into metal stock*

Instead of cannons and wooden stocks, most bells of modern make are bolted into metal stocks which turn with the bell as it swings. One of these is shown in Figure 56. All bells which swing are provided with wheels and ropes.

Meneely Bell Foundry
FIG. 57.   *Showing two ways of ringing the same bell*

Figure 57 shows how a bell may be struck on the

outside with a lever, and Figure 38[1] illustrates the lever attached to the top of the clapper which strikes the bell on the inside. If a double lever is used, with a rope for each hand, the bell may be rung as fast as the clapper can move from one side to the other. A double clapper[2] also makes rapid striking easy. In Figure 57 the bell may be struck either by machinery on the outside or by the clapper pulled by a rope on the inside.

Meneely Bell Foundry

FIG. 58. *Bell hung with both wheel and hammer*

The bells which ring clock chimes are examples of those struck by machinery. The levers are attached to the mechanism of the clock and at certain times they are set free to fall upon the bell.

Nowadays the bells of many city churches "go by machinery," that is, they have clock-like machines which are wound up to strike the bells at certain hours, just as clocks are struck.

In each of the above cases the bell is stationary, and the problem of hanging it is more simple than in those cases where the bells are rung by swinging them.

Some modern bells are made with rotary yokes, as shown in Figure 58. By this method of hanging

[1]Chap. VII, p. 71.     [2]See Fig. 81, p. 180.

the bell it may be turned around while still mounted, to allow the clapper to strike in a different place. When a bell is struck in one place for generations, it becomes worn in that spot and may crack unless it is turned. Many modern bells are hung so that they may either swing or be rung by a lever, as shown in this illustration.

It is not practicable to arrange for the swinging of the heaviest bells. Sometimes even the lifting of a very large bell to a great height is a complicated process.

Bells that are not to swing are hung in a fixed position, bolted to the bell frame, as shown in Figure 57 (p. 122). The English people are still partial to swinging bells, but most of the modern bells in America are stationary.

# CHAPTER XII

## PEALS AND CHANGE RINGING

When bells of different sizes were made, it did not take our European forefathers long to discover the musical possibilities in them. Efforts were then bent toward making a series of bells which could be played in a musical way, and it was soon discovered how they could be made to sound the different notes of the diatonic scale.[1] A set of bells thus tuned was called a "peal" of bells.

The first tunable peal used in England was in 945. The ancient peal consisted of three bells, as the "ding-dong-bell" of the nursery rime reminds us. Such were the peals which the Dublin Cathedral used to the middle of the seventeenth century. In 1456 Pope Calixtus III sent a peal of five bells to Kings College, Cambridge, and for some time this was considered to be the largest peal in the kingdom. At the beginning of the sixteenth century eight bells, tuned to the complete diatonic scale, were hung in a few of the principal churches. Long after, sets of ten or twelve bells were made, but eight was the most popular number for a peal of bells.

The bells were rung by ropes fastened to a wheel, as shown in Figure 53 on page 119, and a separate rope was necessary for each bell. When a bell is

[1]See p. 70.

properly rung by a rope, it must be inverted and swung, first in one direction and then in the reverse, right around above the frame, so that at the end of each swing it is mouth upwards and has performed nearly a whole revolution each time the rope is pulled. In careful peal ringing, a man to each bell is necessary.

The earliest method of peal ringing was to ring all the bells in succession, beginning with the highest tone and repeating this series, over and over. This was called "round ringing." Thus a peal of three bells would be (in number notation) 3-2-1, 3-2-1, etc. If the peal consisted of five bells, the tones would be 5-4-3-2-1, 5-4-3-2-1, etc. In a peal of eight bells the tones would be 8-7-6-5-4-3-2-1, 8-7-6-5, etc., the 8 always following immediately after the 1. The effect of this was pleasing, and it was not difficult to accomplish, for it meant merely taking each note in succession.

In the early days round ringing was a fashionable pastime, especially in England, where gentlemen of leisure found it an interesting and fascinating art. A traveler who visited England in the year 1598 writes in his journal: "The people are vastly fond of great noises that fill the air, such as firing of cannon, drums and the ringing of bells; so that in London it is common for a number of them that have got a glass in their heads to go up into some belfry and ring the bells for hours together for the sake of exercise."

But in time a new way of ringing came into use. Instead of playing the bells in succession, it was permissible to change the order and ring the series in some other succession rather than straight down the scale. This was called "change ringing." It gave much variety to the sound of the scale, having the notes follow in a different order each time. And there were so many ways! Even in a peal of three bells there were six ways of change ringing: 3–2–1, 2–1–3, 1–2–3, 3–1–2, 2–3–1, 1–3–2.

There were 120 ways of playing on five bells, using all five of them each time, and each bell only once! In a peal of eight bells there were 40,320 changes, and upon a peal of twelve bells, no less than 479,091,600 changes! The rule for finding out the number of changes possible on any number of bells is $n(n-1)(n-2)....3 \times 2 \times 1$. For example, the changes on five bells are $5 \times 4 \times 3 \times 2 \times 1$, or 120.

Up to the seventeenth century change ringing was confined to peals on five bells. Since swinging bells require so much space for their swinging, in order that they may not interfere with each other, it is not practicable to use many bells, and eight constitute the average peal. However, ten or twelve bells have often been used for change ringing.

When more than three or four bells are used for change ringing, a leader is required to call out the succession of bells. Sometimes the leader also takes charge of one of the ropes. Figure 59 (p. 128) is from an old drawing from the *Illustrated London*

*News* of 1856, which represents a group of six ringers, and evidently one of the ringers is also conductor.

Round ringing had been very popular; but when change ringing came into vogue it took the ringing world by storm. By the end of the seventeenth century changes were rung on eight bells. The next

From an old drawing by Keene

FIG. 59. *Bell ringers*

century was the golden age of bell ringing, and then, indeed, England deserved the name of the "land of bells." Ringing became one of the most popular forms of sport, ranking with hunting and football. The "country squire, the professional man, the tradesman in the town, and the craftsman in the village," all found entertainment and exercise in change ringing. The custom was encouraged, and books were written with rules and directions for the changes clearly set forth.

A writer who published a book in London about 1796 on *The Art of Ringing* states: "As an athletic exercise or amusement, there are few of so noble a nature, so conducive to health, and employing so many faculties, both mental and corporal, as that of the Art of Ringing." Some of the directions were very intricate, quite like mathematical problems, and challenged the mental concentration of the ringers (or at least that of the leaders) as well as muscular control in the use of the ropes.

In 1880 a book was published in London called *Change-Ringing Disentangled*, by the Reverend Woolmore Wigram, in which the directions were so clearly stated that it seems worth while to quote a few paragraphs from that book:

"*The bell in motion.* Watch the bell while it is being rung. You will see in the first place, that the clapper, which rests on one side of the bell when she is set mouth uppermost [bells are always feminine], moves with her as she is swung round; and at the moment when the bell slackens her motion as she turns mouth uppermost, being about to balance, the clapper flies across, and, striking the opposite side, lies still once more on the place which it struck.

"(2) You will observe that as the bell is set, the stay rests against the slider on one side and on the other alternately; and that the rope at the one position crosses the wheel, merely touching it, but at the other position, the rope is wound round the wheel for the greater part of its circumference. The former position is that of the 'hand stroke'; the ringer then has the tuffing of the rope in his hand, and the slack part lies before him on the floor in a large loop, the extreme end being held in his left hand. The latter position is that of the 'back stroke'; and the ringer then has only the extreme end of the rope within reach, a large portion being gathered round the wheel. [See Fig. 60, p. 133.]

"(3) If the bell be swung too hard, the stay will rebound from the slider, and the bell will return, swinging down again, instead of coming to rest. If the bell be checked too soon, she will fail to balance, not rising sufficiently high; and again she will swing down before she is wanted. But that which is required is knack, not strength — the weight of the bell does the work; the hand of the ringer interferes only at what a mechanic would call 'the dead point'; *i.e.*, the moment at which the bell is on the balance and when a very slight force is required to send her either way.

"The exact position in which a bell is brought to rest admits of some variety. She may be allowed to go right up, and back, until the stay rests against the slider; in which case she has passed the balance; and if the stay broke would swing down on the other side. She may be just balanced, so that the touch of a finger will bring her back again; or she may be held by the rope in some position between these two. In the first case, the bell is said to be 'rung high'; in the second, to be 'rung low.' It obviously will require more time and labor to bring her back from the first position than from the second; hence the former is used in slow ringing, the latter in quick ringing; and the expressions 'high compass' and 'low compass' mean, in the language of ringing, exactly the same as 'slow time' and 'quick time' in the language of music.

"(4) It is thus seen that the bell is a large pendulum, swung through the entire circle; and that in the hands of a good ringer she will be balanced exactly each time she is set, without resting any weight against the stay and slider. . . . . From the time when the bell is pulled off the balance until she goes up and balances again, she is beyond all control, and during that interval the rope must be left entirely free.

"The smallest bell is called the treble, and the largest the tenor, whatever the number of the ring or keynote. The others are called second, third, and so on, counting from treble to tenor.

"*Hand stroke and back stroke.* The bells having been rung up and set mouth uppermost, each is struck twice before it returns to the same position. The first of these blows is called the hand stroke, and the second the back stroke. And when the bell, having been struck twice, has been brought back to the position from which she started, a whole pull has been made with her [see Fig. 60].

"A 'peal' means the full number of changes which can be produced upon the ring, or set, of bells." [In the case of more than seven bells, 5,000 changes constitute a peal. It would take nearly thirty-eight years to ring all the changes on twelve bells —479,001,600!]

"The changes on four bells are called 'singles'; on five, 'doubles'; on six, 'minor'; on seven, 'triples'; on eight, 'major'; on nine, 'caters,' etc. The rule or method by which the changes are produced is called 'the method.' Thus the expression 'a peal of grandsire doubles' means

120 changes in the method called 'grandsire,' and rung upon five bells. 'A peal of grandsire triples' means 5,040 changes in the same method upon seven bells. 'A peal of treble bob minor' means 720 changes in the method called 'treble bob' upon six bells. 'A peal of treble bob major' means 5,000 or more changes in the treble-bob method rung upon eight bells.

"A bell 'hunts' when she leads a whole pull, strikes once in the place of each bell in succession, lies behind a whole pull, and then returns in the same manner step by step to the lead.

"The changes on three bells are all produced by hunting alone. But in the case of four bells, it is necessary to employ in addition, place making and dodging. It is called the 'bob method,' and the rule is as follows: All the bells hunt until the treble leads; the bell which she turns from the lead makes second's place, and leads again; those above second's place making at the same time a single dodge. The whole peal is here given:

| 1 | 2 | 3 | 4 |
|---|---|---|---|

| | | | | | 4 | 2 | 1 | 3 |
|---|---|---|---|---|---|---|---|---|
| 2 | 1 | 4 | 3 | | 4 | 1 | 2 | 3 |
| 2 | 4 | 1 | 3 | | 1 | 4 | 3 | 2 |
| 4 | 2 | 3 | 1 | | 1 | 4 | 2 | 3 |
| 4 | 3 | 2 | 1 | | 4 | 1 | 3 | 2 |
| 3 | 4 | 1 | 2 | | 4 | 3 | 1 | 2 |
| 3 | 1 | 4 | 2 | | 3 | 4 | 2 | 1 |
| 1 | 3 | 2 | 4 | | 3 | 2 | 4 | 1 |
| 1 | 3 | 4 | 2 | | | | | |
| 3 | 1 | 2 | 4 | | 2 | 3 | 1 | 4 |
| 3 | 2 | 1 | 4 | | 2 | 1 | 3 | 4 |
| 2 | 3 | 4 | 1 | | 1 | 2 | 4 | 3 |
| 2 | 4 | 3 | 1 | | 1 | 2 | 3 | 4 |

"The learner will observe that the treble, and she alone, has a plain hunting course throughout. All the other bells have to vary, each taking her turn in making second's place, and in dodging in three-four."

Figure 60, taken from another book published about the same time, shows the position of the bell when it is set at hand stroke and back stroke.

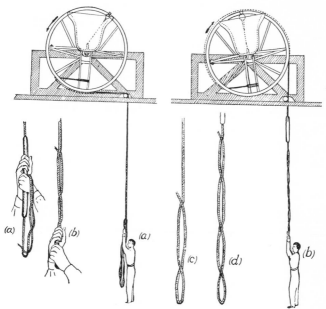

FIG. 60.   *A bell set at hand stroke and at back stroke.   The hands* (a) *and* (b) *correspond to the ringers' positions* (a) *and* (b)

The Reverend H. T. Ellacombe, an English bell authority, writing in 1872 says: "Of all arts and pastimes, change ringing is preëminently one which exercises the mind and body at the same time; . . . usually a strong, steady pull repeated every four or five seconds. . . . In ringing a peal, each ringer must so balance his bell, not once in

half a dozen times, but at every pull throughout
the whole performance, be its duration measured
by minutes or hours.  Besides this mere physical
dexterity, the ringing of changes requires a mental
effort to be made and kept up, conjointly with the
physical exertion and adjustment.

" 'Set' or 'call' changes are very common; but
in change ringing proper, the bells are never sounded
twice in the same order; and this is continued to
the end of the peal, when the bells are brought home
to their regular places.  This end is only to be
attained by each bell being made to follow a certain
course, and to change places with the other bells
by the evolution of certain rules or 'methods.'  To
manage his bell properly in this respect, and guide
it up and down the maze, making it strike now
before, now after this and that other bell, not only
requires much practice and study, but a cool head
and close attention.  And this necessity justifies
the remark that ringing requires a mental as well
as bodily effort.  Its popularity in England is not
to be wondered at."

In Southey's *Life of John Bunyan* an interesting
account is given of Bunyan's attitude toward ringing: "He had taken great delight in bell ringing,
an exercise in which it is now difficult to see any
harm, but which he began to think a vain and sinful
practice, probably from its being connected with
the externals of the Established Church; still he so
hankered after his old amusement, that though he

did not pull a rope himself, he would go and look at the ringers, not without a secret feeling that to do so was unbecoming the religious character he professed. A fear came upon him that one of the bells might fall; to secure himself against such an accident, he stood under a beam that lay athwart the steeple from side to side; but his apprehensions being once awakened, he then considered that the bell might fall with a swing, hit the wall first, rebound, and so strike him in its descent. Upon this he retired to the steeple door, thinking himself safe enough there, for if the bell should fall, he might slip out. Further than the door, he did not venture, nor did he long continue to think himself safe enough there; for the next fancy that possessed him was that the steeple itself might fall, and this so much disturbed him that he dared not stand at the door any longer, but fled for fear the tower should come down upon him."

Southey himself looks with more charity upon the practice. He says: "Great are the mysteries of bell ringing. And this may be said in its praise, that of all devices which men have sought out for obtaining distinction by making a noise in the world, it is the most harmless."

England has long been called "the Ringing Isle," and Handel, who lived for a long time in England, called the bell the English national instrument. Nothing which can be done with bells (says an English writer) "is to be compared with our old

English mode of ringing peals and musical changes. One of the greatest charms is in the effect of the wind carrying the sound, now near, now far, and near again." Although many consider the bells of the continent finer than those of England, yet nowhere in the world have bells been used with such effect as in England.

Mr. E. B. Osborn, an English writer on bells, says in the London *Morning Post*, July 25, 1913: "Why change ringing should be the Englishman's favorite form of bell music is, I think, easily explained. It involves much physical exertion, which tires, but need not overtax, as many muscles as are used in rowing, and is unquestionably one of the finest exercises known. . . . Strictly speaking, change ringing is not music at all; though when the voices of the bells used are mellow and melodious, it decorates the passing time with simple, subtly-varied sound-patterns, and forms an acceptable obligato to the elemental emotions of an individual or the nation."

Various devices have been used for striking bells in a more convenient way than by swinging them, but lovers of bell ringing still cling to the old practice, and claim that the full value of bell ringing is obtained only when the bells are swung with their mouths uppermost, and in peals of six or eight bells managed by as many ringers acting in harmony under a leader.

If bells do not swing when they are rung, they are not properly called "peals," according to one of the best English bell authorities. It is said that only in England are bells rung in peal (with swinging bells), excepting one or two rings in America and in the English colonies. There is a set of genuine peals in St. Matthew's Church, Quebec, Canada. One of the largest and finest peals in England is at Exeter Cathedral; another celebrated one is that of St. Margaret's, Leicester, which consists of ten bells. If bells are struck by iron or wooden hammers while the bells are not in motion, they produce a mournful effect, Starmer says, "but the sound of swinging bells is totally different, and a well rung peal is never mournful, but is always joyful and exhilarating."

Swinging bells, such as are used in change ringing, have not been manufactured in America because there has been no demand for them.

# CHAPTER XIII

## RINGING SOCIETIES

In the seventeenth century change ringing was so popular that ringing clubs were organized, with special conditions for membership, regular meeting times, and strict rules of order. There still exists in England an organization called the Society of College Youths which is said to have been founded on November 5, 1637, and is probably the oldest existing company of change ringers. Sir Richard Whittington, the famous lord mayor, founded a College of the Holy Spirit and St. Mary on College Hill, London. That church contained a ring of six bells, and the neighboring gentry used to amuse themselves by chiming them in rounds. This was said to be the origin of the name "college youths."[1] The society was founded by members of the "nobility and gentry for the purpose of practicing and promoting the art of ringing." At first they rang only rounds and "set" changes; but afterward accomplished a complete peal of 120 changes on five bells. This society can boast, among its founders and members, men in all ranks of life from the peerage downward.

Changes proper were supposed to have been first rung about 1642, but little progress was made until

[1] H. B. Walters, in *The Church Bells of England.*

a book called *Campanologia* was published in 1677 and dedicated to the Society of College Youths. Thus provided with a guide and textbook, the art of bell ringing developed rapidly. Other books were written, and during the next century ringing societies were organized all over the country. Many a town added to its bells in order to keep up with its neighbors in this fashionable amusement, and then, if ever, England justified the name of "the Ringing Isle."

Some of these ringing clubs would travel about the country, ringing peals in different belfries. The College Youths rang in all parts of the country, and even crossed the Channel into the continent to ring in foreign belfries. All the ringing societies took great pride in performing feats of great endurance and precision. One astonishing feat is recorded wherein eight members of the College Youths were locked in the belfry of St. Matthew's Church, Bethnal Green, in 1868, and rang 15,840 changes without stopping. They began at 8:45 in the morning and accomplished this feat in nine hours and twelve minutes.

Other bell-ringing societies were the Cumberland Society of Change Ringers, the Society of Union Scholars, the Society of Eastern Scholars, the Society of London Youths, Westminster Youths, and Prince of Wales Youths.

In former days the College Youths attended the divine service at Bow Church in a body on

November 5 (the anniversary of its foundation) and other occasions. At such times the beadle of the society carried a staff surmounted by a massive silver bell. This bell is now in the possession of the Junior Society of College Youths.

Each ringing society had its own set of rules and by-laws necessary for the orderly and instructive use of the bells. Copies of the old rules may still be seen hanging on the walls in many belfries. Some of them are still read at the annual meetings of the societies. They are often in verse, but the oldest ones are in prose.

The oldest rules known are those from the Society of St. Stephen Ringers at Bristol, and date back to the time of Queen Elizabeth. There are thirty of these rules, in prose, from which the following are taken:[1]

1. None shall be of the said Society save those who shall be of honest, peaceable, and good conversation.

2. They shall at all times be ready to defend the said Society against all charges that may be brought against it.

3. They must endeavor to gain credit by the musical exercise, etc.

12. If anyone of the said Company, after the time that he shall come into the church to ring, shall curse or swear, or make any noise or disturbance, either in scoffing or unseemly jesting, that the party so offending shall pay for his offense threepence (to be divided among the Company).

[1]H. B. Walters, in *The Church Bells of England.*

15. If anyone of the said Company shall speak, or make any manner of noise, when the Bells do ring, so that the ringers or any of them by that means may make a fault, the party so offending shall pay for his offense threepence, to be divided among the Company.

17. If any of the said Company do or shall, after they are come together, quarrel or misuse any of the said Company, before they do depart, the party so offending shall pay for his offense sixpence, to the use of the said Company.

22. If anyone of the said Society shall be so rude as to run into the belfry before he do kneel down and pray, as every Christian ought to do, he shall pay for the first offense, sixpence, and for the second, he shall be cast out of the Company.

At Shillingstone, Dorset, Dr. Raven copied a set of rules headed by the prose injunction: "Praise the Lord with Lowd Symbols: if you curse or sware during the time of ringing you shall pay threepence." Below are the lines:

> There is no musick played or sung
> Is like good Bells if well Rung
> Put off your hat, coat and spurs
> And see you make no brawls or iares
> Or if you chance to curse or sware
> Be sure you shall pay sixpence here
> Or if you chance to break a stay
> Eighteenpence you shall pay
> Or if you ring with gurse or belt
> We will have sixpence or your pelt.

1767.

In a belfry in Hornsey, Middlesex, is a set of rules which may be called the normal type:

> If that to ring you do come here
> You must ring well with hand and ear;
> If that you ring in spur or hat
> A quart of ale must pay for that.
> And if a bell you overthrow
> Sixpence is due before you go.
> And if you curse or swear, I say,
> A shilling's due without delay.
> And if you quarrill in this place
> You shall not ring in any case.

The sexton must have been very watchful for his fee, which seemed to be derived from the fines of these gentlemen members of the ringing club.

Here are some of the "Orders" of the Ringers Regulations at Holy Trinity in Hull:

(1) 6d. for ringing any bell with hat or spurs on.
(2) 1s. for pulling bell off her stay and not set it right again.
(3) 6d. for throwing bell over, and cost of any breakage caused by it.
(4) 6d. for not hanging up the rope when he is finished ringing.
(5) 6d. for cutting on the lead or marking it up in any way.
(6) 6d. for having read the above orders with his hat on.

In some cases the last order includes spurs, "with hat or spurs on."

From a belfry in the Welsh border country were taken the following rules in verse:

### Ringer's Rules

If for to ring you do come here
You must ring well with hands and ear;
And if you ring with spur or hat,
A quart of beer is due for that.
And if the bell you overthrow
A shilling pay before you go:
The law is old, *well known to you*
Therefore the clerk must have his due.

The "jugg of beer" played only too prominent part in the ringers' doings in the Stuart and Georgian eras. In Warwickshire one of the bells, dated 1702, has the words: "Harken do ye heare our claperes want beere," a gentle hint as to how the ringers wished to be refreshed after their efforts.

Briscoe, in his *Curiosities of the Belfry*, gives many of the old ringers' rules that may still be seen in the old belfries. The general ideas seem to be the same throughout the country, though the rules vary as to details. Some of them forbid cursing, telling lies in the steeple, or coming into the belfry intoxicated.

In all cases the fines went to the regular church bell ringer, who had to keep the bells and ropes in good order.

On a board affixed to the wall of a church in Cornwall is this:

We ring the quick to church, the dead to grave,
Good is our use, such useage let us have.
Who swear, or curse, or in a furious mood
Quarrels, or strikes, although he draws no blood

Who wears a hat, or spurs, or turns a bell
Or by unskilful handling mars a peall
Let him pay sixpence for each single crime
Twil make him cautious gainst another time.

At Dundee, one of the regulations reads: "There
shall be one regular practice night every week, on
such a day and at such an hour as the steeple keeper,
with the consent of the authorities of his church or
tower, may appoint.  If in his judgment more practice be desirable, he must exercise a wise discretion,
inasmuch as every residenter is not a lover of bell
ringing, and the tongues of the bells should be tied
if there be more than one night's practice each week.
In fixing practice nights, due regard must be had
to the church services and choir practice; at those
times the belfry should be closed to all.  Also the
feelings and wishes of any sick person in the neighborhood must be tenderly considered."
In All Saints Church in Hastings:


### I. H. S.

This is a belfry that is free
For all those that civil be;
And if you please to chime or ring,
It is a very pleasant thing.
　　There is no music played or sung
　　Like unto bells when they're well rung;
　　Then ring your bells well if you can
　　Silence is best for every man.

But if you ring in spur or hat
Sixpence you pay, be sure of that;
And if a bell you overthrow
Pray pay a groat before you go. — 1756.

At the end of one of the ringers' rules:

These eight Bells rung with care and art
With joy will transport every heart.

In the belfry of Redbourne Church:

All that intend to take these ropes in hand
To ring, mark well these lines and understand,
Which if with care you read will plainly see
What fines and forfeits are the sexton's fee:—
He that doth break a stay or turn a bell,
The forfeit is a groat, it's known full well;
And carelessly to ring with spur or hat,
The forfeit is a groat, beware of that.
And they that fight or quarrel, swear or curse,
Must pay two pots, turn out, or else do worse;
And for unlocking the steeple door,
And for sweeping of the belfry floor,
And to buy oil you know is very dear,
And for my own attendance given here,
If you will well observe such rules as these
You're welcome for to ring here when you please.

Pray remember the sexton, Jos. Brown.
May 1764.

It seems that the bell ringers' societies must have
cultivated the art of poetry along with their music,

to the extent of having poet laureates. The following lines were written by the poet laureate of a bell ringers' guild which was established by charter in 1620:

Then the folks every Sunday went twice at least to church, Sir,
And never left the parson, nor his sermon, in the lurch, Sir.

And in regard to security of property:

Then our streets were unpaved, and our houses were all thatched, Sir,
Our windows were all latticed, and our doors were only latched, Sir;
Yet so few were the folks that would plunder or would rob, Sir,
That the hangman was starving for want of a job, Sir.

There is in Suffolk an epitaph of a ringer who died in 1825 at the age of eighty:

To ringing from his youth he always took delight;
Now his bell has rung, and his soul has took its flight,
We hope, to join the choir of heavenly singing,
That far excels the harmony of ringing.

Figure 61 pictures the members of a ringing society in 1856 ringing the bells in their rejoicing over the close of the Crimean War. Figure 46,[1] drawn for the *Illustrated London News* in November, 1878, shows a group of ringers who were members of the

[1]See chap. IX, p. 93.

From *Illustrated London News*

FIG. 61.  *The peace rejoicings in 1856*

Ancient Society of College Youths in the dedication of the new bells for St. Paul's Cathedral. According to the *News* the service concluded at 5:30, when the bells burst into a joyous peal. Two ringers had to ring the tenor bell, weighing 6,200 pounds and five feet in diameter. The ringing lasted until 7:30, about a thousand changes being executed.

# CHAPTER XIV

## BELLS AS MUSICAL INSTRUMENTS PLAYED BY HAND

The tune-playing possibilities of bells have been known since the earliest civilizations. There are records of the Chinese having used bells tuned to certain scale notes nearly five thousand years ago. It is claimed that once on a time the Chinese could play the entire scale on one bell—a kind of bell that was cast with knobs on the surface,[1] each knob giving a different note of the scale when it was struck. This method, however, was probably unsatisfactory, as it was given up later and separate bells were used for the different notes. The bells found in the tombs of the ancient Assyrians show that they must have been used for melody playing. Numerous bells, varying in size and tone, have been found in the tombs of the Etruscans; and one of their ancient instruments has been found which consists of a row of bronze vessels placed on a metal rod in the same manner in which we place our musical bells today. It is also known that the Romans used bells that were attuned to different pitches.

Nearly all primitive peoples employ the jangling sound of metal for musical effect. As the musical

[1]See p. 302.

sense becomes more and more developed, they contrive more intelligent uses of metal, until, as in the case of the Japanese gongs, music is produced that is melodious and pleasing, even to European ears.

Old illuminated manuscripts show that the Christians used bells for tune playing at a very early date. Figure 62 is copied from an ancient manuscript which is said to date from the time of Charlemagne (768–814), and shows King David sitting on a throne, striking a lyre with his left hand and holding a scepter in his right. He is probably engaged in singing psalms, accompanied by four musical instruments—the pneumatic organ, a sort of violin, a trumpet, and a set of bells.

From an eighth-century MS.

FIG. 62. *King David and other musicians*

A ninth-century manuscript gives an interesting drawing (see Fig. 63) of rote and bell music combined.

The rote—an early Irish instrument—has five strings, and we presume they were tuned to accord

From a ninth-century MS.

FIG. 63.   *Rote and bells*

with the tones of the bells.   The bells were suspended on a rod fastened across an arch in the church.

By the tenth century bell ringing for melody seems to have been practiced extensively in Europe, the sets consisting of four or five bells.   The old manuscripts

which give the pictures indicate that this playing
was connected with the religious services in the
church, and probably accompanied the singing.

Figure 64, from a manu-
script in the Brussels
Library, represents a woman
sitting on a fantastic chair
playing on four bells which
are suspended on a rod
under an arch in the church.

On the capital of a column
in the ancient church of St.
George de Bocherville, Normandy, founded by William
the Conqueror, may be seen
the figure of a king playing
upon a set of five bells. The
figure sitting in front of him

From a tenth-century MS.
FIG. 64.  *A bell ringer*

probably played a rote or harp of some kind, but
it has been broken away (see Fig. 65).

As the church organ developed, bells were attached
to that instrument, and the combination of organ
and bell tones in the church services became very
common.

Aelred, an abbot of Rievaulx,[1] who lived in the
twelfth century, cries in pious horror: "Why such
organs and so many cymbals [small bells] in the
church?  What with the sound of the bellows, the
noise of the cymbals and the united strains of

[1]Rev. Francis William Galpin, in *Old English Instruments of Music.*

the organ pipes, the common folk stand with won-
dering faces, trembling and amazed!"

A monk who lived toward the end of the eleventh
century described the making of these bell cymbals.
They were little hemispherical bells cast in molds
that were carefully prepared and proportioned, the

FIG. 65. *A bell ringer on the capital of an eleventh-century church*

metal being a mixture of tin and copper, with five
or six times as much copper as tin. If the tone
was not right, it was rectified by filing.

Sets of bells suspended in wooden frames are
frequently found in the representations of musical
performances dating from the Middle Ages. In the
British Museum is an ancient psalter in manuscript,
of the fourteenth century, which shows King David
(see Frontispiece) holding in each hand a hammer

with which he strikes upon bells of different sizes suspended on a wooden stand.

In Figure 66 is seen a complete orchestra of the early fifteenth century, consisting of harp, psaltery, triangle, clarion, and chime bells.

The method of playing tunes by swinging bells in the hand is also of ancient date. The Lancashire bell ringers have long been famous in England for this kind of music. Each ringer of the Lancashire ensemble manages two bells, holding one in each hand, so that a group of four ringers may easily play melodies within the range of an octave of the diatonic scale. It is their custom for each ringer to have two other bells which he may substitute whenever required; so that, if they are skillful in the management of their bells, both as to ringing and making the exchanges of bells, seven ringers with twenty-eight bells may produce rather intricate music.

The Swiss bell ringers have a device by which each ringer plays four bells in each hand, one ringer giving the complete diatonic scale. The bells are fastened four on one handle, and the clappers are so fixed that when the cluster is turned in one direction, one bell sounds, and it is turned in a different direction for each of the three other bells to sound. It requires a strong wrist to manage skillfully the weight of four metal bells in each hand.

When the player has only to regulate the stroke of a hammer, it is easier to give the stroke at the

precise moment than when he swings a bell.  It is
difficult to play melodies with varied rhythm on
swinging bells.

Orchestral bells are merely flat bars of metal
tuned to scale notes and arranged on a frame so

FIG. 66.  *An orchestra of the early fifteenth century*

that when they are tapped they have the sound of
ringing bells.  They are properly called gongs, but
the bell effects which they produce have caused
them to be erroneously called bells.  They may be
made of bell metal, steel or aluminum, and tuned to
several octaves, including all the half-steps, and

arranged in the same manner as the piano keyboard. They are played with rubber-tipped mallets.

Metal bars tuned to the chromatic scale are built in modern pipe organs, and arranged to be played mechanically. When properly tuned and adjusted, they are capable of wonderful harp-like effects.

Tubular bells, consisting of cylindrical tubes of bell metal, have come into use in recent years as chimes, to be used both in and out of doors. They are usually suspended from a frame, vertically, by loops of leather or silk cords, and allowed to swing freely. They are struck with hammers, either by hand or by some mechanism connected with a clock or other movement. They are sometimes made nine or ten feet long, with a weight of two hundred pounds or more.

The tubaphone is a smaller form of tubular bells, cut in different lengths for the tones of the chromatic scale, and arranged to lie on a padded frame instead of being suspended. Like the orchestral bells, they may be arranged in piano keyboard form. They are played with a rubber hammer.

Sleigh bells are sometimes tuned to the notes of a chord and allowed to jingle for the harmonious effect. They may be tuned also to the notes of the complete scale, and suspended for melody playing. Sleigh bells should be shaken, one bell at a time, and should not be struck.

The greatest disadvantage of the bell as a musical instrument is the continued vibration of the metal after the bell is struck. Without "dampers" to stop the vibrations that are no longer desired, the sounds become discordant when a rapid succession of notes is played. But in spite of this handicap, bell music can be made most impressive and agreeable to the ear.

The foregoing discussion refers to bells played by hand. Change ringing (by means of ropes) is described in a former chapter; chimes (played by mechanism) and carillons (played by mechanism or keyboard) will be discussed in later chapters.

## CHAPTER XV

## CLOCK BELLS

There was a time when the sun and moon were the only guides which man employed for the measurement of the divisions of the day and night. The sundial was invented to make more exact use of the sun's light for this purpose; and later, burning candles, burning rope, and, in the hourglass, grains of sand were employed to measure definite units of time.

Water was also brought into the service of time measurement, and the clepsydra was invented. This consisted of vessels which allowed water to drip slowly from one to the other. The amount of water which dripped from sunrise to sunrise was taken as a guide, and this was divided into equal parts for the divisions of the day. The clepsydra was used by the ancient Egyptians, Chinese, Greeks, and Romans.

In the early years of the Christian church the day was divided into eight equal parts or "canonical hours," and bells were rung in the monasteries on these hours to call the monks to prayer. The large church bells were also made to serve this purpose, so that the entire community might be notified of the canonical hours. This is, perhaps, the earliest use of the bell as a time marker in Christian countries;

and these bells were, of course, rung by hand, either with or without ropes.

In nearly all European countries there have been town criers and night watchmen who went about the streets ringing a bell and informing the inhabitants of the passage of time. This custom continued, even in some parts of America, until the last century.

Clocks driven by weight were invented in Verona in the ninth century. As bells had been used before this to announce the canonical hours, it was only natural that the inventive mind would turn to connecting the weight-driven machinery with a metallic ring to announce the hours, and striking clocks were developed.

The oldest tower clock mentioned in England was in the former Westminster tower in 1288. Perhaps the earliest tower clock with bell-ringing mechanism was one made by Peter Lightfoot, a monk of Glastonbury, about 1325.[1] Connected with this clock were automatic figures which struck a bell on the hours. These performing figures pleased the public, and during the Middle Ages many of the town clocks of Europe were provided with such figures to ring the hours on bells. They were used for proclaiming time long before the introduction of clock dials.

The famous clock at Strasburg Cathedral, made in the fourteenth century, has (besides a host of

[1] W. W. Starmer, in *The Clock Jacks of England.*

other mechanical figures) a skeleton-like form of Death which strikes the hours on a bell, using a human bone for that purpose! And the traveler

C. Jacobi Eliot

FIG. 67. *Automatic bell-striking figures in St. Mark's Piazza, Venice*

in Venice may see, high above the great clock in St. Mark's Piazza, two automatic figures ready to strike the ponderous bell between them (see Fig. 67).

In England, the figures which strike bells are called "Jacks." Formerly they were usually represented as being clothed in a suit of mail—an idea probably borrowed from the sentries in armor who, in the Middle Ages, were placed in watch towers to

give bell alarms when occasion arose.[1] Two such
figures, striking their bells with swords, are shown
in Figure 68.

In time it became the custom to have the Jacks
strike the quarter hours as well as the hours.[2] This
made it necessary to have some way of distinguish-
ing between the hour and the quarter-hour signals;
so a second bell of different tone was added, their
tones being, in pitch, either a fourth or a fifth apart.
Two Jacks also were required, and their combined
action played a simple "ding-dong." One "ding-

FIG. 68.    *Two old English Jacks of the Clock,*
*Blythburgh and Southwold*

dong" was played at the first quarter, two at the
second, and three at the third quarter; but on the

[1]W. W. Starmer, in *The Clock Jacks of England.*
[2]They are now frequently called "Quarter Boys."

hour only one bell announcing that hour was struck. Figure 69 represents two armored knights who, with their battle axes, used to strike the hours at Wells Cathedral.

The largest and perhaps the best known Jacks in England are "Gog and Magog" at St. Dunstan's Lodge in London. Figure 70 shows a group of three

FIG. 69. *Knights who used to strike the hours at Wells Cathedral*

figures at Russell's Observatory in Liverpool. The large one strikes the hours, and the other two play the "ding-dong" at the quarter hours.

In the seventeenth century a bell called Great Tom of Westminster hung in a campanile opposite Westminster Hall, London, rang for the hours. A story connected with this bell runs thus: During the reign of William and Mary a sentinel at Windsor Castle, named James Hadfield, was accused of sleeping at his post, a crime which incurred the

Fig. 70. *Clock-striking figures at Russell's Observatory, Liverpool*

death penalty. The sentinel insisted that he had not slept, and, to prove his wakefulness, asserted that he heard the Westminster bell strike for midnight, and that it struck thirteen instead of twelve times.

Investigation was made, and his story was verified by Londoners. Thus the bell saved the life of the sentinel. This story is often given as an instance of a bell being heard at a great distance, Windsor Castle and Westminster Hall being several miles apart.

After a time the "ding-dong" quarter bells became old-fashioned, and three bells were used to chime the quarter hours. These were tuned to the first, third, and fifth intervals of the scale. Four is now considered the most desirable number of bells for clock ringing, for with four bells a definite and pleasing tune may be played.

Clock bells are rung by hammers to which wires are attached, these wires being connected with the works of the clock. The wires are so arranged that they hold the hammer up until, at a certain time, the wire is loosened and lets the hammer fall.

In the case of a large modern tower clock, the machinery which operates the clock and its bells is very complicated. Figure 71 shows the mechanism of a large clock made by Gillett & Johnston of Croydon, England. This machinery is in three parts. The center section, called the "going train," drives the hands of four ten-foot dials; the section on the left side, called the "striking train," strikes the hours on a bell weighing one and a half tons; the section on the right, called the "quarter train," chimes the Westminster Quarters (see music on p. 166) on four bells.

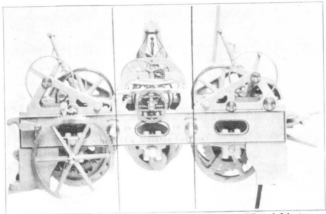

Gillett & Johnston

Fig. 71. *Striking train, going train, and quarter train machinery*

Gillett & Johnston

Fig. 72. *Electric mechanism for striking quarters*

## CAMBRIDGE CHIMES

First quarter

Second
quarter

Third
quarter

Fourth
quarter

Many modern clock bells are rung by electrical apparatus. Figure 72 (p. 165) shows an electrical mechanism by Gillett & Johnston which chimes the Westminster Quarters on four bells.

Sometimes clock bells are arranged so that they may be either swung by ropes and thus rung by hand, or rung by the clock mechanism, as one may choose.

The most famous clock music for four bells is the arrangement known as the Cambridge Chimes, so called because this melody, with bells tuned to suit

it, was first used at the University Church of
St. Mary at Cambridge, in 1793. The author of
the melody was Dr. Crotch, who used a measure
of the opening symphony of Handel's "I Know
that My Redeemer Liveth" as a pattern, and from

Meneely Bell Foundry
FIG. 73. *A Westminster peal, showing ropes and pulleys*

it evolved the series given on the preceding page.
For this music the four bells must be tuned to
numbers one, two, three, and low five of the scale.
Any set of bells tuned in this order, to play this
music, is often called a "set of Cambridge chimes"
or a "Cambridge peal." After their introduction
in Cambridge they were not duplicated until sixty
years later, when Sir Edmund Beckett chose to

have this melody played by the quarter bells of the great clock which he was having made for the Houses of Parliament in Westminster, London. Here they took on the name of the Westminster Chimes, and are known by both names. Being considerably larger than the Cambridge bells, the Westminster bells are tuned to play the melody in a much lower key. Since that time bells tuned to play this music have been used in clock towers of different countries, a notable peal being that of the Metropolitan Tower in New York.[1] Figure 73 (p. 167) shows a Westminster peal made by the Meneely Bell Company of Troy, New York.

In a Cambridge (or Westminster) peal, the hour is often struck on the largest of the four bells, just after the four phrases of melody have been played. This is true in the case of the Metropolitan bells of New York. In some cases, however, an extra bell is provided to strike the hours, as in the case of the Westminster clock. The large bell which strikes the hours for this great clock is Big Ben, to whose history the next chapter is devoted.

[1]See p. 285.

## CHAPTER XVI

## THE STORY OF BIG BEN[1]

Big Ben—the large hour bell which hangs in the clock tower of the Houses of Parliament (Fig. 74)—is perhaps the most universally known bell of modern make. It was first cast on August 6, 1856, at the Warner foundry in the village of Norton. A report of this event in the *London News* states:

"The preparation of the mold had occupied six weeks, and two reverberatory furnaces, capable of

Courtesy of *Mentor*
FIG. 74. *The Houses of Parliament, showing clock tower*
[1]The illustrations, Figs. 75–79, in this chapter are from the *London News* of 1856–58.

melting six tons of metal each, had been built expressly for the purpose of casting this monster bell. . . . The whole of the night previous was a scene of busy industry; and early in the morning the furnaces [seen to the right in the background of Figure 75], having attained the requisite heat, their doors were opened, and the operation of charging, or putting in the metal, commenced, occupying about one hour. In less than two hours and a half, the whole of the metal (eighteen tons) was in a state of perfect fusion. On the signal being given, the furnaces were tapped, and the metal flowed from them in two channels into a pool prepared to hold it, before being admitted into the bell mold. The shutter, or gate, was then lifted, and the metal allowed to flow. In five minutes the casting of the bell was complete, the successful termination of which delighted all present, who cordially joined the workmen in three hearty cheers."

About two weeks later the bell had cooled sufficiently to be raised from the pit. The following inscription appeared on its surface: "Cast in the 20th year of the reign of Her Majesty Queen Victoria, and in the year of our Lord 1856, from the design of Edmund Beckett Denison, Q. C.; Sir Benjamin Hall, Baronet, M. P., Chief Commissioner of Works." The bell was named Big Ben in honor of Sir Benjamin Hall.

It was necessary that the bell should be sent by train from the foundry to West Hartlepool, where

FIG. 75.   *The casting of Big Ben, August 23, 1856*

FIG. 76.   *Big Ben being brought from the foundry to the Houses of Parliament*

FIG. 77. *Experiment with the hammer upon the great bell*

the boat for London could be employed for its
further transportation. The bell was so wide that
it would not admit of other trains passing the car
which carried it; hence it made the journey by
special train on a Sunday, when other trains were
not running and both tracks were free for its passage.

When the bell reached London it was conveyed
on a low truck drawn by sixteen horses over Westminster Bridge (see Fig. 76, p. 171), and was
deposited in the Palace Yard, where the crowd was
so great that the police had great difficulty in
making a passage for it.

Figure 77 shows the experiment with a trial hammer to find out how heavy the striking hammer

FIG. 78.  *Breaking up Big Ben, March 6, 1858*

should be in order to bring the best tone from the
bell.  For some time Big Ben remained in the
Palace Yard, and important visitors were allowed to
hear the wondrous sound of its deep voice.

One day Big Ben suffered an accident.  It was
not able, apparently, to bear up under all the
strokes of the ponderous hammer, and it cracked,
even before it was hung!  Some have laid the blame
on the heaviness of the hammer, some say it was a
fault in the casting, but it is the more general opinion
that the metal contained too much tin, and was,
therefore, too brittle.  The crack was located somewhat as a bicyclist locates a puncture.  "Eight men
were placed round the bell and carefully watched

its circumference. The sound bow was wetted all around, and then the rim of the bell was struck. A minute row of tiny bubbles came out, and at once indicated the location of the crack."[1]

Poor Ben then had to be broken up into pieces so it could be carted away, and the metal melted and cast again. Figure 78 (p. 173) appeared in the *Illustrated London News* with the following explanation:

"The process by which the enormous mass of metal was reduced to fragments may be told in a few words. Ben was simply lowered from the massive framework which supported him in the corner of the Palace Yard, and laid upon his side on the ground. In this position the great weight of the head of the bell caused it to sink into the earth, so as to leave its mouth, instead of being completely vertical, slightly inclined upwards, yawning like an enormous cavern. From the framework above, an ordinary rope and block were fastened, and with them, by the aid of a windlass, a ball of iron weighing 24 cwt. was hoisted to a height of about 30 feet, and when the proper moment arrived, suffered to fall with all its weight upon Ben.

"The instant the heavy ball reached its appointed height, the string was pulled, and down came the mass in the inside of Ben's sound bow, and, with a crazy bellow, two pieces, one of about a ton and

[1]A. A. Johnston, "Clocks, Carillons and Bells," in *Journal of the Society of Arts*, London, 1901.

Fig. 79.  *The recasting of Big Ben, April 17, 1858*

one of some thousand pounds, were knocked out of his side.  After the first blow, the work of destruction went on rapidly, piece after piece was broken out, till scarcely anything but fragments remained of poor Ben, and even these were carted away as fast as possible to Messrs. Mears' foundry in Whitechapel.''

Then began the long process of making another mold (for a different foundry undertook the second casting), melting the old metal, and recasting it. Figure 79 appeared in the *London News* in April, 1858.

Another journey over Westminster Bridge again brought the new bell in great state, drawn by sixteen horses, to the Palace Yard.  The problem of lifting it to its place in the tower was solved by means of a monster windlass and chains forged especially for the purpose.  The dimensions of the bell are: seven and one-half feet in height and nine feet in diameter at the mouth; weight, thirteen tons, ten hundred weight, three quarters, and fifteen pounds, or thirteen tons and 1,765 pounds.

At the time of the second casting an attempt was made to call the bell "Victoria," and later "St. Stephen," but the public would have nothing but "Big Ben," so the old name prevailed.

But an ill fate seems to have kept Big Ben from being perfect.  After the clock had struck on Ben for a few months, some small cracks appeared on the outside of the sound bow, opposite the place where the hammer struck.  A bit of metal was cut from the crack and analyzed, and the casting was pronounced defective, as it was porous and unhomogeneous.  The Board of Works stopped the use of it for two or three years; but so much confusion was caused by striking the hours on one of the quarter bells, that the striking of Big Ben was allowed to be resumed with a lighter hammer (in November, 1863), and the bell was turned a quarter round on the button, or mushroom head, by which it was hung, so the striking hammer would fall in a different place.  The cracks do not seem to get deeper, and many consider that they do not seriously affect the tone of the bell.  However, its "ring" is not perfect, and its tone seems harsh to those whose ears are accustomed to the ringing of more delicately tuned bells. It is a pity that the bell is not as fine as it is famous.

In the spring of 1925 the sound of Big Ben was heard in New York for the first time, by radio, as it struck the midnight hour.

# CHAPTER XVII

## CHIMES

When the enterprising burglar's not a-burgling,
  When the cutthroat isn't occupied in crime,
He loves to hear the little brook a-gurgling,
  And listen to the merry village chime.

—W. S. Gilbert

Any set of bells tuned in definite relation to each
other is called a "ring." A ring of bells may be
a swinging peal sounded by their own clappers when
swung, or a set of stationary bells rung either by
hammers or by clappers. In a swinging peal a
separate ringer is usually employed for each bell,
as in change ringing.[1] Some hymns and slow melodies may be played by a band of ringers under the
direction of a leader, but this is very unsatisfactory
unless the rhythm is steady. Varied rhythms are
not attempted in change ringing. When definite
melodies are played, stationary bells are usually
employed. Bells are often hung so that they may
be either swung or tapped, and have both inside
clappers and outside hammers.

The word "chimes" has been used indiscrimi-
nately to denote any kind of tune-playing bells. In
its proper sense, however, it is understood to mean a
set of *stationary bells, three to twelve or fifteen in number,*

[1]See p. 127.

*tuned to major scale intervals.* A ring which consists
of more bells, and those tuned to chromatic intervals, or half-steps, is properly called a "carillon"[1]

Playing on bells for musical effects, as contrasted
with the practical uses of bells, is called the "art

Meneely Bell Foundry

FIG. 80. *Chime-ringing levers*

of campanology"—whether the bells are struck by
hand, struck by machinery, or pulled over by ropes.

Chimes may be played by means of levers or some
kind of apparatus for hand chiming; or they may be
operated automatically, as in the case of clock bells.

Figure 80 shows a set of levers for ringing chimes
by hand. These levers are attached to wires which

[1]See next chapter.

extend to the belfry, pass over pulleys, and control
the hammers of the bells.    Figure 81 shows a set
of chimes[1] to be rung by pressing levers as shown
in Figure 80.    These bells have double clappers, to

Meneely Bell Foundry

FIG. 81.    *Bells rung by the levers shown in Figure 80*

which the wires are attached.    The pulleys guiding the
wires may be plainly seen.    The largest bell, mounted
also with a wheel and rope, can be swung whenever
it is required for the ordinary uses of a church bell.

The clock bell which first struck the hours was
the ancestor of our present automatic chimes.    The

[1]Made by Meneely Bell Company of Troy, N.Y.

invention, which at first served only a useful purpose in announcing the hours, was gradually developed into a musical as well as a practical instrument. The "ding-dong" of two bells was increased to three tones of the major chord, and was played with pleasing effect on three bells. Or perhaps the bells were tuned to the first three or four tones of the scale. A simple tune, such as "Hot-Cross Buns," may be played on three bells. Below is an old Canterbury tune called "The Voice of the Bells," taken from an ancient psalmody; it is to be played on four bells:

## THE VOICE OF THE BELLS

When will ye to the tem - ple come,

O bless - ed chil - dren dear,

To give the Lord His hon - or due,

With rev - er - ence and fear?

An old Scotch Psalter of 1615 contains the following tune to be played on five bells:

The great-er sort crave world-ly goods,

And rich - es do em - brace;

But, Lord, grant us Thy coun - te - nance,

Thy fa - vor and Thy grace.

It will be seen that in three places a little harmony is permitted. The famous "Turn Again Whittington"[1] was played on six bells.

Chimes with set tunes may be played by the machinery connected with a clock in the same way that "quarters" are rung. When a tune requiring a considerable number of bells is played, an extra piece of mechanism is usually used, consisting of an extra train of wheels, and a "chime barrel" with

[1]See p. 261.

pegs. A chime barrel is a cylinder with rows of holes running lengthwise of the cylinder. Each row consists of as many holes as there are wires connected with bells. Pegs are placed in these holes, and as the barrel turns, these pegs strike wires which

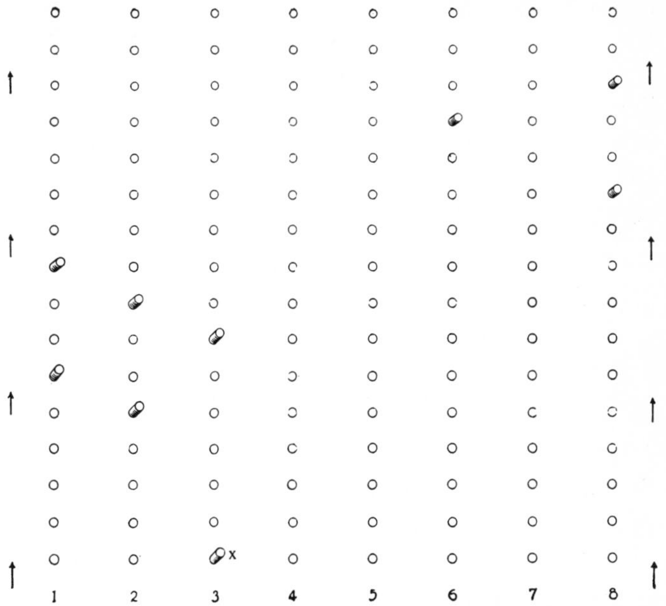

1    2    3    4    5    6    7    8

FIG. 82. *Pegs set for the first phrase of "Suwanee River"*

cause certain hammers to fall upon the bells. The tune is "set" beforehand by arranging the pegs in a certain order; and when the time (which has also been set in the clock machinery) arrives, the barrel begins to turn, the pegs begin to touch wire connections, and the bells begin to ring. Suppose one wanted to set the barrel to play "Suwanee River" on eight bells when the clock reached a certain time. For the first two measures the pegs would be arranged in the holes somewhat as shown on page 183. As the barrel turns in the direction indicated by the arrows, bell number 3 will be the first one struck, the hammer being released by the peg marked *x*. As the melody requires that this shall be a long note, three rows of holes are passed before another peg is reached; then come five in quick succession, ringing bells number 2, 1, 3, 2, 1; one row of holes passes, and then bell number 8 is rung; and so on.

Thus it is easily seen how one may set as many tunes as the barrel can accommodate; and the tunes may be changed as often as one wishes to change the pegs.

The chiming apparatus as described above is said to have been invented in the Netherlands in the fifteenth century, and Belgium claims to have had melody-ringing chimes even earlier. Some kind of chiming machinery was also used in England during that century, for an Englishman, John Baret, who died in 1463, left in his will a provision that the sexton of St. Mary's Church was to be paid "xij d. per annum so he will ring and find bread and ale to his fellowship . . . and so he do the chimes smite Requiem Eternam; also viij s. to keep the clock, take heed to the chimes, wind up the pegs and the plummets as often as need be."[1]

[1] H. B. Walters, in *The Church Bells of England*.

Various European countries adopted automatic chimes during the centuries that followed, and their use has been most marked in the Netherlands and in Belgium, where the more elaborate carillon was developed.[1]

The most modern method of automatic chiming,

John Taylor & Co.

FIG. 83.   *Chime of twelve bells at the University of California*

both in melody playing and in ringing the clock quarters, is by electricity.

Chimes of six, eight, ten, and twelve bells may be found in various parts of the world, especially in Europe and America; and even so far away as Australia. Some are rung automatically, but many are rung by hand levers. Eight is the most popular number of bells in a chime, and these are tuned to the tones of the major scale. Figure 83 shows a ring of twelve bells made by an English foundry

[1] See next chapter.

(Taylor of Loughborough) for the University of California.

Some of the finest chimes in the world hang in English cathedrals. Exeter Cathedral has a very fine ring of ten bells. The ring of twelve bells in Worcester is said to be the grandest peal in England. Peals of twelve are also found at York Minster, St. Mary-le-Bow, St. Paul's Cathedral, and other churches.

Year by year chimes are becoming more numerous in America also, being supplied not only by the English foundries at Croydon and Loughborough, but also made in this country by the Meneely Bell Company of Troy, New York, the Cincinnati Bell Foundry, and other foundries.

# CHAPTER XVIII

## CARILLONS IN GENERAL

A fine carillon is the highest point yet reached in the evolution of bell instruments. The single bell, the clock chime, the swinging peal, musical hand bells, and the stationary chime—each class has its appeal and its definite use. Almost any musical person, with a little training, can do justice to any of the above instruments; but the carillon, to be properly heard, must be played by an artist.

"Carillon" is a French word meaning a series of bells played by mechanism. In reality the carillon is a highly developed and elaborated chime. The underlying principles are the same, and both chime and carillon may be played either automatically or by hand-directed mechanism. The difference between a carillon and a chime is in the number of bells, the tuning of them, and the arrangement of the keyboard. For simple melody playing, the chime has, usually, eight to twelve bells tuned to the major scale; the carillon has at least two octaves (often four octaves), with all the sharps and flats, suited for complicated harmonies as well as for melodies. Chiming levers are arranged in a row; the carillon keyboard in four rows, two rows for the hands and two for the feet. Carillon bells must be tuned with greater care and scientific accuracy

FIG. 84.   *The drum of the Bruges carillon, showing pegs for automatic playing*

than is demanded of chime bells, for imperfect overtones destroy the harmony when several bells are struck at once.   A bell may sound in tune when played in a chime, but when combined with other bells in a carillon it would cause jangling discord if its own overtones were imperfect and the bell not completely "in tune with itself" as well as with the other bells.   So the chime and the carillon, although so closely akin, are vastly different.

The automatic carillon plays music which is set on a barrel in the same manner as the tunes are set on the chime barrel described on page 184.   It is called the *tambour* (barrel) *carillon*.   Formerly the barrel was made of wood, but in modern times it is made of metal, and, like the simpler chime barrel, is punctured with rows of holes. Little spikes are fitted into these holes (according to the music to be played) which make the barrel resemble the cylinder of a mammoth music box (see Fig. 84). In a music box the spikes flip little tongues of metal which make musical sounds. In the tambour carillon each spike lifts a tongue which pulls a wire connected with a hammer, raises the hammer, and lets it fall on a bell. Some bells have as many as half a dozen hammers, each hammer supplied with a separate wire, to be used when one bell is to be struck several times in rapid succession. The spikes, or pegs, are set to play as complicated music as desired, and the barrel is connected with the clock, so that, at certain fixed times, the music plays automatically. A carillon machine is shown in Figure 85 (p. 190). This mechanism is usually set to play just before the stroke of the hour, and at the half and quarter hours.

The other kind of mechanism allows the bells to be played by means of a keyboard. A series of large wooden keys is arranged in the order of a piano keyboard. Each key is connected with a bell by means of a wire which raises a hammer and makes it strike the bell from the inside, when the key is pressed down. By this mechanism nothing is "set," and the performer plays whatever he chooses. This kind is called the *clavier* (keyboard) *carillon*. It has been called a "piano which plays bells instead of strings." The largest bells are usually connected with a pedal keyboard, and the performer who uses both feet and both hands skillfully may play very intricate music. The keys, too large and heavy to be pressed down with one finger, are usually played by blows with the gloved fists. Some-

Gillett & Johnston

FIG. 85. *A carillon machine*

times, however, the thumb and middle finger can press down two keys at once. Figure 86 shows a front view of the keyboard of a carillon in Morristown, New Jersey. The pedal keys show clearly the arrangement like piano keys. The musician who plays a clavier carillon is called a *carillonneur*.

Photograph by Curtiss

FIG. 86. *The keyboard of the Morristown, New Jersey, carillon*

Many carillons are provided with both kinds of mechanism, one connected with the clock and the other for artists' concerts. They do not interfere, as one is arranged to strike from the inside of the bells and the other from the outside.

In a carillon of the first order—one having three or four octaves of bells—the sizes of the bells vary all the way from huge ones weighing several tons down to small ones weighing not over ten or fifteen pounds. In Belgium the bells are always hung in tiers, while in Holland they are often arranged in circles. See Figure 87, showing the arrangement of the bells in tiers in Notre Dame Cathedral in Antwerp.

The carillon is developed to the greatest degree of perfection in Belgium and Holland. Very fine ones are found, however, in Germany and France, and to some extent in a few other countries. "When John V of Portugal visited the Netherlands, about 1730, he was so delighted with the bell music that he determined to have a carillon for his sumptuous palace then being built. The price having been ascertained (it appears to have been something like $43,000 for the completed carillon put in place), the suggestion was guardedly made by his treasurer that, in view of the financial burdens upon the king's purse, this was a large expenditure. The implied criticism is said to have so offended the self-esteem of the monarch that he replied: 'I did not think it would be so cheap; I wish two.' And these he got, for two carillons of forty-eight bells each, played by clavier and clockwork, existed a few years ago, and, so far as I know," says Mr. Rice,[1] "still exist in the twin towers of the convent, formerly the palace chapel, at Mafra."

For some reason carillons have not been heard in England to any great extent until quite recently,

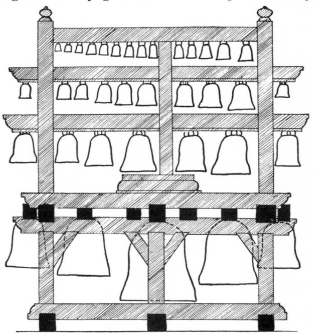

FIG. 87.  *The arrangement of the carillon of Notre Dame Cathedral, Antwerp*

even though England has long been called "the Ringing Isle." This may be because the English

[1]W. G. Rice, in the *Musical Quarterly* for April, 1915.

have found their change ringing so satisfying. Starmer, the foremost English bell authority, is still loyal to the swinging peal. The music from a peal of bells is louder than the music of the carillon. In the former there is an intense blow as the bell swings against the clapper; but in the carillon the hammer strikes the bell from a very short distance — one-quarter of an inch — and consequently there is less volume of sound at any time.

The carillon is particularly suited to flat countries such as Holland and Belgium, where the bell sounds travel with more effect and at far greater distances than in hilly countries, where the sound is closed in, interrupted, and echoed back. Mr. Rice gives the following as the probable course of the carillon's development in those countries:[1] "In Holland and Belgium in the distant years when clocks and watches were more rare than now, and the people were much more dependent upon the town clock for knowledge of the time of day or night, it became the custom to precede the striking of the hour by a short, automatic chiming on three or four small bells in the clock tower, as a premonitory signal. As this and that town sought to surpass its neighbors, the bells were increased in number, and the musical scale of tones and half-tones became complete. Brief melodies began to be heard at the hour and half-hour, and with still more bells, came, at these divisions, whole tunes. All this playing was automatic.

[1]The standard authority on carillons is W. G. Rice's *Carillons of Belgium and Holland*, from which a large part of the material in this and the following chapter has been obtained.

"Then came the point of greatest advance. The keyboard was just beginning to be used with stringed instruments. What was more natural than that bells should have their keyboard, or clavier, and so be made ready to respond to the art of the aspiring musician? Soon pedals were employed with the heavier bells. By these improvements, rapid and quite complicated playing was possible, and almost any composition could be fairly interpreted by a skillful executant, and so regular carillon recitals or concerts came into being.

"Thus in the course of two or three centuries was developed a carillon, a musical instrument of distinct characteristics, and possessing wide possibilities for community service. Not only did the carillon have, by automatic play, constant companionship with time, but beyond this, the master of its clavier could make the town council meeting hour enjoyable, and the market (ever a feature of the life of the Low Countries) additionally gay for old and young.

"Carillon recitals which the traveler often hears in Belgium and Holland take place at a fixed time on the market day, and on each Sunday, and in the greater cities on some regular weekday evening in summer. The latter are called 'program concerts.' The carillon recitals of this kind are announced by widely distributed posters; and the music to be given and the carillonneurs who are to play are announced months in advance by means of elaborately printed and illustrated booklets.

"The carillon is indeed a very beautiful and majestic musical instrument. Only those who have heard Chopin's Funeral March on this instrument can conceive how impressive that music can be. The carillon can reach, instruct, and give joy to thousands assembled out of doors, and in this it surpasses any other instrument."

A Belgian writer of the nineteenth century (Van der Straeton) says: "A good bell is not made by chance, but is the result of a wise combination of qualities and thought, and a fine carillon is as precious as a violin by Stradivarius."

Starmer[1] also agrees that "the carillon with its clavier is the finest musical instrument in existence for educating the people and cultivating their love for folk songs, and in teaching them the great melodies of their fatherland; for the music best suited to the carillon—excepting music specially written for that instrument—includes the folk music which has successfully stood the test of time."

The most famous makers of carillons in the olden days were Franz Hemony (1597–1667) and Pieter Hemony (1619–1680) of Lorraine; Pieter van den Gheyn of Holland and others of his family, dating back to the middle of the sixteenth century and covering several generations. The Dumery family of Antwerp is also famous as makers of carillons, besides many others. The founders of the present day who make carillons are Felix van Aerschodt of

[1] W. W. Starmer, in *The Musical Standard* for Feb. 16, 1918.

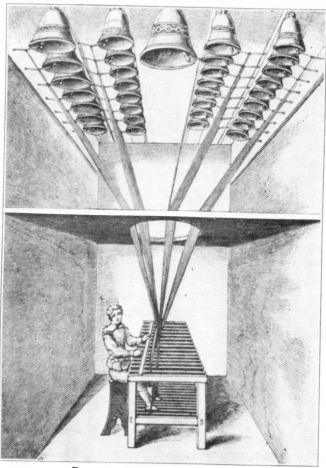

FIG. 88. *A carillon of former days*

Louvain (the representative of tne van den Gheyns), John Taylor of Loughborough, England, and Gillett & Johnston of Croydon, England. According to Rice, "the Hemonys, the van den Gheyns and the Dumerys were the great founders of former times. Hemony's bells, generally speaking, are the best; they are bright, clear, and true—epic in character. Van den Gheyn's bells are similar. Dumery's are velvety, soft, and true—elegiac in character. . . . Carillons today by makers such as van Aerschodt at Louvain and Taylor at Loughborough are even more perfect than those of former times."

Every prosperous community of Belgium in the early days had a belfry crowned with a carillon. The community felt, and still feels, such a deep interest in its carillon that no matter where it is placed the bells belong to the town, and the bell master is a municipal officer.[1] Perhaps one reason the carillon is so beloved by the town is because it is so democratic, and can be enjoyed by the whole town at once, the rich and the poor, and with no one having to take the trouble to go to any particular spot to hear it. For this reason bell music has been often called "the poor man's music."

The carillon seems especially fitting as an instrument for the celebration of national feelings, both as reminders on anniversaries or as giving expression to national emotion; but, better still, "it sends out from its aërial heights an influence which lightens

[1]W. G. Rice, in *Carillons of Belgium and Holland*.

routine, and to happy occupation adds enchanting accompaniment."

An Englishman[1] who was cruising in a fishing boat off the coast of Holland heard a carillon for the first time. He writes: "I guessed that a living artist, not a mechanical contrivance, was making music—music as magical as it was majestical—in his far-off unseen tower across the moonlit levels of the still sea, and the low-lying shore hidden by fog-drifts. I think now (but am not sure) that it came from the belfry of Gouda. At the time, I thought it was music from the moon which the moonlight made audible, so strange and other-worldly were its fugal cadences, flight after flight of prismatic sounds."

Musical melodies floating down through the air from a high tower, with an invisible performer, can hardly help lifting the thoughts of men above sordid things, and must play a definite part in the molding of character. A graduate of Delft wrote from a foreign land, says Mr. Rice, of his "many memories of enchanting music heard unexpectedly in the stillness of a winter night. Many a night my friend and I, on our walks through the quiet snow-covered city, have stood still and listened, and had our whole trend of thought changed and lifted by this wonderful music."

[2]E. B. Osborn.

# CHAPTER XIX

## IMPORTANT CARILLONS

Belgium is the home of the most celebrated carillons in the world, there being at least thirty important ones in that small country. Holland has about twenty. All together, there are more than a hundred carillons in Belgium and Holland, and until recently there were perhaps not that many in all the rest of the world combined.

The Bruges carillon is, of all bells, the most celebrated in verse. The bell tower is shown in Figure 89. In 1842 Longfellow visited Bruges, and his diary at that time foreshadows his now well-known poems, "Carillon" and "The Belfry of Bruges." These poems are given on pages 416 and 419. The diary states:

"*May 30.* In the evening took the railway from Ghent to Bruges. . . . It was not yet night; and I strolled through the fine old streets and felt myself a hundred years old. The chimes seemed to be ringing incessantly; and the air of repose and antiquity was delightful. . . . Oh, those chimes, those chimes! how deliciously they lull one to sleep! The little bells, with their clear, liquid notes, like the voices of boys in a choir, and the solemn bass of the great bell tolling in, like the voice of a friar!

FIG. 89.   *The bell tower of Bruges, Belgium*

William Thompson

FIG. 90. *St. Rombold's Tower, Malines (Mechlin), Belgium*

"*May 31.* Rose before five and climbed the high belfry which was once crowned by the gilded copper dragon now at Ghent. The carillon of forty-eight bells; the little chamber in the tower; the machinery, like a huge barrel-organ, with keys like a musical instrument for the carillonneur; the view from the tower; the singing of swallows with the chimes; the fresh morning air; the mist in the horizon; the red roofs far below; the canal, like a silver clasp, linking the city with the sea,—how much to remember!"

The first Bruges carillon, consisting of thirty-eight bells, was made in 1662 by Franz Hemony. This was destroyed in 1741. Two years later the present carillon of forty-seven bells was made by Joris Dumery of Antwerp. The drum for automatic playing is seen in Figure 84.[1]

The Mechlin carillon in St. Rombold's Tower (see Fig. 90) has had the reputation for many years past of being the finest in the world. It consists of forty-five bells, made at various times, the oldest one dating back to 1480. There are several Hemony bells of the seventeenth century, some of the eighteenth century made by A. van den Gheyn, and others by makers of less renown. The largest bell is "Salvator," weighing nearly nine tons, and until recently the heaviest bell in any carillon. The bells hang two hundred feet from the ground.

During the French Revolution this carillon was saved from destruction by the diplomacy of Gérard

[1]See p. 188.

Gommaire Haverals, the carillonneur at the time.
"The revolutionary council had decreed that the
Mechlin bells should be melted and made into
cannon, when Haverals by his eloquence and cleverness persuaded the French authorities that one
carillon should be preserved. Otherwise, he asked,
how properly could be celebrated 'la gloire de la
république'? A few years later the reaction came,
and he was given a sharp reprimand by the town
council because of the republican songs he had
played. His beloved bells, though, were safe, and
so again he changed his tunes to suit changed times
and endured patiently the municipal castigation.
Happily his devotion and skill were so compelling
that even political passions were subdued and he
continued as carillonneur until he died in 1841,
being on the verge of fourscore years, and having
played bells in St. Rombold's Tower continuously
since he was seventeen."[1]

The drum for mechanical playing (see Fig. 84),
made nearly two hundred years ago, is of gun metal,
five feet three inches in diameter, and has one hundred and eighty longitudinal rows of holes. It is
wound twice a day, and about sixty thousand notes
are played by this drum every twenty-four hours.

But the daily mechanical playing of the Mechlin
bells is not their chief glory. The concerts of the
renowned carillonneur, Joseph Denyn, are without
equal in the world. At Mechlin, under the direction

[1]W. G. Rice.

of Mr. Denyn, is the only existing school for carillon playing, founded in 1922. One of Denyn's concerts has been thus described by Mr. Rice:

"After the bell ceased striking (the hour), and the vibration of its deep and solemn tone had died away, there was silence. So long a silence it seemed, so absolute, that we wondered if it was to be broken. Then pianissimo, from the highest, lightest bells, as if not to startle us, and from far, far above the tower, it seemed—indeed as if very gently shaken from the sky itself—came trills and runs that were angelic! Rapidly they grew in volume and majesty as they descended the scale until the entire heaven seemed full of music. Seated in the garden we watched the little light in the tower, where we knew the unseen carillonneur sat at his clavier and drew the music from his keys, and yet as we watched and listened, we somehow felt that the music came from somewhere far beyond the tower, far higher than that dim light, and was produced by superhuman hands. Sometimes in winter after icicles have formed, there comes a thaw, and one by one they tinkle down, gently and timidly at first; then bolder in a mass they come till, like an avalanche, they crash down with a mighty roar. All of this the music suggested. It was low, it was loud; it was from one bell, it was from chords of many bells; it was majestic, it was simple. And every note seemed to fall from above, from such heights that the whole land heard its beauty. It was as if a

great master had said: 'I am no longer content
to sit at my cathedral organ and give pleasure to a
few hundreds only; I must give joy to thousands.'
So he mounts the cathedral tower, and plays his
sonata, or his prelude, or his songs upon the great
clavier, so that all the world may hear.   With
this feeling we listened that evening to van den
Gheyn's Prelude and to the Andante and Allegro
from Rossini's 'Barbier de Séville,' and to old Belgian and French folk songs.   Here was no pretty
cleverness, but a splendid masterhand ringing out
from his mighty instrument not alone grand, sub-
lime effects, but also the tenderest shades of feeling
that awaken both memory and aspiration.   Indeed,
the tower seemed a living being, opening its lips in
the mysterious night to pour out a great and noble
message of song to all mankind.

"As the hour passed, daylight died, but the tower
grew more distinct in the light of the full moon rising
over the trees.   We had programs which we passed
in silence to one another, and if there was occasion
to speak, we spoke in whispers.   It seemed that if
we moved or spoke aloud, the tower, the far-away
light, and the music might all vanish.   Nothing we
had ever experienced had been like this.   Sometimes
the sounds were so low that we found ourselves bend-
ing forward to hear them.   They seemed to come
from an infinite distance, so faint and delicate were
they.   Then at other times, great chords, in the
volume of many organs, burst forth rapturously!

"The concert ended promptly at nine with the national air of Belgium. Directly after this the great bell slowly, solemnly struck the hour."

In speaking of Mr. Denyn's concerts, an English gentleman[1] writes: "It was surprising to see how attentively the audience followed this concert in the sky. The vast majority had to stand the entire time, and they stood motionless, speaking not a word, and not even clicking their wooden shoes until the tower had ceased singing. The people of Mechlin and its trim countryside take so great a pride in their vast singing tower that one can easily understand why they ran to put out a fire when the red harvest moon shone through the great open windows of the bell loft.

"If that tower had been finished according to the original plan, it would have been the loftiest in the world. But the stone for completing it was carted off into Holland between 1582 and 1584 to build the fortress town of Willemstad. The theft has never been forgotten nor forgiven. Yet the tower is well enough as it is; Vauban calls it the eighth wonder of the world. And to the people of Belgium it is more than that, for they see in it a fixed forefinger of their elder faith, an upright scroll of national history, and a leaping fountain of many-colored music."

The Antwerp Cathedral is famous for its beauty of form and line (see Fig. 91). Napoleon compared

[1] E. B. Osborn, in *The Nineteenth Century and After*.

the tower to Mechlin lace. The cathedral carillon consists of forty-seven bells, thirty-six made by Hemony in the seventeenth century, and others by Dumery and Aerschodt. The largest bell was cast in 1459, and it is said that Emperor Charles V stood sponsor at its baptism. Mr. Brees is the well-known carillonneur. In the cathedral tower is another carillon of twenty-six bells, made in the seventeenth century, but these bells are not now used.

In the Ghent carillon are fifty-two bells, four and a half octaves. The largest of these is Roland, one of Europe's most famous bells, dating back to 1314 (see p. 239). The smallest bell of the Ghent carillon is only eight inches high.

Many of the injured carillons of Belgium and French Flanders are being restored and others are to be built. A fine carillon, housed in a magnificent tower, is planned for the new library at Louvain.

The carillon of Middelburg, Holland, consists of forty-three bells, made in the eighteenth century. William G. Rice designates this carillon as "among the best and much the busiest of carillons. It plays for nearly two minutes before the hour, a minute before the half, a few measures at the quarters, and some notes every seven and a half minutes, besides a warning ripple before each quarter hour. The butter and egg market place, crowded with peasants in costume at the market hour (Thursday noon), is perhaps the most interesting place to hear the bells. They blend with the activity of the

W. G. Rice

FIG. 91. *The spire of Antwerp Cathedral*

William Thompson

FIG. 92. *"Boston Stump," St. Botolph's Cathedral,
Boston, England*

marketing most agreeably." A graceful compliment was paid to these busy bells when Lucas said: "One cannot say more for persistent chimes than this,—at Middelburg it is no misfortune to wake in the night!"

Amsterdam has five Hemony carillons, all hung in circles in as many towers, and the bells may be seen from the street.

Delft has a Hemony carillon of forty bells in the tower of Nieuwe Kerk, 375 feet high. Utrecht has forty-two bells, most of them of Hemony's make.

In the Rotterdam Town Hall is a fine carillon of forty-nine bells recently cast by Taylor, the English founder. They are said to be perfectly in tune, accurate to a single vibration per second. The Taylor foundry has also made carillons for several other towns in Holland.

Germany has several carillons, those of north Germany being especially fine. Belgium's neighbor, France, also has had good carillons for a long time.

The first carillon in England was hung in the celebrated "Boston Stump" in 1868. This is a picturesque church tower 365 feet high on the Lincolnshire shore, facing the North Sea (see Fig. 92). The carillon consisted of forty-four bells, founded by Gillett & Johnston of Croydon.

In the War Memorial Campanile in Loughborough, England (see Fig. 93, p. 212), a carillon of forty-seven bells, cast at the Taylor foundry, was installed in 1923 in memory of those who fell in the

World War. There is also a carillon of forty-two small and perfectly tuned bells in the tower of the Taylor foundry (see Fig. 94). This foundry has also

John Taylor & Co.

FIG. 93. *War Memorial carillon tower, Loughborough, England*

made carillons for Cobh (Queenstown), Ireland (forty-two bells, shown in Fig. 95, p. 214); Armagh, Ireland (thirty-nine bells); Flushing, Holland (thirty-three bells); Parkgate, Cheshire (thirty-seven bells); Bournville, Birmingham (thirty-seven bells), and Capetown, South Africa (thirty-seven bells).

A carillon recently made by Gillett & Johnston for Toronto, Canada, consists of twenty-three bells. A weight-driven tower-clock movement chimes the Cambridge Quarters and strikes the hours, and, after the last stroke of each hour, releases the starting switch of an automatic electro-pneumatic

John Taylor & Co.

FIG. 94. *Carillon tower, John Taylor & Company bell foundry at Loughborough, England*

machine, which then plays some well-known air; and in addition there is the hand clavier for the carillonneur.

John Taylor & Co.
FIG. 95.　*Carillon at Cobh (Queenstown), Ireland*
*The largest bell weighs 6,772 pounds*

Not until recently have carillons been known in America. In the past few years several have been installed in various parts of the country, and a remarkably fine carillon was made for New York by the Croydon founders in 1925 (see p. 289).

The popularity of this instrument is growing so rapidly, in all parts of the world, that any complete list of important carillons would in a few years be out of date.

## CHAPTER XX

## DOCTOR BURNEY ON CARILLONS
(1775)

More than a hundred and fifty years ago
Dr. Charles Burney, a learned English authority on
music, made a tour through the Netherlands and
other countries to collect material for a general history of music. This *History of Music* was, by the
way, the first ever written by an Englishman, was
very complete up to that time, and is still considered
a work of great value. In 1775 Dr. Burney published in London a book called *The Present State of
Music in Germany, the Netherlands, and the United
Provinces*, and his impressions of the carillon, as
given in this book, are so interesting and amusing
that they seem worth quoting in their entirety:

"When I came to Ghent, I determined to inform
myself in a particular manner concerning the *carillon*
science. For this purpose I mounted the town belfry, from whence I had a full view of the city of
Ghent, which is reckoned one of the largest in
Europe; and here I had not only an opportunity
of examining the mechanism of the chimes, as far
as they are played by clock-work, but could likewise
see the carillonneur perform with a kind of keys
communicating with bells, as those of the harpsichord and organ do with strings and pipes.

"I soon saw that the chimes in these countries
had a greater number of bells than those of the
largest peals in England; but when I mounted the
belfry I was astonished at the great quantity of
bells I saw; in short, there is a complete series or
scale of tones and semi-tones like those on the
harpsichord and organ.  The carillonneur was liter-
ally *at work*, and *hard* work indeed it must be.  He
was in his shirt with his collar unbuttoned, and in
a violent sweat.  There are pedals communicating
with the great bells, upon which, with his feet, he
played the bass to several sprightly and rather
difficult airs performed with his two hands upon the
upper species of keys.

"These keys are projecting sticks, wide enough
asunder to be struck with violence and velocity by
either of the two hands edgeways, without the
danger of hitting the neighboring keys.  The player
has a thick leather covering for the little finger of
each hand, otherwise it would be impossible for him
to support the pain which the violence of the stroke
necessary to be given to each key, in order to its
being distinctly heard throughout a very large town,
requires.

"The carillons are said to be originally from Alost,
in this country, and are still here and in Holland,
in their greatest perfection.  It is certainly a Gothic
invention, and perhaps a barbarous taste which
neither the French, the English nor the Italians
have imitated or encouraged.  The carillonneur at

my request played several pieces very dexterously in three parts, the first and second treble with the two hands on the upper set of keys, and the bass with the feet on the pedals.

"  .   .   .   As to the clock-work chimes, or those worked by a barrel, nothing, to my thinking, can be more tiresome; for night and day, to hear the same tune played every hour during six months, in such a stiff and unalterable manner, requires that kind of patience which nothing but a total absence of taste can produce.  .   .   .

"*In Amsterdam.*   At noon I attended M. Pothoff (organist), who is not young, and totally blind, to the tower of the Stad-huys or town-house, of which he is carillonneur; it is a drudgery unworthy of such a genius;  he has had this employment, however, many years, having been elected to it at thirteen. He had very much astonished me on the organ, after all that I had heard in the rest of Europe; but in playing those bells, his amazing dexterity raised my wonder much higher; for he executed with his two hands, passages that would be very difficult to play with the ten fingers; shakes, beats, swift divisions, triplets, and even arpeggios he has contrived to vanquish.

"He began with a psalm tune, with which their High Mightinesses are chiefly delighted, and which they require at his hands whenever he performs, which is on Tuesdays and Fridays.   He next played variations upon a psalm tune, with great fancy and even taste. When he had performed this task he was so obliging as to play a quarter of an hour extempore in such a manner as he thought would be more agreeable to me than psalmody; and in this he succeeded so well, that I sometimes forgot both the difficulty and defects of the instrument. He never played in less than three parts, marking the bass and the measure constantly with the pedals. I never heard a greater variety of passages in so short a time; he produced effects by the *pianos* and *fortes*, and the *crescendo* and the *shake*, both as to loudness and velocity, which I did not think possible upon an instrument that seemed to require little other merit than force in the performer.

"But surely this was a barbarous invention, and there is barbarity in the continuance of it. If M. Pothoff had been put into Dr. Dominicetti's hottest human caldron for an hour, he could not have perspired more violently than he did after a quarter of an hour of this furious exercise; he stripped to his shirt, put on his nightcap, and trussed up his sleeves for this execution; and he said he was forced to go to bed the instant it is over, in order to prevent his catching cold, as well as to recover himself; he being usually so much exhausted as to be utterly unable to speak.

"By the little attention that is paid to this performer, extraordinary as he is, it should seem as if some hewer of wood, and drawer of water, whose coarse constitution, and gross habits of body, required frequent sudorifics, would do the business, equally to the satisfaction of such unskillful and unfeeling hearers.

". . . Besides these carillons à clavier, the chimes here, played by clock-work, are much celebrated. The brass cylinder, on which the tunes are set, weighs 4,474 pounds, and has 7,200 iron studs fixed in it, which, in the rotation of the cylinder, give motion to the clappers of the bells. If their High Mightinesses' judgment, as well as taste, had not failed them, for half the prime cost of this expensive machine, and its real charge for repairs, new setting and constant attendance, they might have had one of the best bands in Europe. But those who can be charmed with *barrel music* certainly neither want, nor deserve better. There is scarce a church belonging to the Calvinists in Amsterdam, without its chimes, which not only play the same tunes every quarter of an hour for three months together, without their being changed; but by the difference of clocks, one has scarce five minutes quiet in the four and twenty hours, from these *carols for grown gentlemen*. In a few days' time I had so thorough a surfeit of them, that in as many months, I really believe, if they had not deprived me of hearing, I should have hated music in general."

# CHAPTER XXI

## THE BELLS OF RUSSIA

There were no bell foundries in Russia until the 16th century. Before that time the bells used in the churches were brought from Italy. But when the bell-founding art once started in Russia, it spread very rapidly, and before the end of the 16th century there were said to be more than five thousand bells in Moscow and its suburbs. On fête days, when they all rang at the same time, it was said that people could not hear each other speak in the streets. Whenever the czar left the city, the largest bell announced his departure and also heralded his return.

It came to be regarded as a deed of great merit for any citizen or royal personage to donate a bell to a church, and the larger the bell, the greater the merit.

Ivan Veliki had a great bell tower built near the Cathedral of St. Nicholas for the proper hanging of the bells that were donated to that church. This tower still stands, serving its original purpose (see Fig. 96). Each story is a belfry. In the first story, hanging in solitary grandeur, is a huge bell given to the cathedral by the Czar Boris Godunov in the early seventeenth century. Its weight is given by most writers as one hundred and twenty-eight tons, though some say it is one hundred and

FIG. 96.   *Tower of Ivan the Great, Moscow, Russia*

ten, and others less. A writer of 1850 refers to this bell sending out its mighty voice three times a year, "which produces a tremulous effect through the city, and a noise like the rolling of distant thunder."

Gramstorff Bros., Inc., Malden, Mass.

FIG. 97. *The "Great Bell of Moscow"*

The clapper of this bell is so heavy that it requires several men to sway it from side to side by pulling on ropes. It is the largest *ringing* bell in the world.

The second story of the Ivan Tower contains two huge bells, and each story contains bells arranged according to their size. There is one which weighs seventy-two tons, another fifty-nine tons, another seventeen tons, and many others of exceptional size and weight. As one climbs the steps of the tower, one passes thirty-three bells of various sizes placed at different heights in the tower.

The tower of Ivan Veliki stands inside the walls of the Kremlin—a fortified inclosure in the heart of Moscow—and contains the famous Cathedral of the Assumption, where all the sovereigns of Russia for several hundred years have been crowned, and many other revered and ancient buildings besides the Ivan Tower.

Within the Kremlin and near the Ivan Tower stands the largest and perhaps the most universally known bell in the world,—the Czar Kolokol, or king of bells, usually called the "Great Bell of Moscow." It is sometimes called Czarina Kolokol, or queen of bells. It weighs about two hundred tons, and still rests over the spot where it was cast nearly two hundred years ago (see Fig. 97). It is also seen in Figure 96.

In 1701 a very large bell of Moscow was destroyed by fire; and in 1733 the Empress Anna Ivanovna ordered a great bell to be cast to replace the old one. Usually the bell tower is made first, and the bell hung in it afterwards. But according to the empress' plan, the great bell was to be cast in the ground immediately beneath the place where it would be hung, and after it was completed the tower should be built around and above it, and thus the only moving it would require would be to lift it. In this way an enormous bell could be managed. The tower which was planned would be a mate to the great tower of Ivan Veliki, and the two buildings were to be connected with passageways at various heights, and thus both towers would be strengthened.

All Moscow was deeply interested in the new bell, and when it was being cast the nobles and other devout Russians, both rich and poor, threw into the molten metal all kinds of jewels, and plates of gold and silver. At last the bell was cast.

Then a terrible accident occurred. Writers disagree as to just how it came about that the great bell cracked; but they all agree that the great fire of 1737, which demolished so much of the city of Moscow, was the occasion of the break. Some say that the bell was still in the casting pit in the earth, and not yet cool, when the fire came, and that the water which was poured on the burning wood above the pit found its way down to the bell, which, still being hot, was cracked by the cold water. Others say that the bell was suspended from beams which, being destroyed by the fire, permitted the bell to fall and break and sink into the ground of its own weight. Still others say that the blazing wooden rafters which had been put up around the bell, fell upon it and heated the metal, and when water was poured on the burning timber above, it reached the bell and cracked it. In any case, in spite of the fact that the metal of the bell was nearly two feet thick, a great piece was broken out of it which made the bell dumb even before anyone had ever heard its voice! The severed piece weighs eleven tons (see Fig. 97).

For over a hundred years the mighty bell remained in the ground. In 1797, says Starmer, "a mechanician named Guirt made an attempt to raise this colossus; but his plans, though well conceived, were never carried out, as it was thought that in raising it, the bell would break into pieces." Again, in 1819, the raising of the bell was considered, but nothing was done until 1836. By order of Czar Nicholas the First, Aug. de Montferrand, an engineer of repute, was given instructions to raise the bell from its pit. The manipulation of such an enormous weight at that period was a problem of great difficulty. It was successfully done by means of twenty capstans, manned by a large number of soldiers, on July 23, 1836.

Montferrand gives the following description of the ornamentation on the bell: "Considered as a work of art this bell is remarkable for the beauty of its form and for its bas-reliefs. These represent portraits at full length and of natural size, although not finished, of the Czar Alexis Michaelovitch and the Empress Anna Ivanovna. . . . The upper part is ornamented by figures representing Our Lord, the Virgin, and the Holy Evangelists. The upper and lower friezes are composed of psalms, treated in a broad style and with a great deal of art."

On top of the bell is a ball upon which rests a Greek cross of gilded bronze, the total height being thirty-four feet. On one side of the pedestal is an inscription cut in a marble slab. Translated, it reads:

THIS BELL

CAST IN 1733, UNDER THE REIGN OF THE EMPRESS
ANNA IVANOVNA

AFTER HAVING BEEN BURIED IN THE EARTH FOR MORE THAN A
CENTURY WAS RAISED TO THIS PLACE

AUGUST 4, 1836

BY THE WILL AND UNDER THE GLORIOUS REIGN OF
THE EMPEROR NICHOLAS THE FIRST

Montferrand gives the particulars of the bell as follows; height, 20 feet, 7 inches; diameter, 22 feet, 8 inches; and weight, 193 tons. Other writers have computed its weight as 185, 200, and 220 tons. Its circumference has been given variously as 66 feet, 67 feet and 4 inches, 63 feet and 11 inches. Within the bell, it is said, forty people can assemble at one time, and the cavity beneath it has been used as a chapel.

One of the large bells in the Ivan Tower was cast in 1817, and called the "New Bell." It is twenty-one feet high, eighteen feet in diameter, and its tongue weighs 4,200 pounds. Like the Great Bell, the New Bell was also made to replace another large bell. In 1710 a bell called Bolshoi (the big) was cast weighing sixty-two tons, and was hung with thirty-two smaller ones in the Ivan Tower. During the French invasion of 1812 the belfry was almost destroyed, and the Bolshoi thrown down and broken. Five years later the bell was broken up and additional metal was given by the emperor to found a new bell, which should weigh seventy-two tons. The new bell was cast with great ceremony in the presence of great throngs of people and of the archbishop, who gave his benediction. Nearly all the inhabitants of Moscow assembled and proved their devotion by throwing gold, jewelry, and silver plate into the molten metal.

Later the New Bell was moved on a large wooden sledge from the foundry to the tower. A Te Deum was sung, and the labor of dragging the sledge was given over to the multitude, who disputed the honor of touching a rope. "The movements were regulated by little bells managed by Mr. Bogdanof, the founder, who stood on a platform attached to the bell. Part of the wall was taken down to admit its passage, and, as soon as it reached its destination, the people leaped upon Mr. Bogdanof, kissing his hands, cheeks and clothes, and showing by every means in their power the gratitude they felt at the restoration of their old favorite. Some days after this, the New Bell was slowly raised to the place of its predecessor and properly suspended." It is said that this bell sounds during the entire time that the words of the Nicene Creed are chanted.

Figure 98 shows a bell belonging to the cathedral at Leningrad which is made of worn-out and reclaimed coins.  The diameter is about eight feet.

FIG. 98.　*The great bell of the Cathedral of St. Isaac, Leningrad, Russia*

It is richly ornamented with four large medallions, one of Catherine II, one of Peter the Great, and two of other emperors.

There are many other large bells in Russia, particularly at Trotzk and Novgorod.  A most interesting peal of ancient bells still hangs in the campanile near the cathedral at Rostov

The bells of Russia are never rung by swinging, as is the case with English bells.  They are fixed immovably to their beams, and the clappers alone are movable.  The clapper is swung by means of leather bands which are pulled by ropes in such a manner as to cause it to strike the bell in different places. An old writer (of 1698) states that when the first Czar Kolokol was rung, forty or fifty men were employed, half on each side of the bell, who, by means of ropes, pulled the clapper to and fro.

Russia is second to no other country in its appreciation of bells. In spite of the sameness of Russian ringing, an accustomed ear easily learns the meanings of the various sounds that issue from the belfry. The different sized bells used, the number of rings, the length of time between the rings, the

Brown Bros.

FIG. 99. *Bell market at Moscow, Russia*

grouping, etc., all have definite meanings to the inhabitants, just as the clicks in the telegraph office are understood by those who know the code. How much the Russians love bells is shown by the display of bells for sale at their fairs. At the great fair in Nijni-Novgorod there were bells for sale which weighed a number of tons. Figure 99 (p. 229) is from a photograph of a bell market in Moscow.

The impressive bell tones which occur at the close of Tschaikovsky's 1812 Overture afford an instance of the soul-stirring effect of bells even in art. It was the awe-inspiring sounds of the great bells of Moscow which were uppermost in Tschaikovsky's mind when he composed that magnificent finale.

# CHAPTER XXII

## OTHER EUROPEAN BELLS

Italy is the birthplace of Christian church bells, and, as one would suppose, there are numerous old bells in that country. Figure 100 shows one in the cathedral at Siena, made in 1159, one of the oldest cast and dated bells in existence. This old bell is still in use. It has only two cannons (or loops), is about three feet high, and is shaped like a barrel. There are bells in Pisa dated 1106, 1154, and 1173; one in the Leaning Tower dated 1262, and one in Verona cast in 1149. Figure 101 (p. 232) shows an Italian bell dated 1184, now in a museum in Florence.

FIG. 100. *Italian bell, cast in 1159, now in Siena*

The famous artist Benvenuto Cellini made for Pope Clement VII, in the sixteenth century, a silver bell covered with designs of serpents, flies, grasshoppers, and other insects. This bell was used by the pope to give a papal cursing of the creatures represented whenever they became too numerous in the land. The curse, aided by the ringing of this bell, was supposed to have a powerful effect in checking the depredations of those

231

creatures which sometimes "covered the earth like a crawling blanket."

The great bell in St. Peter's Church at Rome,

made in 1786 and weighing over nine tons, has been considered the most beautiful bell in the world.

There are several very old bells still existing in France. Figure 19[1] shows an old bell of the seventh century from a church in Noyon. It is not cast, and the rivets may be plainly seen. Bells were hung in the various cathedrals of France as early as the tenth century, probably the oldest

FIG. 101. *Italian bell, cast in 1184, now in Florence*

cast bell now existing in France being an old bell of Normandy, cast in 1202, and now in the Museum of Bayeux (see Fig. 102).

By the thirteenth century large bells were being made. Figure 103[2] shows a thirteenth-century bell and Figure 104[2] a fourteenth-century bell of

[1]Chap. IV, p. 37.                    [2]See p. 235.

France. The "Jacquelin" of Paris, cast in 1400, weighed twelve and a half tons, and the celebrated "Ambroise Bell" at Rouen, cast in 1501, weighed over eighteen tons! In 1786, when Louis XVI visited Rouen, amid the public rejoicings this bell cracked, which incident was afterward considered an omen of the fate of that unfortunate king. In 1793 the bell was converted into cannon.

The famous city of Avignon in the south of France in its palmy days had three hundred bells, and was called the "Ringing City." In the cathedral was a

FIG. 102.   *French bell from Fontenailles, dated 1202*

silver bell which was especially famous for its supposed ability to ring of its own accord.[1]

[1]See chap. XXIII, p. 250.

In 1547 Francis the First, king of France, imposed a tax on salt. This caused a rebellion, and at Bordeaux the rebels murdered the king's lieutenant, Tristram de Moneins, and filled his body with salt. Henry II sent the constable, Anne de Montmorency, who with the help of the Duke de Guise caused one hundred and fifty persons to be executed, and he obliged the nobles of the city to exhume, with their own nails, the buried body of De Moneins; then the man who first sounded the tocsin was condemned to be hanged from the clapper of the bell. All the bells which had been used to rouse the people to rebellion were destroyed, and the others were carried to different towns. This deprivation of its bells was a punishment very humiliating to the city. Two years later, however, Henry II pardoned the people of Bordeaux, and one of the happy results of the pardon was the restoration of bells in the churches.[1]

The large clock bell at Notre Dame in Paris was cast in 1682, and is eleven feet in diameter. There is also a fine Bourbon bell in Notre Dame called "Emanuel." This bell was cast in 1685, weighs more than eight tons, and is eight feet and seven inches in diameter.

In former days the bell ringers of France and Spain often rang the bells by jumping ape-like from one bell rope to another, to the great uneasiness of all onlookers.

[1]Rev. H. T. Ellacombe, in *Church Bells of Devon*, Exeter, 1872.

FIG. 103. *A French bell dated 1273*

FIG. 104. *A French bell of the fourteenth century*

Germany is not lacking in bells, both old and new. Figure 20 (chap. IV) shows one which was made in Cologne in the seventh century. There is one in Bavaria dated 1144, and one at Freiburg dated 1258.

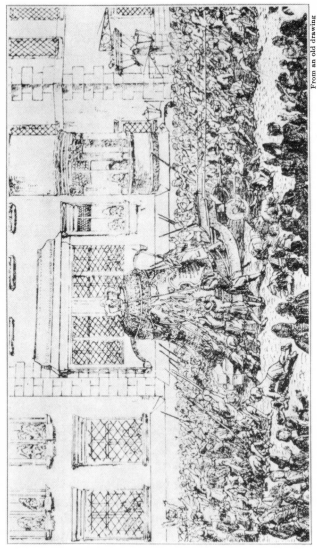

FIG. 105.   *Big bell on its way to St. Stephen's Church, Vienna, in 1711*

In the fourteenth century bell foundries were set up in most of the principal towns, and the art spread over the country.

One of the most famous bells of Germany is in Erfurt, Saxony. In 1451 a large bell was cast for the Erfurt Cathedral, but in 1472 a fire in the cathedral melted the bell. In 1497 another great bell was cast, which bears the name of "Maria Gloriosa." It is supposed to weigh fifteen tons, and has a diameter of eight feet, seven and one-half inches. Its tone is fine and pure, and in clear weather it may be heard at a distance of three miles. It is considered a very fine example of bell founding.

In the Church of St. Stephen at Vienna is a large bell weighing over seventeen tons, with a diameter of nearly ten feet. It was cast in 1711 by order of Emperor Joseph from the cannon left by the Turks when they raised the siege of that city. Figure 105 is from an old drawing which represents this bell being carried through the streets of Vienna on the way from the foundry to the church. The following news concerning this bell appeared in a New York paper of March 5, 1925, with the heading: "Vienna's 17-Ton Bell is Rung, 200 Years Old, Silent for 50."

"The big bell of famous St. Stephen's Cathedral, weighing seventeen tons, that has been silent for fifty years, was rung again today.

"The bell was made two hundred years ago. It has not been rung for the last five decades because of the tower being thought unsafe."

Figure 106 is a very ornate bell cast in Saxony about 1860.

Two famous bells, the "Maria Gloriosa" and the "Emperor," hung for many years in the twin towers

FIG. 106.  *Bell at Stargard, cast about 1860*

of the Cologne Cathedral.[1]  They were cast from the metal of forty-two French cannon captured by the Germans in the War of 1870.  In the late World War they were again made into cannon.  A massive new bell was made for this cathedral in 1924.  Figure 107 shows this bell as it was being moved from the foundry.  The same bell is also pictured in Figure 47[2].

The oldest dated bell in Denmark is at Odense, cast in 1300.  In Norway many large bells were destroyed at the time of the Reformation, and

[1]See Fig. 156 on p. 360.          [2]See p. 94.

others were, from time to time, melted down and turned into money for the wars. However, there are several bells in Scandinavia with Runic inscriptions. Figure 108 on page 240 is a drawing of the "Dref Bell" in Sweden. The Runic inscription is read from right to left. Translated, it means: "Brother Sbialbuthi made me. Jesus Christus. Ave Maria Gracia."

One of the most famous bells of Europe is the great alarm bell "Roland," which hangs in the belfry of Ghent in Belgium. It was cast in 1343, recast in 1659, and bears the following inscription: *"Meester Jan van Roosbeke, clock-meester. Ick heete Roelandt: Als men my slaet, dan is't brandt; Als*

Gilliams Service, N.Y.

Fig. 107. *Moving the big bell for the Cologne Cathedral*

*men my luyd, is't zegen of storm in Vlaenderland.''*
Translated, this means (following the name of the maker): "My name is Roland; when I toll, there is fire; and when I ring, there is victory in the land." It was badly cracked again in July, 1914. For many generations Roland has called the citizens of

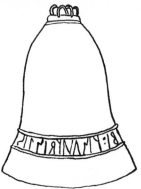

FIG. 108.   *The "Dref Bell" of Sweden*

Ghent together to defend their town, and there are few bells in the world that have been so beloved.

Above the belfry is a gilded copper dragon which was made at Ghent at the close of the fourteenth century. For a time the people of Bruges possessed this dragon, but it later came back into the possession of the Ghent burghers, who placed it above the belfry tower. There is a legend that the Crusaders brought this dragon from Constantinople to Bruges, but this is probably only a myth.

The bell fame of Belgium and Holland lies in their carillons.[1]

There is a bell in the cathedral of Toledo, Spain, which is said to weigh seventeen tons, and has long been celebrated for its size and for the stories connected with it. One writer says that fifteen shoemakers could sit under it and draw out their cobbler's thread without touching. Another story about this bell runs thus:[2] A rich count of Toledo had a son who, having killed a man in a duel, sought refuge in the cathedral while his father went to Madrid to petition the king for his pardon. "No," said the king; "he who has killed a man must die!" The count continued to petition and the king to refuse, until at length the king, wishing to get rid of him, said: "When you can make a bell at Toledo that I can hear at Madrid, I'll pardon the young man." Now Toledo is nearly sixty miles from Madrid. The count went home, and some time after, as the king was sitting in his palace at the open window, he heard a distant roll. "Volgame Dias," "God help me!" he cried. "That's the bell of Toledo!" and the young man obtained his pardon.

Many bells of Spanish make were brought to America during the time of the Spanish missions, and some of them are still in existence in this country. Some of these are shown in Figures 117 and 118.[3]

[1] See chap. XIX.
[2] Rev. H. T. Ellacombe, in *Church Bells of Devon*.
[3] See pp. 281 and 282.

With the possible exception of Russia, no country of Europe has attached more importance to church bells than has Great Britain. Ireland claims the oldest Christian bells in existence.[1] Figure 109 shows three modern bells of Ireland, cast by an English founder. They are the largest and the smallest bells of the carillon of the Armagh Cathedral.

John Taylor & Co.

FIG. 109.  *Three bells of the carillon in Armagh Cathedral, Ireland*

The oldest dated bell in England is one at Claughton, Lancashire, bearing the date 1296, but with no other inscription. There is one, however, in Surrey which is said to date from 1250 or earlier. "Great Peter" of Exeter has been traced back to the middle of the fourteenth century, but, like most of the old bells, it has been recast,—once in

[1] See chap. v.

1484, and again in 1676. It is used now as a clock bell, for curfew and matins.

St. Dunstan's bell at Canterbury Cathedral was cast in 1430.

"Great Peter" of Gloucester has the distinction of being the only medieval *signum*, or great bell, now remaining in England. It was probably cast about the middle of the fifteenth century. Every evening at nine o'clock it is struck with a hammer forty-nine times.

Sir Henry Vernon of Tong, in Shropshire, once lost his way in a forest and was guided home by the sound of the bells of the village. In gratitude he gave a bell in 1518 to the parish church of Tong, and ordered that it should be tolled "when any Vernon came to Tong." It weighs two and one-half tons, and is called the "Great Bell of Tong." In 1720, and again in 1892, it had to be recast.

In the reign of Henry VIII there stood in St. Paul's churchyard a lofty bell tower containing four bells called "Jesus Bells," the largest in London. In a gambling game with one of his courtiers, Sir Miles Partridge. King Henry staked the bell tower and its bells. Sir Miles won, and had the tower pulled down and the bells broken up. A few years afterward this gentleman was hanged; and some of the old writers have said that it was a judgment sent upon him for gambling for bells.

"Great Tom" of Lincoln is a very old and well known bell. It was probably made during the reign of Queen Elizabeth, and recast in 1610. It suffered a severe crack some two hundred years later, and was again melted and recast, with an additional ton of metal, in 1835, and now weighs five tons. It is used as a sermon bell on great festivals, and tolls for the funerals of church dignitaries and members of the royal family. It is also used as a clock bell, and is sometimes rung on Good Friday.

"Great Tom" of Oxford hangs in a belfry called Tom's Tower over the gateway to Christ Church College. The bell has a long inscription beginning "Magnus Thomas Oxoniensis." It is the descendant of one of the bells of Osney Abbey given to the college. This old bell was christened Mary at the beginning of Bloody Mary's reign. It was damaged and recast in 1612; was again broken and recast in 1680, and is now called Tom. It still tolls one hundred and one strokes every night at nine o'clock, as a signal that all the undergraduates must return to their colleges. The one hundred and one strokes is a time-honored custom, that being the number of students enrolled the first year of the college. It is claimed that the two Toms (of Oxford and of Lincoln) owe their names to the fact that they give out a sound which resembles that name

The hour bell of St. Paul's Cathedral in London is one of England's famous bells, cast in 1716, and weighing over five tons. The ancestor of this bell was old "Great Tom" of Westminster,[1] which hung in a campanile opposite Westminster Hall until 1698, when the campanile was pulled down and the bell moved to St. Paul's. It cracked soon after, and was recast in 1716. It is struck every hour by machinery connected with the clock, and the clapper hangs idle except when the bell is tolled to announce the death or funeral of a bishop of London, a dean of St. Paul's, a member of the royal family, or the Lord Mayor of the year.

"Great Peter" of York is one of England's largest bells, being over seven feet high and weighing ten and three-quarters tons. When it was cast, in 1845, it required fourteen days to cool. Every day at noon it is struck twelve times, and it is tolled

Fig. 110. *"Great Paul" of St. Paul's Cathedral, London, being lifted into the tower*

occasionally for deaths or funerals. It is also given twelve strokes at midnight on New Year's Eve.

[1]See p. 162.

The largest bell in England is "Great Paul," in St. Paul's Cathedral. It was cast in 1881 by Taylor of Loughborough, and weighs seventeen and one-half tons, is nearly nine feet high, and nine and one-half feet in diameter. Its tone is low E flat. Figure 110 (p. 245) shows the bell being lifted into the tower of St. Paul's Cathedral.

Perhaps the most widely known of England's bells is "Big Ben," a bell of thirteen and one-half tons which hangs in the bell tower of the Houses of Parliament in London. The complete story of this bell is given in chapter XVI.

The third largest bell in England was made recently by the Taylor bell foundry for Bristol University, and weighs something over twelve tons.

England's carillons have been mentioned in another chapter. The rapidly growing interest in carillon music will probably result in more and finer bells being made, not only for Great Britain and the Continent, but for all other countries as well.

# CHAPTER XXIII

## EUROPEAN BELL LEGENDS

When Clotaire II, king of France (615 A.D.), was at Sens in Burgundy, he heard a bell in the church of St. Stephen which pleased him so much that he ordered it to be taken to Paris. The bell was so distressed at being carried away from home that it turned dumb on the road and lost all its sound. When the king heard of this, he was much concerned. A few years before this the French army had been frightened away by the ringing of the bells in St. Stephen's Church, and now the king was perhaps no less frightened by the silence of this one. He commanded that the bell should be carried back to Sens. No sooner did the bell approach the town than it recovered its voice, and rang so loudly that it was heard at Sens while it was yet seven miles away!

Many stories are told of bells which would not allow themselves to be taken away from the churches to which they belonged, or where they were baptized. In some cases, bells which were removed were thought to take nightly trips to their old homes unless they were securely tied with chains and ropes. In Wiltshire there is a legend of a tenor bell having been conjured into the river; but when night came the bell returned, having overcome the fiend that conjured it. The ringer says, in relating the incident in rime:

> "In spite of all the devils in hell
> Here comes our old and faithful bell."

Not only the Celts[1] but other Europeans also believed in the power of bells to work miraculous punishments upon wrongdoers. The incident of Charlemagne's bell which would not ring (probably because the clapper was not rightly adjusted, or the bell not properly hung) will be recalled.[2] This bell was ever afterward looked upon with great veneration as the discoverer and punisher of the dishonest bell founder.

The bishop of Bangor offers another case of miraculous bell punishment. This bishop sold his cathedral bells, and became blind while they were being shipped.

There is a story of a band of robbers who went into a monastery, stole what they wished, and then, out of mere bravado, went to the bell ropes and began to ring a peal upon the bells. The priest prayed, a miracle was wrought, and the robbers were unable to let the ropes go. The story does not state how long these robbers were forced to swing in the air.

Cruikshank, one of the old English artists, has made this legend famous by his drawing of the robbers' uncomfortable plight (see Fig. 111).

[1]See chap. VI.            See p. 38.

Another thief who was brought to justice by a
church bell is well known.  This thief broke into
a small church in Scotland where he hoped to reap
a rich harvest by stealing the communion plate.  He
heard steps outside the building and, fearing that
he might be discovered, looked about for a place
to hide.  In a corner of the church he espied a long

Fig. 111.  *Cruikshank's drawing of the robber band*

rope hanging from the dark shadows above and
dangling to the floor.  "Aha," he said to himself,

"I'll just climb up there and be out of sight," and laid hold of the rope. His weight rang the bell so loudly that his pursuers came at once to the spot. The thief, being caught, turned to the bell which had brought him to justice, saying: "If it had not been for thy long tongue and empty head, I should not have been in my present predicament!"

According to many legends, bells have refused to sound at times, and have also rung of their own accord upon suitable occasions. A bell in the monastery of Meinulph was said to ring unaided whenever any of the nuns died. It is also recorded that the church bells rang without human assistance when Thomas à Becket was murdered. In 1062, when a great famine raged in Flanders, a certain man was found dead of hunger at Ardenburg, near Bruges. It is recorded that while he was being buried the parish priests forbade the tolling of the bells, because he was unknown; and to the wonder of all, the bells sounded forth of their own accord.

A silver bell in the cathedral at Avignon was famous for its power to ring of its own volition. It rang to announce the accession of a new pope, and when a pope died it was said to toll without stopping for the space of twenty-four hours.

Saint Hilda died at Whitby in the year 680. Bede, the historian, states that "one of the Sisters named Bega, in the distant monastery of Hackness (13 miles away), while she was in the dormitory, on the night of Hilda's death, on a sudden heard in the air the well known sound of the bell which used to call the Sisters to prayers when any one of them was being taken from this world. Opening her eyes, she saw, as she thought, the top of the house open and a strong light pour in from above. Looking earnestly into the light, she saw the soul of the departed Abbess attended toward heaven by angels. She told of her vision to the Sisters who presided over the monastery, and they assembled the Sisters in the church. They were engaged in praying and singing songs for the soul of St. Hilda when the messenger came to report her death."

There are many legends of buried churches from which the bells may be heard to ring from the interior of the earth and from under water. In some of the mountainous districts of Europe the peasants collect in the fields or valleys to hear the bells which, as they believe, "are sure to sound out for joy on Christmas Eve from beneath their feet." In Germany there is a legend of a church lost in a thick forest. The German poet Uhland refers to this in his lines which read, when translated:

> Oft in the forest far one hears
> A passing sound of distant bells;
> Nor legends old, nor human wit,
> Can tell us whence the music swells.
> From the lost church 'tis that soft though
> Faint ringing cometh on the wind:
> Once many pilgrims trod the path,
> But no one now the way can find.

Much poetry hangs about these legends, relating how, "through the silent night—whether to the fisher or the sailor or the miner—they speak of a city or a temple that is buried, or a life that has passed away into darkness, yet lives, and with its pure and tender sound calls from the deep." "The Sunken Bell" by Hauptmann is a well-known poem which was inspired by these legends. Even musical composers have made use of them, a notable example of which is Debussy's "Disappearing Cathedral."

There is a valley in Nottinghamshire, England, said to have been caused by an earthquake several centuries ago which swallowed up an entire village together with the church. Formerly the people assembled in this valley regularly, every Christmas Day, to listen to the ringing of the bells in the church beneath them. It was positively asserted that these sounds could be heard by putting the ear to the ground and listening very attentively. Even now on Christmas morning the old men and women tell their children and young friends to go to the valley and stoop down to listen to the Christmas bells ringing merrily beneath them.

Two fine bells once hung in a church tower in the town of Lochen, Holland. These bells, however, had not been baptized; so one day the Evil One appeared and suddenly carried them away from the church tower and hid them in two ponds near the town. This was many years ago, they say, but the peasants still believe they hear the bells ringing from these ponds of stagnant water every year on Christmas Eve, precisely at twelve o'clock.

A little chapel is said to have been submerged in one of the lakes at Crose Mere, England; and the villagers will tell of how the bells may be heard ringing constantly beneath the still water.

Near the end of the seventeenth century Port Royal, in the West Indies, was submerged. For many years the sailors in those parts would tell wonderful stories of how they anchored amongst the chimneys and church steeples of the city beneath the sea. They also declared that at times the sound of the church bells, as they were agitated by the waves, could be plainly heard.

The legend of the Jersey bells is well known among the people of that island in the English Channel. Many years ago the twelve parish churches in Jersey each possessed a beautiful and valuable peal of bells; but during the long English civil war the states determined on selling these bells to defray the heavy expenses of their army. The bells were accordingly collected and sent to France for that purpose. But on the passage the ship foundered, and everything was lost, to show the wrath of heaven at the sacrilege. Ever since then, just before a storm, these bells ring up from the deep; and to this day the fishermen of St. Ouen's Bay always go to the edge of the water before embarking, to listen for "the bells upon the wind." If those warning notes are heard, nothing will induce them to leave

the shore; if all is quiet, they fearlessly set sail.
As a gentleman who has versified the legend says:

> 'Tis an omen of death to the mariner,
> Who wearily fights with the sea,
> For the foaming surge is his winding sheet,
> And his funeral knell are we;—
> His funeral knell our passing bell,
> And his winding sheet the sea.[1]

The bells of Bottreaux which were lost on the
Cornish coast have furnished a legend similar to
that of the Jersey bells. The Bottreaux bells had
arrived in a goodly ship to within sight of the town
in which they were to be hung. But before the ship
landed the captain used such blasphemous language
that, as a punishment (according to the legend),
the vessel was driven on shore, and foundered
amidst the rocks, with all its freight on board. The
bells, however, may still be heard ringing from the
bottom of the sea with a warning voice amidst
the breakers when a storm is about to rise.

Once Peter Gyldenstierne, of Jutland, in Denmark, in some war with the Swedes was so struck
with the tone of two bells that hung in a Swedish
church tower that he determined to obtain them and
take them to Jutland. He consulted all the villagers as to how he might get the bells down without
injuring the church tower, but no one could assist
him. Finally a man came to him and said: "Provide for my wife and children, and I will show you

[1] Rev. H. T. Ellacombe.

how to obtain the bells." Peter agreed. The peasant then had two lofty hillocks of sand erected at the side of the tower; then cutting the chains that held the bells, he let them roll down gently, one after the other. They reached the ground safely, the tower was not injured, and the peasant forthwith claimed his reward. "Yes," answered Gyldenstierne, "I will keep my promise, and provide handsomely for your wife and children. But for yourself, a traitor to your country, you shall take the place of the bells." And the peasant was strung up to the church tower.

One of the bells arrived safely in Jutland and was hung in the tower of Thim Church. The other one was shipwrecked off the coast by "Missum Fiorde." It fell tongue uppermost, however, and according to the story, it still lies embedded in the sand. On a summer's evening when the tide is low, "the music may still be heard by the fishermen who ply their crafts in the water, music so beautiful, they say, the like was never heard. As for the other bell, her tones are sad and melancholy; no wonder—she wants to come down to her sister."

Many of the peasants of Europe preserve the tradition that the baptized church bells wander every year to Rome for confession. They leave on Thursday in Passion week, and return on Easter morning. In some places the children gaze into the sky and imagine they see in the clouds the figures of angels bringing the bells home after they have received the pope's blessing. The fact that the bells were not rung during the three days before Easter probably gave rise to this belief. Figure 112 shows a detail of the celebration in Spain on the occasion of the bell's return from Rome, when the people dance in the streets and the young men perform gymnastic feats on the bell ropes.

In Florence and other places in Italy the oil that dropped from the framework of church bells was regarded as a valuable remedy for various ailments. People who suffered with rheumatism and other complaints were rubbed with this oil, and they fully believed that it helped them.

In the *Lay of the Last Minstrel*, Walter Scott relates an incident of the wondrous Michael Scott:

> A wizard of such dreadful fame
> That when in Salamanca's cave,
> Him listed his magic wand to wave,
> The bells would ring in Notre Dame!

According to the story, Michael Scott was sent upon an embassy to the king of France, and for this trip he called forth by magic a huge black horse that flew through the air to France with Michael on his back. When he arrived in Paris he tied his horse at the royal gate, entered the palace, and stood before the king. The king was about to refuse the request when he was asked to postpone his answer until he had seen Michael's horse stamp three times. The first stamp shook every steeple in Paris and made all the bells ring. The second stamp threw down three of the towers of the palace; and before the horse had stamped a third time the king granted Michael's request and told him to begone.

Countless stories have been told of bells which pronounced words, and even sentences, when they rang. These stories take hold on the imagination of simple peoples, if, when they are told, bell sounds are imitated in repeating the words the bells are supposed to pronounce. Such a story is told of a bell in the old church at Krempe, in Holstein. While this bell was being cast the people from all the country around brought silver coins and trinkets to be thrown into the fusing metal, for it was thought that the mixture of silver in bell metal improved the sound of the bell. The avaricious founder decided to keep these valuable offerings for himself, so he put them

FIG. 112. *Celebrating the return of the bells at Easter*

all aside; but during his temporary absence the apprentice took all the silver and threw it into the melting mass. When the master returned the apprentice told him that he had applied the silver to the purpose for which it was presented by the donors; at this the master grew very angry, and killed the lad.

When the bell was cast, and hung in the tower of the church, its tone proved to be very fine, but also mournful; and whenever it was rung it distinctly sounded like "*Schad' um den Jungen! Schad' um den Jungen!*" ("Pity for the lad! Pity for the lad!")

"The church bell of Keitum, on the Isle of Silt in the North Sea, off the coast of Denmark, distinctly says '*Ing Dung!*' which are the names of two pious spinsters at whose expense the old bell tower of the church was erected long ago. There exists an old prophecy in the place that, after the bell shall have fallen down and killed the finest youth of the island, the tower will likewise fall, and will kill the most beautiful girl of Silt. A fine youth was actually killed by the fall of the bell in the year 1739; and since that time the young girls of Silt are generally very timid in approaching the tower, for each one thinks that she may be the destined victim."[1]

The church at Dambeck, in northern Germany, is so very old that the oldest inhabitants of the place affirm that its outer walls, which only are now

[1]Carl Engel, in *Musical Myths and Facts*.

remaining, were built before the deluge. The tower with the bells is sunk in the Lake Müritz; and in olden time the people have often seen the bells rising to the surface of the water on St. John's Day. One afternoon some children, who had carried the dinner to their parents laboring in an adjacent field, stopped by the lake to wash the napkins. These little urchins saw the bells, which had risen above the water. One of the children, a little girl, spread her napkin over one for the purpose of drying it; the consequence was that the bell could not descend again. But though all the rich people of the town of Röbel came to secure the bell for themselves, they were unable to remove it, notwithstanding that they brought sixteen strong horses to draw it from the place. They were still unsuccessfully urging the horses when a poor man happened to pass that way from the fields with a pair of oxen. The man, seeing what the rich people were about, at once told them to put their horses aside; he then yoked his pair of oxen to the bell, and said: *"Nu met God foer Arme un Rieke, all to geliekel!"* ("Now with the help of God, alike for poor and rich.") Having pronounced these words, he drove the bell without the least difficulty to Röbel, where it was soon hung in the tower of the new church. Whenever a really poor man dies in Röbel, this bell is tolled for him free of charge, and it distinctly says "Dambeck! Dambeck!"[1]

[1]Carl Engel, in *Musical Myths and Facts.*

The prophetic words chimed by the bells of Bow Church to Dick Whittington are known in all English speaking countries. According to the story, Dick was a poor orphan who found his way to London and worked in the house of a rich merchant named Fitzwarren. Dick slept in a garret where the rats were very troublesome until he acquired a cat to keep him company. This cat was the only thing he possessed in the world.

One day Mr. Fitzwarren prepared a ship to sail to foreign countries, loading it with valuable things to sell. All the servants in the house were allowed to send something of their own to be sold, to try their luck in the field of foreign trade. Dick, since he owned nothing else, sent his beloved cat.

Some time after the ship had sailed, Dick was treated so unkindly by the other servants in the merchant's family that he decided he could stand it no longer, and ran away. He walked as far as Halloway, and there sat down on a stone to rest and to think which road he should take. While he was thinking, the bells of Bow Church in London began to ring the tune given on the opposite page. As he listened, it seemed to him that the bells were saying, "Turn again, Whittington, Lord Mayor of London! Turn again, Whittington, Lord Mayor of London!"

"Lord Mayor of London!" he said to himself. "Of course I will obey the bells and turn back if that is what they promise me! I am willing to

## THE BELLS TO WHITTINGTON

Turn a - gain, Whit - ting - ton,
Lord Mayor of Lon don;
Turn a - gain, Whit - ting - ton,
Lord Mayor of Lon - don.

endure anything if I may only be Lord Mayor when I am a man!'' So Dick turned back and again took up his work among the Fitzwarren servants.

Meanwhile, the ship landed on the shores of Barbary at a time when the queen's residence was overrun with rats. The cat was sold to the queen of Barbary for enough gold to make Dick a rich man. The story relates that he married the merchant's daughter, became a great merchant himself, was three times Lord Mayor of London, and was made a knight by King Henry V.

The latter part of this story is probably true, for the Sir Richard Whittington of history was three times Lord Mayor of London, was very wealthy, and famous for his acts of charity and public helpfulness. He died in 1423. In truth, however, Sir Richard was never a poor boy, and the famous legend of Dick and his cat is probably a myth. The story has been associated with the bells of Bow Church for hundreds of years, and the song on page 261 is placed among the old English folk songs.

Many stories are told of great and lifelong affection for certain bells. Such a story is associated with the bells of St. Mary's Church in Limerick, Ireland. These bells were made by an Italian founder, who spent so much care and thought upon them that by the time they were finished he had come to love them almost as if they were human beings. He sold them to a convent for enough money to buy for himself a little home near by, where he hoped to spend the rest of his days within sound of their daily ringing. But his peaceful content did not last long. The convent was destroyed, and the bells were carried away to Ireland.

Various misfortunes sent the poor bell maker wandering about the world, seeking some place of quiet happiness. In his old age he found his way to Ireland—to Limerick, where in the steeple of St. Mary's Church hung the bells which he had made. One day, as he sailed up the River Shannon, he heard the bells ringing as he looked at the church steeple. After all these years he remembered their tones, and knew they were his bells. His joy at hearing them again was so great that his feeble frame could not bear it, and he died while yet the bells were ringing.

A peasant bell ringer of earlier days in Italy was so devoted to the large bell which he rang every day that when orders were given for this bell to be kept silent for a time (as a punishment to the city) his grief was unbearable. He climbed to the belfry, threw his arms about the bell, and wept. Leaning against the bell, he wailed so bitterly and so loudly, and the sound of his voice was so intensified by the metal, that his wailing was heard like the mournful ringing of a bell all over the city and far out into the country beyond. There he died, so the story goes, broken hearted, still clinging to his beloved bell.

Another story of lifelong affection for a bell is told in chapter I, pages 1–8.

Bells have been blamed for the disappearance of the dwarfs and other mysterious inhabitants of fairy-tale days. These curious traditions may still be found among the country folk of northern Europe—it being such an easy way to explain the absence of those small beings who could not bear the sound of bell ringing!

According to one of these legends,[1] a large number of mountain dwarfs of Holstein were so troubled

[1] Carl Engel, in *Musical Myths and Facts*.

by the sounds of the many new church bells introduced there, that they made up their minds to leave
the country. So they arranged their affairs, set
out in a body, and traveled northward until they
came to the River Eider. There they found a
ferryboat, but, it being late at night, the ferryman
was asleep. They knocked at his door several
times, and finally he appeared with a bludgeon in
his hand ready to punish the disturber of his sleep.

As he walked in the direction of the river he saw
before him, to his great surprise, a multitude of
gray-looking dwarfs, who moved restlessly to and
fro, like ants when an anthill is opened. One of
them, a very old dwarf with a long white beard,
approached the ferryman and asked that he ferry
the company across the river.

"You will be paid for your services," said the
dwarf with the long beard. "Just place your hat
upon the bank of the river for our people to throw
the money into as they enter the boat."

The ferryman did so, and the boat was soon
crowded with the little beings, who scrambled about
like insects. There were so many that he had to
make the trip several times before he had carried
all of them across the river. He noticed that each
of them threw what seemed to be a grain of sand
into the hat; but he did not mind that; his one
thought was to be finished with these strange people,
for he felt very uncomfortable among them. The
dwarf with the long beard had told him that they

were compelled to migrate to some other part of the world on account of the church bells and the hymn singing, which they could no longer endure. This, in the mind of the ferryman, seemed to prove their connection, in some way, with evil spirits, and he was greatly relieved when the last load was on the other side. Then, looking across the river, he saw the whole field glittering with lights which flitted about in every direction. The little travelers had lighted their lanterns. When he came to the bank and took up his hat, how he opened his eyes! The hat was full of gold!

Long ago, in Sweden, it was thought to be the common practice with pagan giants to hurl stones at the churches, though they never hit them. The sound of the church bell was very hateful to these giants. Near Laga[1] is a mountain celebrated as the former domicile of a giant, who lived there until the time of the Reformation, when the church of the place was provided with bells. One morning the dejected giant addressed a peasant from Laga whose name was Jacob and who happened to be at the foot of the mountain. "Jacob," said the giant in a subdued tone of voice, "come in, Jacob, and eat of my stew!"

But Jacob, alarmed at the kind invitation, replied rather hesitatingly: "Sir, if you have more stew than you can consume, you had better keep the rest for tomorrow."

[1]Carl Engel, in *Musical Myths and Facts*.

Upon this sensible advice the dejected giant complained: "I cannot stay here even till tomorrow! I am compelled to leave this place because of the constant bell ringing, which is quite insupportable!"

Whereupon Jacob, getting a little courage, asked him: "And when do you intend to come back again?"

The dejected giant, hearing himself thus questioned, replied whiningly: "Come back again? Oh, certainly not until the mount has become the bottom of the sea, and the sea itself arable and fertile land. If this should ever happen, then I may perhaps come back again." So the church bells banished paganism from Sweden!

The bells of justice which were used ages ago in China[1] and later in other countries have given rise to several legends. One of these is called "The Stone of Gratitude," which runs as follows:

Once a Roman emperor became blind, but he still wished to govern his people wisely, and not allow them to suffer from his loss of eyesight. So in his palace he had a bell hung with a long rope fastened to it and extending to the outside of the palace so that the rope could be pulled and the bell rung by any sufferer from injustice. When this bell was rung, one of the emperor's officers went down to hear the complaint and right the wrong.

It happened that a serpent had her home in the ground under the end of the bell rope. Here she

[1]See p. 306.

kept her little serpents safe from harm. One day an ugly toad came into her home, frightened her little ones, and refused to go out. Then the serpent, in desperation, coiled her tail about the bell rope and rang the bell. The judge came down, and after he had finally discovered the serpent and the toad, he reported the case to the emperor.

"The toad is in the wrong," said the emperor. "Kill it, and let the serpent keep her home." The judge did as he was told.

A few days later, as the emperor lay in his bed, the serpent came into the room and crawled toward him. The servants were afraid lest it do some harm to the emperor, but he said, "It will do me no harm. I have been just to it. Let us see what it will do."

The serpent glided up the bed and laid upon the emperor's eyes a precious stone which it carried in its mouth. Then it slipped out of the room and disappeared. But no sooner had the stone touched the emperor's eyes than his sight was restored.[1]

"The Bell of Atri," another justice-bell story, from Longfellow's *Tales of a Wayside Inn*, is given in the chapter on "The Poetry of Bells."[2]

[1]From Horace Scudder's *The Book of Legends Told Over Again*.
[2]Pp. 404-8.

## CHAPTER XXIV

## THE BELLS OF AMERICA

America's early colonists were too greatly occupied with more serious problems to practice the bell-founding art, and the first bells used by the colonies were brought from Europe. Only a few of these have been preserved. In the confusion and rapid changes of those early days, they were lost, or broken by bad handling, or destroyed by fire.

Records show that Harvard College had a bell in a turret in 1643.[1] Reference is made to it in 1650 in the rules and regulations of the "tolling of the bell." A second bell was acquired about 1658. In 1667 the college had regular bell ringing, with specially stated times for ringing, and instructions as to the manner of "ringing" and "tolling."

Probably the oldest English bell in this country now is one in the courthouse at Barnstable, Massachusetts, dated 1675.[2] In 1685 William Penn imported a bell to Philadelphia, where it probably hung in the crotch of a tree and summoned the people to church and to other meetings. This bell was hung in the town hall in 1705.

A bell now preserved in a church at Passaic, New Jersey, was cast in Holland in 1700.[3] The

[1]A. H. Nichols, in *The Bells of Harvard College*, Boston, 1911.
[2]A. H. Nichols, in *New England Genealogical Register* for 1916.
[3]Passaic church tablet.

original bells of Trinity Church in New York were cast in England about 1700, and were said to have been the gift of Queen Anne to that church.[1] There is now in Trinity Church of Newport, Rhode Island, an English bell cast in 1702, bearing an inscription which states that it was donated to the church by Queen Anne in 1709. It has been recast, however, and made much heavier than it was originally. The chimes of Christ Church, Philadelphia, are also claimed to have been a gift from Queen Anne. During the Revolution they were removed from the church and sunk in the Delaware River to prevent their being destroyed by the British. These well-known chimes are among Philadelphia's greatest treasures. In the Dutch Reformed Church of New York there is a bell cast at Amsterdam in 1731.

A ring of eight bells was ordered from England for Christ Church, Boston, in 1744, and the cost was met by subscribers.[2] They are said to be the first set of bells cast for America. They were used for change ringing, after the English custom, as is shown by a circle of eight deeply worn depressions, noticed many years ago in the floor boards of the ringing chamber, where the circle of ringers stood. For more than a century and a half these bells have mingled their voices with every popular ovation in all public rejoicing and sorrowing. "In 1894 the bells were overhauled[3] and new supports, etc., provided.

[1] A. H. Nichols, in *New England Genealogical Register* for 1916.
[2] A. H. Nichols, in *Christ Church Bells*, Boston.
[3] *Ibid.*

FIG. 113.   *Liberty Bell, in Independence Hall, Philadelphia*

The restoration was celebrated by a memorial service held in the ancient church, when the pealing of the bells by a trained band of English ringers revealed to the present generation the prodigious volume and sweetness of their sound. No more precious heirloom has been transmitted from our forefathers, and it is to be hoped that they may be preserved for many centuries as examples of the superior handicraft and kindly feeling of our English ancestors."

By far the most famous bell in America is the Liberty Bell, which hangs at the head of the stairway in Independence Hall, Philadelphia (Fig. 113). It was the first bell cast in America. It was dedicated to the cause of liberty, and later it actually "proclaimed the liberty" of the thirteen colonies. A writer in the *New York Herald* several years ago gave its early history as follows:

"In 1751 Mr. Speaker Joseph Parker Norris of the Assembly of Pennsylvania wrote to Robert Charles, then in London, to procure a good bell of two thousand pounds' weight, at a cost of about one hundred pounds sterling, to be cast by the best workmen and to contain in well-shaped letters around it: 'By order of the Assembly of the Province of Pennsylvania, for the State House in the city of Philadelphia, 1752,' and underneath, 'Proclaim Liberty throughout all the land to all the inhabitants thereof. Levt. xxv–10.'

"The bell arrived in August, 1752, but was cracked while being tested, 'upon which,' writes

Mr. Norris, 'two ingenious workmen undertook to cast it here, and I am just now (March 10, 1753) informed they have this day opened the mold, and have a good bell, which I confess pleases me very much that we should first venture upon and succeed in the greatest bell cast, for aught I know, in English America.'

"This bell was hung in 1753, but the metal was too brittle (so said the judges), for it cracked. Another was attempted, but with no better results. On July 8th (not 4th), 1776, it announced to all the world that a new republic had been born a few days before." When the British approached Philadelphia in 1777 the bell was taken down and carried to Bethlehem for safekeeping. After the British left Philadelphia it was brought back, and it rang from Independence Hall for many years.

One authority says the bell cracked when sounding a fire alarm; another states that it cracked in 1835 while being tolled in memory of Chief Justice John Marshall, and that on February 22, 1843, the crack was so enlarged as to destroy the sound of the bell. In any case, the crack renders it useless for all purposes except as a highly treasured and nationally revered emblem of our liberty.

It has been loaned to various exhibitions, and in 1915 it was carried across the continent to an exhibition at San Francisco. The railway company built a special car for it, with buffers to prevent severe jolts. Greater honor could hardly have been given

to any person than was shown to this bell when it
arrived in San Francisco. A holiday, a great procession, flowers, fifty thousand children singing the
national anthem in the streets as it passed, and a
roar of salutes from the cannon on the fleet in the

Gramstorff Bros., Inc., Malden, Mass.

FIG. 114. *The old belfry in Lexington, Massachusetts*

harbor! This was its last journey, for the fear of
further accident to this great national treasure
caused the enactment of a law to the effect that it
should never again leave Philadelphia.

Figure 114 shows the old belfry in Lexington,
Massachusetts, from which the village bell rang out

the alarm on the morning of April 19, 1775, calling the minutemen together.

The first bell foundry in the United States was established by the Hanks family, ancestors of Abraham Lincoln on his mother's side. The first tower clock in New York was in the old Dutch Church (at Nassau and Liberty streets), and was built by Jonathan Hanks and operated by an ingenious windmill attachment. The Hanks family continued the making of bells through the generations, and the art is still pursued by the present representatives of the family, the Meneely Bell Company in Troy, New York.

The name of Paul Revere is known to all readers of American history as the patriot who took a memorable midnight ride to give his countrymen notice of the coming of the British soldiers. A few years after the Revolutionary War was over, Paul Revere built a furnace in Boston (on what is now Commercial Street) for the casting of bells. Here he made not only small bells, but large church bells also, and his business was successfully carried on until he died, in 1818, at the age of eighty-nine years. His foundry cast more than two hundred bells. Several of them are still in existence, though many have been lost, and at one time fifty of them were destroyed by fire. One of Paul Revere's bells hangs in King's Chapel, Boston, and others in various churches in the country are exhibited with great pride.

In many of the early settlements there were no bells to call the people together, and various other signals were used. Often a drum or a horn was employed for that purpose. "In 1759[1] South Hadley, in Massachusetts, voted to have a sign for meeting on the Sabbath, and a large conch shell was procured, and for the faithful blowing thereof the town meeting ordered that the sum of three pounds should be paid yearly.

"The following lines were written in Dorchester in 1719:

> Well, that night I slept till near prayer time,
> Next morning I wondered to hear no bell chime,
> At which I did ask, and the reason I found,
> 'Twas because they had ne'er a bell in the town.

Later, when a bell came, it was hung on a pine tree until a place could be prepared to receive it. The bell was placed in the center of the roof, and the rope hung down in the broad aisle, where the ringer stationed himself. He remonstrated when, besides the nine o'clock bell every night, he was required to toll the day of the month. One of the Dorchester by-laws read: 'Constables are to take up loose people who do not heed the ringing of the nine o'clock bell.'"

The antique chapel bell at Yale College was described as about as good a bell as a fur cap with a sheep's tail for a clapper!

The chimes in the tower of St. Michael's Church in Charleston, South Carolina, have had a most

[1]From *Bells, an Anthology*, by Mary J. Taber.

eventful career. Their story is quoted by permission of the publishers of the Everyday Library,
*Marvels of Industry*,[1] as follows: "Cast in London,
installed in the steeple of St. Michael's Church
in 1764. When the British evacuated Charleston
in the Revolutionary War, they took possession
of the bells and carried them to England. A
merchant of Charleston bought them and sent
them home. When they were unloaded and hung
in the belfry, there was great rejoicing that the city
had its voice back again.

"But the bells' adventures had only begun. In
1823 it was discovered that two of them were
cracked. After local workmen had made several
unsuccessful attempts to restore the tones, the two
damaged bells made a second trip to England, this
time to be recast in their original molds. In 1839
they were again hung in their place, and, to the great
joy of the people, rang until the time of civil strife
and discord came.

"In 1862, during the bombardment of Charleston,
the chimes were taken down and moved to Columbia, South Carolina, to escape injury, but this was
a most disastrous move, for during the occupation
of Columbia by Sherman's army the bells were
burned in the fire of February 17, 1865. They
were so loved by the people, however, that the
precious fragments were sacredly guarded, and when
the war was over they were sent to London to be

[1]Copyright, 1916.

recast. Strange as it may seem, the original molds into which they had been poured a century before, had still been preserved. In February, 1867, the eight bells came back once more to their home in the steeple of St. Michael. The entire set had crossed the Atlantic five times, and two of the bells, seven times. On March 21st, they rang out joyously the tune: 'Home again, home again, from a foreign land.'

"Since then, they have passed unharmed through many dangers. In spite of a cyclone and an earthquake that nearly demolished the church, they still swing, uninjured, high up in the steeple.

"At the close of the eighteenth century, the church narrowly escaped destruction by fire. It was saved only by the courage of a negro sailor who climbed to the top of the tower and tore off the blazing shingles. As a reward for his bravery, the slave received his liberty, a sum of money, and a fishing boat equipped with nets."

Among the most important of America's bells are those which have hung in the missions of California and the Southwest. When the Southwest was under the rule of Spain, missions were built along the California coast, and a line of them extended through a part of Texas all the way to the Rio Grande. No less than seventy of these missions were founded by the monks of the Franciscan, Jesuit, and Dominican orders. The devout Spanish monks who had charge of the missions had one definite purpose—

FIG. 115. *San Luis Rey Mission, founded in 1798*

that of Christianizing the Indians and bringing them under the wing of the Catholic Church. The patience and gentleness of the *padres* (as the monks were called), their wisdom and fair treatment of the Indians, and the success of their missions, furnish an interesting page of American history, and one which reflects credit upon Spain.

One of the first Spanish missions, San Francisco de la Espada, founded in 1689, still stands in Texas. The mission of San Jose de Aguayo, also in Texas, was founded in 1720, and is, perhaps, the most beautiful of all the missions. The mission architecture was on the Moorish style, with long arched porches which afforded shade from the sun. Luxurious fruit trees and shaded gardens surrounded them. The bell tower was a very important part of the mission, and it usually added much to the beauty of the building.

Figure 115 shows the San Luis Rey Mission of California (founded in 1798) as it is now. This was one of the most prosperous of the old Spanish missions; the building is a hundred and sixty feet long, and its walls four to five feet thick. The two-story belfry contained eight bells, one in each archway.

The less wealthy missions were content with fewer bells. "The chime of bells[1] was ever an important feature with the *padres* in the founding and life of a mission. These bells were brought from Spain, and were of the best Castile metal and workmanship. Their tones called the Indians to assemble at the mission, and marked the hours for labor. By the melodies which they chimed, the *padres* and their Indian followers chanted hymns of praise and songs of thanksgiving. Serra (the pioneer of the California mission founders) often said that he would have their ringing sound from the mountains to the sea, as it was God's invitation to the souls of heathen men and women to flee to Him and escape the wrath to come. These bells were of silver and bronze and other metallic mixtures, to give variety to their tones. They performed all kinds of service in mission work and worship, and were indispensable to the *padres*."

[1] From *The Missions of California and the Old Southwest*, by Jesse Hildrup. Published, 1907, by A. C. McClurg & Co., Chicago.

FIG. 116. *The belfry of Pala Chapel, near San Diego, California*

Figure 116 shows the picturesque belfry of Pala Chapel, which is, perhaps, the only one of its kind in the world. It is separate from the main building. Nature, assisted by birds, no doubt, has conspired to make this belfry even more picturesque by the cactus spire growing on its summit.

Courtesy of *The Mentor*

FIG. 117. *The cross and bells of San Diego Mission, California*

In Figure 117 are seen the cross and bells of the first mission of California, that of San Diego, founded in 1769. The bells were brought from Spain, and hauled overland from Veracruz. They were at first hung from the branch of a tree until a permanent place was built for them. They hung in the original San Diego Mission until it was destroyed.

FIG. 118.   *Bells of San Gabriel Mission, San Gabriel, California*

The well-known belfry of the San Gabriel Mission
is pictured in Figure 118.   Here again is a belfry of
an unusual type.   The open arches in the masonry
were made to suit the sizes of the bells.

When Spain lost her holdings in America, Mexico
assumed control of California and Texas; and in
1833 the Mexican government confiscated the properties of the missions.   "The religion and morals
of the missions were swept away at this time, with
their material progress and the monuments thereof.
The better life of the Indian neophyte passed into
oblivion with the wreck of his mission home.   The
*padres* could protect him no longer.   The hand of
spoliation was laid upon the rich properties which

the Franciscans had created through toil, privation, and danger.   The old *padres* fled like the Indians."[1]

In 1876, the hundredth anniversary of the birth of the republic, a bell weighing thirteen thousand pounds, to represent the thirteen original states, was cast at the Meneely foundry for the tower of the old State House in Philadelphia.   It is called the "Independence Hall Bell."   Like the original

Meneely Bell Foundry

FIG. 119.   *Independence Hall bell, cast in 1876*

State House Bell, it bears the inscription: "Proclaim Liberty throughout all the land unto all the

[1]Jesse Hildrup, in *The Missions of California and the Old Southwest.* Published, 1907, by A. C. McClurg & Co., Chicago.

inhabitants thereof." It is in constant use, sounding the hours of the day (see Fig. 119, p. 283).

Another bell of national interest is the "Columbian Liberty Bell," cast in 1893 for the World's Fair at Chicago, and made to be rung only on the liberty anniversaries of the nation. It is estimated that more than two hundred thousand people of America contributed to the making of this bell by giving either money or pieces of gold and other jewelry. Some gave valuable relics, gold watches and even wedding rings and thimbles, and hundreds gave silver spoons. Over two hundred and fifty thousand pennies were sent in. These were all melted in the bell metal. The inscription runs: "Glory to God" and "A new commandment I give unto you, that ye love one another."

The four bells that ring the chimes from the Metropolitan Clock Tower in New York are known as the world's highest bells. They are mounted on pedestals between the columns outside the forty-sixth story of the Metropolitan Life Insurance Tower (see Fig. 120), and were placed in position 650 feet high, in 1909. They ring the famous Cambridge Quarters,[1] though in a much lower key than the original. The largest one weighs three and one-half tons and strikes the hours as well as its part in the chime. The sound of the four bells is heard many miles out at sea, and inland also. They were made at the Meneely foundry.

[1]See p. 166.

FIG. 120. *The Metropolitan Life Insurance Building, New York.*
*The chime consists of four bells, weighing respectively seven thousand,*
*three thousand, two thousand, and fifteen hundred pounds, and tuned*
*to D flat, E flat, F flat, and G.*

FIG. 121. *Bell tower of Springfield, Massachusetts, containing a chime of 12 bells placed 247 feet above ground*

There are many rings of excellent chimes in the United States, some of them cast at the Meneely Bell Foundry in this country, and others imported from abroad. Not only the churches, but many universities have been provided recently with chimes for daily and weekly ringing. Cornell University has a chime of fourteen bells; the University of

Meneely Bell Foundry

FIG. 122.   *The chimes in City Hall Tower, Minneapolis, Minnesota*

California, twelve bells; the State College of Iowa, ten bells; the University of Chicago, ten bells; West Point Military Academy, twelve bells; and doubtless many other colleges and universities are supplied with chimes. Figure 122 shows a chime of ten bells in the City Hall Tower of Minneapolis, Minnesota.

No attempt will be made here to list all the church chimes in the country; there are too many. The

John Taylor & Co.

FIG. 123.  *First carillon made for the United States, cast
at the Taylor foundry for Gloucester, Massachusetts*

Photograph by Curtiss

FIG. 124.  *Carillon of St. Peter's Church, in Morristown,
New Jersey*

most famous chimes in the New York City churches
are those of St. Patrick's Cathedral (nineteen bells),
Trinity Church, and Grace Church, which has sixteen bells.

### AMERICA'S CARILLONS

The interest of the American people in bell music
has already led to the building of many "singing
towers," as Mr. Rice calls the carillon towers, and
the founding of many carillons. Unfortunately, the
bell makers of this country have not yet practiced
the art of carillon making, and all our carillons are
at present imported from one of the two English
foundries at Croydon and Loughborough.

The first city in America to obtain a fine modern
carillon was Toronto, Canada. The first carillon
in the United States was hung in the Church of Our
Lady of Good Fortune at Gloucester, Massachusetts,
and dedicated in 1922. A picture of the bells before
they left the Loughborough foundry may be seen in
Figure 123.

The same founders made a carillon of thirty-five
bells for St. Peter's Church in Morristown, New
Jersey, dedicated in 1924. Figure 124 shows these
bells as they hang in the church tower. The keyboard of this instrument is shown in Figure 86.[1]

The largest carillon in the world at present (fifty-
three bells), and said by many to be the most perfectly tuned, was made in 1925 at the Croydon

[1] See p. 191.

foundry for the Park Avenue Baptist Church in
New York City.   It was given by John D. Rockefeller, Jr., in memory of his mother.   Before the
carillon left the English foundry it was set up with
its keyboard and all the wire connections, and
was played by different carillonneurs of Europe.

FIG. 125.  *Chevalier Jef Denyn, famous carillon player of St. Rombold's
Cathedral, Malines, Belgium, testing the set of 53 bells to be
sent to the Park Avenue Baptist Church, New York*

Figure 125 is a photograph of Mr. Denyn, world-renowned carillonneur of Mechlin, at the keyboard, testing the bells before they were shipped to America.

FIG. 126.  *Largest bell of New York's carillon of 53 bells on its arrival at the dock in New York City*

Figure 126 shows the largest bell of the carillon on its arrival at the dock in New York Harbor. This is the largest bell in the United States, and weighs nine tons. Its tone is low E. The smallest bell of the carillon is high A, and weighs only fifteen pounds.

The bells were hung in the summer of 1925 in the tower of the Park Avenue Church where, for several months, superb evening concerts were given by Anton Brees of Antwerp. These concerts were heard not only by great throngs in the streets, but were broadcast by radio and enjoyed by the people of distant cities in their own homes. This carillon will later be removed to the tower of the new church on Riverside Drive, with the bell chamber three hundred feet from the ground. The bells will be heard many miles away, and will probably be heard at their best from boats on the Hudson River.

During the past few years carillons have been acquired also by Plainfield, New Jersey (23 bells); Andover, Massachusetts (37 bells); Cohasset, Massachusetts (43 bells); Birmingham, Alabama (25 bells); Detroit, Michigan (28 bells); Cranbrook, Michigan (30 bells), and St. Chrysostom's Church, Chicago (43 bells). There is also a carillon at Princeton University, and other educational institutions are planning to have them. Albany, New York, is to have forty-two bells in the City Hall Tower. Two other carillons are planned for New York City, and Washington, D. C., is to have three. Mercersburg, Pennsylvania, will soon have one of forty-three bells, and Germantown, Pennsylvania, one of thirty-five bells. In fact, according to William Gorham Rice, America's foremost carillon authority, "there is every indication that in two years' time this country will have twice as many carillons of large compass and perfect tune as are to be found in either Belgium or the Netherlands.

"Even before the New York carillon is moved to its new home uptown, Ottawa, Canada, will have equally noble bells in a tower already constructed, at a height no less. The fifty-three bells of this memorial crowning the Victory Tower of the new Houses of Parliament will be slightly heavier than those in the Park Avenue carillon, New York. The commanding situation of this Canadian tower, set on a picturesque bluff above the Ottawa River, together with the surrounding open space, the dignity of the belfry itself, and the beauty of the whole group of buildings of which it is a part, combine to place it in the very front rank of the singing towers of the world."

# CHAPTER XXV

## CHINESE BELLS

From the earliest ages bells in China have been the most esteemed of instruments. They were used as standards for the tones of the Chinese scale, and it is said that the bell was the first instrument to be played at musical performances.

Supposedly in the year 2697 B.C., or thereabouts, the Emperor Hoang-ti ordered Ling-lun to make a standard by which the tones of the scale might be fixed. These tones, the Chinese claim, had been given to their ancestors by a phoenix bird which was born in the heart of the Sacred Fire. There are many legends told of how he acquired the various pitches that were to form the pattern for the scale, and no two of these legends seem to agree. After he had established these tones, however, Ling-lun went back to the emperor's court and there fixed the pitch of each note in the Chinese scale. Musical stones were tuned and bells were made according to this official pitch, so that the scale might be easily perpetuated.

Chao-hao came after Hoang-ti, and originated the custom of marking the divisions of the night by strokes of a drum. Chao-hao also had made a set of twelve copper bells, to represent the twelve divisions of the year.

In the year 2284 B.C. Emperor Chun established uniformity of weight and measure, as well as uniformity of the musical scale throughout the empire, and tried to have all the bells in the empire made so that their tones were in correct relation to each other.

Yu the Great, who reigned long before the time of Confucius, made use of some of the musical instruments of that day in a very wise and practical way. Wishing to deal justly with his subjects, and to be easily accessible to all of them, he had five instruments of percussion placed outside the gate of his palace. These instruments were to be struck by anyone who wished to speak to the emperor, the different ones to be used according to the nature of the business with the sovereign. These instruments were a large bell, a small bell, a gong, a drum, and a tambourine. If the applicant wished to complain of injustice, he rang the large bell; if he wished to see the emperor on private or confidential business, he rang the small bell. If he wished to report a public or private misfortune, he struck the gong. The drum was to signify a message concerning the manners of the empire; and when the tambourine was used, it meant that an accusation of crime was appealed from some lower tribunal to the judgment of the emperor.

In about 245 B.C. the emperor of that time commanded all ancient books to be burned, excepting works on agriculture and medicine. New models were designed for musical instruments, and new standards for the pitch of notes; and all musical instruments were ordered to be destroyed and made over after new models. The bells which had, up to that time, given the standard pitch, were melted down, and the metal in many of them was used to make colossal statues to deck the entrance to the imperial palace.

Some of the bells, however, were saved. It seems that the emperor's decree was more rigorously carried out with respect to books than to musical instruments, and many of the bells and musical stones escaped destruction by being buried in the earth, whence they could later be exhumed, uninjured.

Then came a long period in which music and the other arts in China made little progress.

Under the Song dynasty (about A.D. 960 to 1279) music took a new impetus. Many books were written, but there was so much uncertainty about the ancient music (which, in Chinese eyes, was the only correct music) that there was much confusion, and apparently no way in which the matter could be adjusted so that the musicians could agree. Very few considered the bells which gave the official scale to be correct. So a new set was made, and this new set pleased the emperor so much that he ordered his own official bells to be melted and recast. The musicians were not at all pleased with the new system, and determined that all trace of the ancient scale should not be lost. So they connived with some of the officials, and when the bells were removed from the tribunal of music and rites one complete set, instead of being thrown into the furnace as the emperor had ordered, was buried in the courtyard of the palace, and long afterward exhumed.

The Chinese very early acquired great skill in the making of bells, and it is quite possible that the art of bell founding began with these people, and from the East extended into Europe. There are now in China perfect bells which were cast many centuries before the Christian era. The bell and the caldron were considered the most valuable treasures among the bronze vessels in China.

It is a notable fact that many of the Chinese bells, both ancient and modern, are made with a hole in the top, and it has been claimed that this is the reason that they never crack.

Their bell metal is six parts of copper and one of tin. When melting,[1] the alloy appears to be of an impure dark color, soon changing into a yellowish white, which gradually passes to a greenish white, and when this last has become green the metal is ready to be poured into the mold. Most of the bells of China are ornamented, some with characters, some with designs and symbols.

The Chinese foundries are not only prepared to make bells of all sizes, but other bronze figures. A French missionary who visited some of the

[1]Van Aalst, in *Chinese Music.*

foundries in Tartary years ago, wrote: "The magnificent statues in bronze and brass, which issue from the great foundries of Tolon-noor, are celebrated not only throughout Tartary, but in the remotest districts of Tibet. Its immense workshops supply all the countries subject to the worship of Buddha, with idols, bells, and vases, employed in that idolatry."

In ancient times the Chinese employed a bell for the same purpose for which we use a tuning fork or pitch pipe; and this bell served also to give two other standards besides that of tone. Being somewhat of a cup shape, it was used as a measure for bulk (as we use quart measures); and being heavy, it was used as a standard for weight. One specimen of this triple-standard bell (for tone, bulk, and weight) appears to have been kept in a royal hall or temple, to be referred to whenever desired as a standard for others.

Although the original use of bells in China was for tone and other standards, they very soon came to be used, either singly or united into chimes, in court and religious ceremonies, and their use gradually pervaded Chinese life in general.

The Chinese name for bell is *tchung* or *chung*. There are two general classes, those with clappers and those without. The name *chung* usually refers to the kind requiring to be struck from the outside. Most of the oldest Chinese bells had no clappers. They had not the round form of our present bells, many of them being nearly square in shape. Some of the finest of the ancient bells are oblong, and oval-shaped at the lip.

### BELLS WITHOUT CLAPPERS

At an early period the Chinese had a somewhat square-shaped bell called the *te-chung*. It was also known by the name of *piao*, and was principally

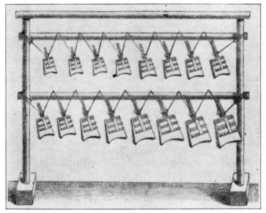

FIG. 127. *Pien-chung, or chime of 16 bells*

used to indicate the time, and divisions in musical performances. It had a fixed pitch of sound. When a single bell was used, it was suspended in a frame.

The *pien-chung* (see Fig. 127) was an arrangement of sixteen *te-chung* or *piao* attuned to a certain order, their tones corresponding exactly to the tones of the *pien-king*, an instrument made of musical stones. These two instruments are always found together in the Confucian temples. They are necessary one to the other; the bell chime sounds, and the stone chime replies.

The *po-chung* (see Fig. 128) is a single bell suspended upon a frame, and corresponds to the

FIG. 128. *Po-chung*

*tse-king*, or single sonorous stone. When this bell sounds, the *tse-king* must answer. There are twelve of them, corresponding to the twelve *lus*, or standard tones of the ancient Chinese, and are intended to meet the changes of key which occur according to the seasons. At the Confucian ceremonies the *po-chung* is placed outside the temple on the right of the "Moon Terrace." It has to give the note at the beginning of each verse, in order to "manifest the sound" (or give the pitch), by being struck with a wooden hammer. During the Middle Ages it was called *sung-chung*.[1] Figure 129 shows a remarkable Chinese jade *po-chung* from the Field Museum, Chicago.

A very ancient form of bell is the *hiuen-chung*, of peculiar oval shape, with crescent mouth (see Fig. 130, p. 302.) It was ornamented with symbolic figures in four divisions, each containing nine raised knobs of metal. Every figure had a deep meaning referring to the seasons and to the mysteries of the Buddhist religion. The largest *hiuen-chung* was about twenty inches long. This instrument was sounded (as was the *te-chung*) by means of a small wooden mallet with an oval knob. It is said that the raised knobs of metal on these bells were made so that, by striking them successively with a wooden mallet, the

Courtesy of Field Museum

FIG. 129. *Po-chung made of jade*

[1]Van Aalst, in *Chinese Music.*

notes of the entire musical scale could be obtained. According to tradition, the *hiuen-chung* was included with the antique instruments at the time of Confucius, and again came into popular use in the

Han dynasty (from 200 B.C. until 200 A.D). This instrument has long since passed entirely out of use. Ten very beautiful specimens of the *hiuen-chung* are photographed and described in a handsome volume in the library of the Metropolitan Museum, and one who reads Chinese characters may find out all about them.

FIG. 130. *Hiuen-chung*

The *yung-chung* is a large bell in the temple of Confucius which, the Chinese say, is made to correspond with the very big drum. The one is not used without the other. The drum gives the signal to begin, and the bell announces the end of the hymn at the ceremonies. It is interesting to note that the Chinese use, in so many instances, their musical instruments in pairs, — bells and stone instruments, or drums and bells, balancing each other.

None of the large metal bells in China at the present day have clappers. They are meant to be struck from the outside, usually by the ends of long beams hung by chords or chains. When a priest strikes a large bell with this battering-ram-like hammer, there is given off a deep majestic boom which may be heard for miles around. The sound is made more solemn and impressive by the use of the wooden beam instead of an iron clapper.

Figure 131 shows four different kinds of temple bells with their stands; Figure 132 (p. 304), a temple bell from an ancient temple, Chen-seng. These Chinese temple bells may be seen in the Crosby-Brown collection of musical instruments in the Metropolitan Museum of New York.

Metropolitan Museum

FIG. 131. *Chinese temple bells in ornamental stands*

### BELLS WITH CLAPPERS

At an early period the Chinese had some kind of bell with a wooden clapper or tongue. This bell, called *to*, was used for military purposes, and for calling the people together to hear the commands of the emperor as announced by his herald. It is recorded that Confucius wished to be "a wooden-tongued bell of heaven," meaning a "herald to proclaim the divine purposes to the multitude." One would judge that the wooden tongue must have brought out the best tone of the metal, since the Chinese used it for such noble purposes. But at present, it is said, the *to* is used only by "bronzes to mark the rhythm of their prayers." Not only

FIG. 132.  *Lotus-shaped bell from an ancient Chinese temple*

the priests in the temple beat upon wooden bells as they pray, but beggars also tap small wooden

bells as they go from house to house saying their
Buddhist prayers and asking alms.

The *wei-shun* (see Fig. 133) is a very ancient bell

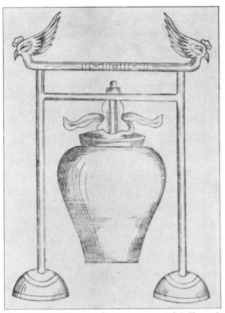

FIG. 133.    *The wei-shun, ceremonial bell used
in the Temple of Ancestors*

of the Chou dynasty.[1]    Its shape was. somewhat
like that of a balloon, and it was hung singly upon
a frame.    The *wei-shun* was used mostly for the
ceremonies in the Temple of Ancestors, where it
corresponded to a kind of drum which is no longer
to be found.    It has been said that this instrument

[1]Van Aalst, in *Chinese Music.*

is simply a large bell with small round bells suspended in it to act as a tongue, the sound produced
thereby being exceedingly shrill.

It must have been bells with clappers which were
used as justice bells by the Chinese.  It is said that
during the ninth century these bells were used in all
parts of China (the custom having started with Yu
the Great, many centuries before), and two Arabs
who traveled through China in that century have
given us an account of them.  In every town there
was a large bell fastened to the wall above the head
of the prince, or governor, and to the bell was
fastened a rope a mile or so in length.  This rope
was laid so temptingly along the thoroughfare that
the humblest sufferer from injustice might pull it
without fear.  When the bell rang, the governor
sent for the petitioner, and demanded just treatment for him.  Even above the head of the emperor
himself such a bell was hung, and he who rang it
without good cause was thoroughly switched.[1]

This custom of using justice bells was probably
adopted by some European countries in later times,
as is indicated by such legends as "The Bell of
Atri"[2] and "The Stone of Gratitude."[3]  This is
only one of the many ideas which are often accredited
to Europeans, but which were really original with
the Chinese.

Another tongued bell of China is the *feng-ling*,
or wind bell.  Small wind bells are hung at the

[1] W. S. Sparrow, "A Dissertation on Foreign Bells," in the *Magazine
of Art*, 1894.                [2] See p. 404.                [3] See p. 266.

eaves of houses and pagodas, and made with light silk streamers hanging to their clappers so that the softest breeze swings the clappers and awakens the musical sounds. For the sake of this pleasing effect, wind bells are often hung in halls and corridors. The pagodas have them hanging from their

FIG. 134. *A Chinese bell tower*

roofs, and as there are many corners to the roofs of most pagodas, there is an opportunity for great variety in the tones which one little breeze may evoke. On the famous Porcelain Tower in Nanking (built by Emperor Yung-lo in the fifteenth century; destroyed in 1853), which was built of white bricks and had the appearance of porcelain, a number of bells with clappers were fastened to the projecting

corners of its different stories. In the Chinese bell
tower shown in Figure 134 (p. 307), the wind bells
at the corners of the roof may be seen.

One writer describes a Chinese pagoda in the
vicinity of Shanghai, octagonal in shape, and consisting of eight stories, each of which "is provided
with a covered veranda having a projecting roof,
at the corners of which are hung small bells of
different tones, and as there are sixty-four of them,
which are kept in almost constant motion by the
wind, the sound they produce is exceedingly pleasing,
greatly resembling the wild melody of the Aeolian
harp." The bell is still the never-failing adjunct
of the pagoda; and bells, either real or imitated,
form a very common architectural ornament for
the shop or joss house.

Bells are found hanging in the temples and bell
towers in all parts of China. They are of all sizes,
ranging from a few inches in diameter to the enormous bell in the temple at Peking.[1]

Not only are bells used in the temples and shops,
but also at home, where even the baby wears little
jingling bells fastened to his garments. In the
streets bells are used in processions of all kinds.
Sometimes many bells are carried on one large
frame; or perhaps they hang by dozens round the
waists of the dancers, to increase the deafening noise
of drums and gongs and crackers.

[1] See next chapter, p. 310.

# CHAPTER XXVI

## CHINA'S BIG BELLS AND
## THEIR LEGENDS

The Chinese claim to have possessed bells even before they had a knowledge of how to hang them. This important secret (according to the legend) was unfolded for them by a monkey with a forked tail which enabled him to acquire the habit of hanging, during the rainy seasons, upon a limb of a tree, with a fork of his tail in each nostril, thus completing the circle. Some of the very ancient bells, when hung, somewhat resembled swinging animals, and this resemblance probably gave rise to the legend.

The most popular legends, however, are formed about the great bells. The two largest bells in China (at Peking and Canton) are even yet believed by the superstitious to have miraculous power.

A native account of Canton states that Canton's "tabooed bell," as it is called, was cast about the middle of the fifteenth century; but because of a prophecy which foretold calamity to Canton whenever it should give forth sound, it was deprived of a striker, and all means of access to it were removed.

Finally, cne day, a rash official directed a man to strike it. "No sooner had its reverberating boom been heard, than upwards of a thousand male and female infants died within the city." As the people explained it, evidently some evil spirit had been irritated by the bell being rung. So in order to ward off his influence, or appease his wrath, infants have ever since worn bells upon their clothing.

Another incident has been related of how the prophecy held good at a much later period. When the English forces were bombarding Canton, in 1857, it was suggested to the commander of one of the English ships to aim a shot at the bell. The result was that the unwonted boom was heard again, a portion of the lower rim of the bell was fractured, and calamity, indeed, befell the city.

During the reign of Yung-lo (1403–1425) of the Ming dynasty the capital of China was moved from Nanking to Peking. In order to make Peking a city worthy of the glorious presence of the emperor and his court, stately buildings were erected, and lookout towers were built on the outskirts of the city. One of these was the Drum Tower, furnished with an enormous drum of such size that "the thunder of its tones might be heard all over the city, the sound being almost enough to waken the dead."

Another one of these lookout towers was the Bell Tower which was to have a bell to correspond with the monster drum. Yung-lo ordered five great bells to be cast, and the bell which still hangs in this tower is one of them. It weighs forty tons, and hangs one hundred and thirty feet above the street level. It is rung every evening at 8:30, when the watch is changed, and can be heard in all parts of Peking (see Fig. 135, p. 313).

The most famous bell in China is the one which hangs in a Buddhist temple called the Big Bell Temple, west of the city of Peking (see Fig. 136, p. 313). This also is one of the five bells which Yung-lo ordered to be cast. Its weight is claimed by some writers to be fifty-three tons; by others, sixty tons. It is fourteen feet high, thirty-four feet in circumference at the rim, and eight inches thick. The bell has no clapper, but is struck with a wooden hammer on the raised square which may be seen in the picture,—and is struck only upon imperial order. It was cast about 1420 where it now stands. The ground was excavated from beneath it, and later it was covered with a temple.

There are five volumes of the classics inscribed upon the bell, covering it, inside and out, with Chinese characters. It is said that this voluminous inscription was not cut, but was cast with the bell.[1] If so, it was indeed a remarkable casting. It is a common belief in Peking that if any foreigner should succeed in translating this inscription, the bell would melt immediately.

There are many varian oɪ the legend connected with the Great Bell of Peking, but they are all centered around the ever popular idea in China that self-sacrifice is necessary to insure some public good. It seems that Yung-lo ordered a mandarin

[1] Carl Crow, *Handbook for China*, Shanghai, 1921.

named Kuan-yu to cast a bell which, upon the least alarm, could be heard all over the city. Two attempts were made to carry out the order, at intervals of some months, but without success. In both cases the casting was "honeycombed." The enraged emperor declared that if the third attempt failed he would behead the unfortunate Kuan-yu.

"Now Kuan-yu had a beautiful daughter, aged sixteen, named Ko-ai, to whom he was tenderly attached, and who did all she could to comfort her distressed parent. One day it struck her that she would go to a celebrated astrologer to ascertain the cause of her father's failures, and what means could be taken to prevent their recurrence. From him she learned that the next casting would also be a failure if the blood of a maiden were not mixed with the ingredients. She returned home full of horror at the information, but resolved to immolate herself sooner than that her father should fail."

Ko-ai obtained leave from her father to be present at the casting, and the catastrophe is thus described:

"A dead silence prevailed through the assemblage as the melted metal once more rushed to its destination. This was broken by a shriek and a cry of 'For my father!' and Ko-ai was seen to throw herself headlong into the seething, hissing metal. One of her followers attempted to seize her while in the act of plunging into the boiling fluid, but succeeded only in grasping one of her shoes, which came off in his hand.

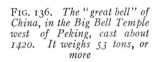

FIG. 135. *The bell which hangs in the Bell Tower in Peking, cast in the fifteenth century. It weighs 40 tons*

FIG. 136. *The "great bell" of China, in the Big Bell Temple west of Peking, cast about 1420. It weighs 53 tons, or more*

"The father was frantic, and had to be kept by force from following her example. He was taken home a raving maniac. The prediction of the astrologer was verified, for on uncovering the bell after it had cooled, it was found to be perfect; but not a vestige of Ko-ai was to be seen. The blood of a maiden had indeed been fused with the ingredients."

The sequel recounts how the sonorous boom of the bell, when struck, was followed by a low, wailing sound like the cry of a human female voice in great agony, distinctly saying the word *hsieh*, the Chinese word for shoe, a sound still heard after every stroke; and to this day people, when they hear it, say, "There's poor Ko-ai calling for her shoe."

The above legend is sometimes told in connection with the Tower Bell. This is only a recent association, and the legend properly belongs to the great Temple Bell.

The belief regarding the miraculous power of the Peking bell is more mild than the uncanny power attached to the Canton bell. It is believed that if the great Temple Bell in Peking is struck by an unauthorized hand it will at once bring down unneeded rain. N. B. Dennys wrote,[1] in 1875, that when he and some friends visited the great Bell Temple outside the city, the priests refused to strike the bell lest the rain god should be offended. A small present from one of the party, however,

[1] In "Folk Lore of China," in *China Review*.

induced them to let the visitors draw back the heavy wooden ram which did duty as a clapper. Strangely enough, as the first blow was struck a heavy rainstorm came on, and the shaven-pated attendants roared out in high glee, "We told you so!" For once, says Mr. Dennys, superstition carried the day.

## CHAPTER XXVII

## THE BELLS OF JAPAN

Travelers have written much about the "great bell of Kyoto," a mass of green bronze that hangs in the Jodo temple of Chion in Kyoto. It is the second largest bell in Japan, and one of the great bells of the world (see Fig. 137). The bell tower which houses it was completed just before the bell was cast, in 1633, and was partly restored in 1911. The bell is ten feet, ten inches high, nine feet in diameter, eleven inches thick at the lip, and weighs seventy-four tons. Near it hangs a long tree trunk, clamped with bronze and iron, which is used to bring forth the tone of the bell. The great beam is pulled back and allowed to hurl itself against the bell on the rebound. It is said to require seventy-five men to ring it so that the full effect of this great mass of metal is obtained.

The largest bell in Japan (and the second largest in the world) was cast in 1902 for the ancient Buddhist temple, Shi-tenno-ji. It hangs ten feet from the belfry floor, is twenty-six feet high, thirty-four feet in circumference, sixteen feet across the mouth, eighteen inches thick at the rim, and weighs over one hundred and fifty-five tons. It is inscribed with extracts from the Buddhist classics and the names of people who contributed to the expense of its casting. Its voice shatters the air for miles around, but the tone is not good. Some one has said that it "sounds like the crack of doom accompanied by a million angry bees heard through a megaphone." Its only claim to fame is its colossal size.

One of the oldest and finest bells in existence is at Nara, the ancient capital of Japan. Near the

Courtesy of *Asia*

FIG. 137. *The "great bell of Kyoto"*

Second Moon Temple (dating from 750 A.D.) stands
a time-worn belfry which contains this monster bell,
cast in 732, when Shōmu was on the throne.　It

is thirteen and one-half
feet high, over nine feet
in diameter, ten inches
thick at the rim, and
weighs forty-eight tons.
It is a companion piece
to the great bronze Bud-
dha.　Its tone is very
fine, and we still marvel
at the art which produced
it.　Pilgrims who wish

FIG. 138.　*Ancient Japanese bells*　to hear the tone of the
bell have been allowed, upon payment of one *sen*,
to swing the great beam which strikes it.

Another large bell is that of Engakuji in Kamakura, made in 1301.　It is about eight feet high,
six feet in diameter, and its metal is six inches thick.
This bell, like most Japanese bells, has almost the
same diameter from top to bottom.　It hangs from
massive timbers in an open belfry on a hillside.
The metal is a lovely hue of green, with an inscription in Chinese.　This bell is also rung by a rope
which swings a beam, and the beam (when swung
with sufficient velocity) strikes a lotus molding on
the side of the bell, and "a great note quivers forth,
deep as thunder and rich as the bass of a mighty
organ."　In former days this bell was supposed to

be the dwelling place of a spirit, and the bell was considered sacred. When its thunder rolls into the valleys, and throbs and quivers between the hills, one can understand the spirit superstition. The temple of Zōzōji and its belfry were burned in 1874 by a fanatic incendiary. For two hundred years the great bell had summoned the people to their devotions and sounded alarms. "On the night of the fire the old bell ringer leaped to his post, and in place of the usual solemn monotone, gave the double stroke of alarm, until the heat had changed one side of the bell to white, the note deepening in tone, until in red heat, the ponderous link softened and bent, dropping its burden to the earth."[1]

Long ago, bells came with Buddhism from China to Japan. Many old bells have been dug out of the ground in Japan which have the indications of being very ancient, and may have been brought from China. Figure 138 shows drawings of two ancient hanging bells, and Figure 139 (p. 320) another antique bronze bell.

It is said that the Koreans were Japan's teachers in bell founding, though the Chinese also claim that honor. Certainly some of the finest bronze gongs and bells in the world are from old Korea, brought to Japan by Japanese pirates who ravaged the Korean shores. Figure 140 (p. 321) shows a very ornate Korean bell in Japan.

[1] William E. Griffis, in *The Mikado's Empire.*

Wherever the Japanese learned the art, in their hands bells have become remarkable specimens both in construction and decoration, and may easily

Metropolitan Museum
FIG. 139.   *An antique bronze bell from Japan*

be classed among the finest in the world. The success of their ancient castings (the Nara bell, for instance) is one of their unexplained achievements. "In Europe[1] the method of producing a really fine toned bell was evolved by ages of empirical trials; but in Japan, bells of huge size and exquisite note were cast in apparent defiance of the rules elaborated with so much difficulty in the west." Such bells are found in the temples and swing in handsome belfries throughout the country.

During the Middle Ages "the casting of a bell[2] was ever the occasion of rejoicing and public festival.

[1]Brinkley's *History of the Japanese People.*
[2]From *The Mikado's Empire,* by Griffis.

When the chief priest of the city announced that one was to be made, the people brought contributions in money or offerings of bronze, gold, pure tin, or copper vessels. Ladies gave, with their own hands, the mirrors which had been the envy of lovers, young girls laid their silver hairpins and *bijouterie* on the heap. When metal enough in due proportion had been amassed, crucibles were made, earth furnaces dug, the molds fashioned, and huge bellows, worked by standing men at each end like a see-saw, were mounted; and, after due prayers and consultation, the auspicious day was appointed. The place selected was usually a hill or commanding place. The people, in their gayest dress, assembled in picnic parties, and with song and dance and feast, waited; while the workmen, in festal uniform, toiled; and the priests, in canonical robes, watched. The

Courtesy of *Asia*

FIG. 140. *A Korean bell from the island of Kyushu. Japanese pirates who ravaged the shores of Korea in the olden times brought back bells to Kyushu as trophies*

fires were lighted, the bellows oscillated, the blast roared, and the crucibles were brought to the proper heat and the contents to fiery fluidity,—the joy of the crowd increasing as each stage in the process was announced. When the molten flood was finally poured into the mold, the excitement of the spectators reached a height of uncontrollable enthusiasm. Another pecuniary harvest was reaped by the priests before the crowds dispersed, by the sale of stamped kerchiefs or paper containing a holy text, or certifying to the presence of the purchaser at the ceremony, and the blessings of the gods upon him therefor. Such a token became an heirloom; and the child who ever afterward heard the solemn boom of the bell at matin or evening, was constrained by filial as well as holy motives, to obey and reverence its admonitory call."

The belfry was usually a separate building, apart from the temple, and often the roof and cornices were very elaborate. The beam of wood, or tree trunk, which struck the bell, swung loosely on two ropes or chains. In nearly all bells of Japan there was a raised spot upon which the blow was supposed to fall. After each blow the bell man held the beam on its rebound, until the bell almost ceased to vibrate (see Fig. 141). The tones thus produced were (and are) more impressive than the European bell tones, though the variety in tempo and expression practiced by European bell ringers is not possible with the Japanese mode of ringing. The Japanese love the solemnly sweet sound of their temple bells, and regard them as dear and sympathetic friends.

H. W. Colby

FIG. 141. *The Japanese method of striking a large bell. A medallion is cast in the bell at the spot where bell and striker meet*

Another frequent adjunct to the Japanese bell is the dragon which usually surmounts the bell, and forms the hook by which the bell is hung. In fact the hook is called *riud-zu*, or dragon's head.

The Japanese employ large bells in their Buddhist worship. The priests also use small bells while officiating in the temple, as is also the case in China, Tibet, and other Asiatic countries.   Figure 142 is a bronze temple bell in the Metropolitan Museum.

Metropolitan Museum

FIG. 142.   *A bronze temple bell from Japan*

Not only in the temples have bells been used, but also to serve purposes of ordinary life.   In the seventh century laws were enacted to keep the upper classes from oppressing the lower classes. The use of public horses was not permitted except by one who traveled on state business.   Everyone who had a right to use the public-service horses was required to show a token of his right by carrying small bronze bells, and the shape and number of his bells showed how many horses he might rightfully use.

Jingle bells were also used as pennants for horse trappings, even in those early days.

When temple bells came into existence[1] "the hours were struck on them for public information. The method of counting the hours was influenced

[1]Brinkley's *History of the Japanese People.*

by the manner of striking them. Whether bronze bell or wooden clapper was used, three preliminary strokes were given by way of warning, and it therefore became inexpedient to designate any of the hours one, two, or three. Accordingly, the first number was four, and the day being divided into six hours instead of twelve, the highest number became nine."

The Japanese pilgrim who climbs Fujisan rings a long-handled bell as he climbs, and chants an invocation which says: "May our six senses be pure, and the weather on the honorable mountain be fair."

A string of bells is at all times worn about the ankles of the dainty Japanese dancing girl. It is a symbol of her profession, which she never lays aside. This practice has suggested the proverb, "You have tied on the bells," which means, "The die is cast."

Bells with fish pendants are very much in evidence in Japan and Korea on May 5, the boys' Flag Feast, and on other holidays. These bells have each a swinging fish attached to the clapper, so that when a breeze strikes the fish it makes the bell ring.

# CHAPTER XXVIII

## JAPANESE BELL LEGENDS

There are several legends connected with the bell at Engakuji. Once a king's son named Sadotoki became a priest and wanted very much to have a large bell for the monastery. So he traveled in great state to the shrine of Benten and implored the goddess there to tell him how he could obtain a bell.

"Go, Sadotoki," she said, "and explore the lake beyond the temple." Sadotoki did so, and found at the bottom of the lake a great quantity of metal. This was brought to land and used to make the great bell of Engakuji.

Some two hundred years later the bell was miraculously given the power to toll of its own accord, when no human being was near. Anyone who doubted this power of the bell was doomed to be attended by bad luck and evil fortune. But all who believed this with proper faith and reverence were sure to meet good fortune and prosperity.

In the village of Tamagawa lived a man whose name was Ono. While he was still a young man Ono fell ill and died, and descended to the underworld, into the presence of Enma, Lord of Death.

"Why do you come here, Ono? You are still young, and have not lived out the span of years planned for you. Go back to the upperworld, and finish your work." Ono replied, "It is impossible, Enma. Alas! I know not the way, and I cannot find the road in the shadows." Then Enma instructed Ono, saying: "Go from here to the south. There you will hear the sound of a deep-toned bell. It will be the great bell at Engakuji, whose sound-waves penetrate even into the darkness of the underworld. Follow that sound, Ono. It will lead you safely to the upperworld of living men."

So it did; and Ono took up his life again with his family. From that day to this, he and his descendants have cherished a deep reverence and affection for the bell of Engakuji, whose ringing had guided homeward the lost soul of Ono.

One of the Japanese legends is very similar to the Chinese story of the Great Bell of Peking. It runs thus: "A Japanese bell founder was bidden to cast a new set of bells which were to give forth the sweetest tones ever rung from a bell, and to this end they were to be cast of mingled metal, gold and silver. The bell founder melted the metals together, but for some reason they would not blend. Hotter and hotter he made his furnace, but all in vain; the metals, though molten, kept distinctly separate. Then a sage told him that only when the metals were fused within a maiden's glow, would they blend. The bell founder's daughter, who had followed her father, always watching in anxiety his weary disappointment, heard the words of the sage, and flung

herself into the melting pot. The gold mingled
with the silver, and the silver with the gold, and the
bells were cast. When taken from their molds they
were smooth, coherent, and well tempered; then
they flung out upon the air notes so sweet and
strong that all men paused at their work, and even
the children at their play, to listen to their entrancing
music."

Another legend seems to explain the presence of
the dragon on the top of nearly all Japanese bells.

It seems that a Buddhist priest left his temple
one day, and happened to see a beautiful tea-house
girl who lived across the river, and fell in love with
her. The priest conquered his love, but unfortunately not until after he had won her affection in
return. The girl was grieved to lose her lover, and
tried in every way to win him back. But she failed.
So she went to a magician and implored him to
teach her how she might become a serpent in order
to work her revenge. After months of practice, she
finally learned how to convert her lovely body into
a great, scaly monster which shot fire from its nos-
trils. Now she was ready for her vengeance.

On some pretext she inveigled the priest to come
across the river, and tried her utmost to win his love
again. When this failed, presto! a great hissing
serpent writhed before him! In terror the priest
fled, swam across the river, and hid in the big temple
bell. But the serpent came right behind him, and
crawled up the bell. The weight of the monster

broke the bell down from its hangings; but, still
poised on the top of the bell, the serpent, with its
fiery breath, melted the metal until the poor priest
beneath it became a part of the molten mass.    The
writhing form of the serpent seems to appear on
the top of almost every bell in Japan.

Several legends are told of the bell at Mii-dera.
Once there lived on the wooded heights of Hiei-zan
a giant called Benkei.   A great fighting giant he
was, whose greatest ambition was to capture a thousand knights and keep their swords.   One day he
went down the hill to Mii-dera and stole the great
bell out of the temple there.   He put it on his back
and started off toward Hiei-zan with it.   As he
toiled wearily along over the hills he came to a
temple and, being very tired, he asked the priests
for refreshment and permission to rest for a while.
The priests offered their hospitality, and the giant
sat down at once and swallowed the contents of a
soup kettle five feet in diameter.   After this he felt
somewhat friendly, and offered to let each one of
the priests strike the bell once.   Cautiously the
first priest came near the great giant and gave a
tap to his bell.   Instead of his usual boom, there
came from the bell the sound of a human voice
saying, "I want to go back to Mii-dera."   Each of
the priests struck it in turn, and every time it said,
"I want to go back to Mii-dera."   The perplexed
giant tried it himself, and the only response to his
heavy blow was the shout, "I want to go back to

Mii-dera!" and Benkei, in great wrath, kicked the bell down the hill. Down it rolled, bumping over great stones and roots and bushes, and knocking against the sides of trees, all the time clanging out its cry of "I want to go back to Mii-dera! I want to go back to Mii-dera!" so loud that people from Mii-dera heard it and rushed out in time to see their beloved bell come plunging down the hill!

The monks of the temple tried their best to lift the bell, but it was too heavy. As they were discussing the ways and means of getting the bell hung up in the temple again, Benkei appeared in the form of a great knight eight feet tall, and offered to hang the bell in its place if the monks would feed him all the soup he could eat, cooked in a caldron the size of the bell. The monks agreed, and Benkei lifted the bell to its accustomed place. Then he began his feast, and did not stop until he had eaten all the food in the monastery. As he drained the last drop of soup from the caldron he bit into the iron rim, and the dent of his teeth may still be seen in this great caldron, still preserved at the Mii-dera monastery.

The bell, also, carries to this day the dents and scratches in its surface which it acquired in the plunge down the rough and wooded hillside.

This same bell at Mii-dera has, in its side, a dent which, they say, appeared when the metal shrank from the touch of a vain and presumptuous woman. The bell was once a woman hater, and would allow no woman to touch it. Women might admire it from a distance, but none were bold enough to incur the bell's displeasure by coming near enough to touch the metal. Finally, one day, there came a very beautiful woman to look at the bell, and also to look at her own lovely face as it was reflected in the shining surface of the bell. The bell looked so warm and friendly, and her own image was so lovely, that she thought surely the bell must be kindly disposed to her, at any rate, even if not to other women. She could not resist the impulse to touch it, gently, with one finger. At once there was an angry clang, and the bell quivered away from her finger, that spot lost its brightness, and a dent was left in the metal as a reminder to all Japanese damsels who may wish to meddle with things too sacred for them.

# CHAPTER XXIX

## THE BELLS OF INDIA

India also claims to have used bells long before the Christian era. Small bells found in ancient burial mounds in India indicate their great antiquity in that country. Figure 143 shows a bell with a clapper attached to it found in a very ancient cairn. It had been cast, and was of good finish when found, and the metal is even yet very resonant. Two others (Figs. 144 and 145) found were of wrought copper, and were evidently used as cattle neck bells.

According to Hindu history, Krishna, one of the principal deified incarnations, was once a cowherd, and for this reason the cowherds have been highly privileged characters among the Hindus. The

FIG. 143.[1] *A cast bronze bell found in a cairn in India*

FIG. 144. *A wrought copper bell found in a cairn in India*

[1]Figs. 143, 144, and 145 are from *Transactions of Royal Irish Academy,* Dublin, 1874.

Hindus have their sacred herds of cattle, and each herd has its queen cow, which is looked upon as a sacred object by the people and is known from the rest by a bell attached to its neck. The milk from this cow is so revered that the common people will not touch it. These animals are generally mottled black and white, the udder being black. When an animal of this color is born, the natives do not keep it, but give it away to the Brahmin priests, either when young or after it has grown up. The animal itself is also privileged, and petted by all, and allowed to roam and browse wherever it wishes without molestation. Every morning before the temple doors are opened, this sacred cow, with the bell suspended from its neck, is led forth by the Brahmin priest to the front of the sacred portals. No mortal dare peep into the *sanctum sanctorum* of the temple before this highly revered animal has first viewed the deity and the interior of the temple; after which the doors are thrown open, and the regular morning service begins.

FIG. 145.   *A wrought copper bell found in a cairn in India*

Cows do not thrive in the trying climate of the hills in southern India, so the hill tribes, or Todas, keep buffaloes instead, and look upon the buffalo with the same reverence that the northern Hindus look upon the cow. With the Todas the buffalo is the focus of all village life. Milk is the divine fluid, and the buffalo the chief gift of the gods and the fountain of all milk. Hence the care and milking of these animals and the charge of the dairy are among the highest and most respected of offices. No Toda will eat buffalo flesh.

Among these people the bell which is (for a short time only) hung around the neck of the sacred buffalo is worshiped as a god. It is called Hiriadeva, or "bell god."

Every village does not own a bell, but certain bell cows of the sacred herds only, which are attached to the holy Mands or *tiriêris* (holy place). One to three bell gods belong to each Mand having from ten to sixty cows (buffaloes). The bell cows are not selected, but are the descendants in direct female line from certain originals whose history has been lost. If a mother should leave no female descendant, a bell cow would be procured from one of the other Mands; or the holy Mand would be broken up, and the entire herd joined to that of some Mand still possessing a bell cow.

A new bell cow is installed or dedicated in the following manner. Twice a day, morning and evening, for three successive days, the priest with his right hand waves the bell round and round the head of the bovine heiress, talking to it meanwhile after this manner:

> "What a fine cow your mother was!
> How well she supported us with milk!
> Won't you supply us in like manner?

"You are a God amongst us!
Don't let the tirièri go to ruin!
Let one become a thousand!
Let all be well!
Let us have plenty of calves!
Let us have plenty of milk!"

During three days and nights the bell is kept fastened around the cow's neck.  On the morning of the fourth day it is removed from her neck and lodged in the priest's house, or in a niche in the temple.  It is never worn again during that cow's lifetime.

No one but a priest is allowed to touch the bell or even to see it.  And though the common people may not look upon it, they pour out libations of milk to it and pay it great reverence.  These bells originally came from Amnor, and are of great antiquity. Their age adds to the veneration which they inspire among the Todas.

Bells not only identify the sacred cattle, but also hang in the Hindu temples where those who pray may call the attention of the gods by beating upon the bells which hang from the temple roofs.  They are used extensively in Hindu ritual, being employed at intervals to attract the attention of the worshipers and to emphasize certain parts of the ceremonies.

The little hand bells or *ghuntas* which the Brahmin priests use have a counterpart in the *sanctus* bell of the Catholic Church.  The *ghuntas* have been used from time immemorial, and are often elegantly

FIG. 146.   *A bell with a Hindu deity for a handle*

FIG. 147.   *A bell from India formed of a cobra and a lotus flower*

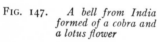

Metropolitan Museum

ornamented. The pre-
siding deity or his em-
blem is usually worked
into the ornamentation.
A Hindu deity forms the
handle of the bell in Figure 146. The snake (co-
bra) is frequently found
curled around the base,
the head forming a can-
opy (see Fig. 147).

Monkeys fill a most
important place in the
poetry, mythology, and
religion of India. Many
of the bells of India
embody representations
of the legendary monkey
god, Hanuman. Figure
148 shows a prayer bell
with an elaborate handle
full of symbols. The fig-
ure of Hanuman on the
handle is supposed to
add greatly to the power
and efficacy of the bell
when it is rung before
the image of this mon-
key god. Long before
they were known in

From a drawing by Mignon Hoffner
FIG. 148. *A prayer bell of India,
with a monkey god for a handle*

Europe, bells were used in Hindu temples to frighten away evil spirits. So that idea was probably not original with our Anglo-Saxon ancestors.

In India the elephants wear bells. They are often made of very hard wood, and each bell has two hardwood clappers tied outside the bell. A cord runs through the clappers and the bell, and is tied around the elephant's neck. As he walks, the clappers beat against the side of the bell. Metal bells are also employed. Elephants are used in India for service, as we use horses. They are turned loose at night to forage for themselves, and if it were not for the bell which each elephant wears, the native would not be able to locate his elephant in the jungle next morning. It is said that every elephant driver knows the tone of his own elephant's bell, and that he never makes the mistake of hunting down the wrong animal. In Ceylon elephants are trained to work in the lumber industry, and here, too, bells are worn on their necks.

These elephant bells are also useful in keeping away bears and other wild animals. A case is reported[1] "where an isolated camp had been repeatedly attacked by bears, which were with some difficulty driven off. The servants eventually adopted the habit of carrying an elephant bell in their hands, which so alarmed the bears by the supposed presence of elephants, that they retired from the vicinity of the camp altogether."

[1]R. T. Kelly, in *Burma Painted and Described*, London, 1905.

All the cattle in the field also wear bells. These
are sometimes made of bronze, but usually of hardwood, "made in the form of an oblong box in which
hang four or more clappers. These serve the double
purpose of locating the cattle as well as frightening
away the snakes as they browse." Sometimes
bells are fastened to the horns of bullocks, and hang
between the animals' eyes.

FIG. 149.   *Wind bells of Burma*

As in other countries, bells have a part to play
in the social life of the people of India. Like the
dancing girls of Japan, those of India also wear bells
as a symbol of their profession. A string of small
brass bells is tied around each leg immediately
beneath the ankle.

Small wind bells, resembling those of China, are
also popular in India. A group of these bells, with
their silken "sails," may be seen in Figure 149.

The bull carts and peddlers' horses of India have bells to announce their coming; and the "magic show" on the street collects its audience, not by signs or advertising, but by ringing a bell in front of the tent.

CHAPTER XXX

BURMESE BELLS

Bells are dear to the heart of every Buddhist, and the Burmans (people of Mongolian blood living in the eastern part of India) are very fond of huge ones. The casting of a large bell has been for a long time a favorite way of "winning merit," for which the Burmese hope to gain reward in a future existence. It is a ceremony of religious importance, and great preparations are made for it. Burmese bells[1] "are cast by the ancient and artistic method known as *cire-perdu*. When some wealthy man has decided to 'win merit' by presenting a bell to the pagoda, the occasion is one that interests the whole neighborhood. The great clay model is made, coated with wax, and covered on the outside with a layer of clay. The crucibles containing the bubbling amalgam of copper and tin are placed upon the open furnaces around. Bands of musicians fill the air with music, and songs are sung in chorus by the crowd; the excitement and enthusiasm become intense; women take off their golden bangles and necklaces and throw them into the melting pots; the hot metal hisses and splutters as it is poured into the mold, the melted wax flows out, and the bell is cast. The Pali inscription, in which the

[1] *Picturesque Burma*, by Mrs. Ernest Hart.

donor's name, his works of charity, and his hopes
of reward are set forth, is then chiseled in the
surface.''

In all Burmese pagodas bells figure largely, and
some of the temples have more than one large bell.
In the Shwe Dagon Pagoda at Rangoon, for instance,
there are bells in every corner of the temple.  Some
of these bells are of enormous size, covered by a
handsome *pyathat*, which is a canopy of several roofs
one above the other, diminishing in size toward the
top, and finally ending in an elongated finial.  Other
bells of smaller size hang out in the open, suspended
by handsome metal work between highly ornamented
posts.  Beside each bell there usually hangs a deer's
antler with which to strike it.  When Buddhists
pray, it is their custom to strike the ground and the
bell in alternate strokes, in order to call the attention
of the "Nats" of the under and upper worlds to their
act of piety.

In one of the corners near the Shwe Dagon
Pagoda is the shrine of the great bell, or Maha
Ganda, "the great sweet voice," fourteen feet high,
over seven and a half feet in diameter, and with
metal fifteen inches thick.  It is said to weigh over
forty-two tons.  Pali inscriptions cover its surface.
In 1579 an Italian traveler wrote of having seen this
bell, saying that at that time no one remembered
where it came from, or how it came there; and that
"there was no nation that could understand its
inscription."

Near another corner of the platform of the Shwe Dagon Pagoda hangs another large bell weighing over eleven tons, which has had a very interesting history. During the war of 1826 the British conquerors seized this bell when they captured Rangoon, and tried to transport it to Calcutta. The boat upon which the English had placed it capsized in the Rangoon River, and the bell fell to the bottom. All their efforts to raise it were futile, and it was finally abandoned.

Some years later the Burmese asked if they might have the bell if they could get it out of the river. The official reply was, "*If* you can raise it, you may have it." After immense efforts, the huge mass of metal was at last lifted and borne away in triumph to their sacred pagoda, where it remains as a lasting tribute to Burmese determination.

Conflicting reports have been given as to how the bell was removed from the river. One writer (in 1827) relates that the natives raised the bell "by attaching two cables to it, which at low water were made fast to a brig moored over it. When the tide rose, so did the bell, and it was hauled ashore."

A recent writer says: "Now the Burmese had no heavy tackle; but they had a small idea whose application solved the problem. They made a heavy disk of solid teak, the exact size of the bell's greatest diameter at the lip, and fastened it firmly to the other end, or ear of the bell, and in that manner made a double wheel of it. They were then able, by passing ropes around the center, to roll the bell out of the river and replace it on the temple platform."[1]

This story has been told of the great forty-two ton bell, Maha Ganda, but it is a mistake. It was the eleven-ton bell that was dropped in the river.

Even the Maha Ganda is small compared to the Great Bell of Mandalay, or the Mingon Bell. It is located on the bank of the Irrawaddy, almost opposite the city of Mandalay. The bell is twelve feet high to the crown, and twenty-one feet high to the top of the monsters. Its diameter is sixteen and one-quarter feet at the lip, and it weighs between eighty and ninety tons. It is the third largest bell in the world, and for a hundred years was second only to the Great Bell of Moscow.

The Mingon Bell was cast toward the end of the eighteenth century by order of King Bodoahpra, who wished to be remembered as the king who had built the largest pagoda and cast the largest bell in Burma. King Bodoahpra's reign is famous as having extended over thirty-six years, and his memory is revered as the sovereign during whose time Burma flourished and extended its limits to distances never before attained. It is said that in the masonry of the enormous unfinished pagoda near the bell, lie entombed a hundred images of solid gold, life size, each image representing one of the members of King Bodoahpra's family. The story relates that the

[1]Walter Del Mar, in *The Romantic East*, London, 1906.

members of the royal family (sons and daughters) amounted to ninety-nine, and that the king was

FIG. 150. *The Great Bell at Mingon, Burma, before it was lifted*

obliged to adopt one child into his household to make up the round number of one hundred.

There was an old prophecy to the effect that the completion of the Mingon Pagoda would bring disaster to King Bodoahpra's dynasty. So it was never finished. In 1838 the shock of an earthquake brought the edifice to a heap of ruins. At the same time, the supports of the bell gave way and it sank to the ground, and remained in that position for half a century (see Fig. 150, p. 345). It was originally suspended on three massive beams of teak, placed horizontally, one over the other. At some time during the last half century it was raised and stones inserted below the lip. In recent years it has been lifted so that it swings free, and an ornamental shed has been erected over it.

In the temple at Moulmein low bronze bells stand at each corner for the people to smite with staghorns when they come to pray. Near the Moulmein Pagoda a famous bell hangs from a beam supported by four pillars. The Burmese, in order to protect this bell from their European aggressors, have placed a threat on the inscription. Besides an inscription in Burmese characters, there is a sentence in poor English, running thus: "This bell is made by KooNaLinnGahjah the priest, and weighs 600 viss [about 1,100 pounds]. No one body design to destroy this bell. Maulmain March 30, 1885. He who destroyed this Bell, they must be in the Great Heell, and unable to coming out."

Another bell in front of an adjacent shrine bears this inscription: "Maulmain 6th March 1887 at 2 P.M. cast a bell by the name of Madoothara made in the quiet reign of Queen Victoria. The dimensions 3 ft. 6 in. in diameter 4 ft. in height 10 ft. 6 in.

in circumference 4 inches in thickness weight 1028 viss. . . . Do not destroy this tremendous bell."

In an obscure temple in the northwestern part of India there is a large bell about three hundred years old, made in Burma, and almost covered with an inscription in Burmese characters. Figure 151 shows the bell, and Figure 152 shows a part of the inscription which gives the story of why the bell was cast.

It seems that early in the seventeenth century the king of Pegu, invaded by his neighbor, the Burmese ruler of Pugan, called upon his ally, the king of Martaban, for help. After gaining his object and driving out the invader, the king of Pegu then tried to destroy his ally. But he became justly the victim of his own treachery, and was defeated by the Martaban king, who took possession of Rangoon, "the abode of royalty, learning, jewels and warriors." Later Martaban, having established peace among the people whom he had conquered, had this bell, weighing about 3,130 pounds, cast to serve as a justice bell for the people, and a "work of merit" for himself. The Burmese inscription, when translated, thus describes the conflict and the events that follow:

"When the king of Martaban arrived in the kingdom of Pegu, he mounted the elephant Airawon, and attacked the armies of Pagahm with such firmness and resolution that it was impossible for them to withstand the shock. The king of Martaban, with his nobles, generals and victorious army

FIG. 151. *A Burmese bell, found in India, cast about three hundred years ago*

FIG. 152. *Burmese inscription on the above bell which relates the story of why the bell was cast*

မောင်မှတ်သဒီး မောင်နံုသည္။ သန္၍။ ဘီလ္။ သုတ။ဝါဂ။ဗ
သော သူတတ်ကောင်းတို႔ဧတရား။ ရွှေမွေးလျှပ်သည်ျဖင်ရှိချ
ၐ်ပြကြည်လင်စွာသမ္ဘာဝိကိရှိလျှက်။ သမ္မတ္႔ၐ္႔ၐခည္ဝတိပြ
ည်ကြီးဝယ်ရေဒီးအရံငသောတန္စိုးဗ္ာၐိတ္ဟာ ၿပြါဗျသော
ေၐင်ျပည်တတ်ဝသောၐတ္နင္ၐျပည်ၐုံတတ္မူသောမွတတ်
ၐတ္တတ်တို႔ၐ္ၐိန္း ဝပ်ၐဝၐး ၐုဃဟာဝတိဘုရား ရွှေကြး
ၐိ္ၐ္ ၐ ၐၐသောင္း ၍ၐေါင်းဒေဝိင်းၐ္ကိုအပေါင်းၐရေၿေမြသုၐ္ၐၐရ
အား သက္ၐသောည်ထားထိုင်ကြားဤ႐ါန္ၐပါၐ။ ဤၐ္ဆို္ၐ္ၐ
ၐသောကုၐ္ၐိုလ္အ႒ိၐ္ကိုၐည္း ရေၿမေသၐင်။ လက်ၐ္နက်ဝ
ၐ္ၐြ္အၐ္ၐ္ၐ္ၐၐၐ္ဆည္ၐ္ၐၐ္ၐိင္ း သၐၐ္အၐ္ၐ္ၐ္ၐသဝၐ္ၐ္ၐၐ္ၐ္ၐ႐ိ္ ၊ တ
ရား ကြီၐ္ၐ္ၐ္ၐၐ္ၐ္ ၊ ၐိၐ္ၐၐ္ၐၐ္ၐၐ္ၐ္ၐၐ္ၐ္ၐ္ၐ္ၐ္ၐ္ၐ္ၐ္ အ႐ု
ဝ ၐ္ ၐ္ၐ္ၐၐ္ၐ္ၐ္ၐၐ္ၐ္ၐ္ၐ္ၐ္ၐ္ၐ္ၐ္ၐ္ၐ္ၐ္ၐ္ၐ္ၐ္ၐ္ၐ္ၐ္ ၐ္ၐၐ္ၐ္ၐ္ၐ္
ၐ္ၐ္ၐ္ၐ္ၐၐ္ၐ္ၐ္ၐ္ၐ္ၐ္ၐ္ၐ္ၐ္ၐ္ၐ္ၐ္ၐ္ၐၐ္ၐ္ၐ္ၐ္ၐ္ၐ္ၐ္ၐ္ၐ္ၐ္
ဝဝၐ္ၐ္ ၐ္ၐ္ၐ္ၐ္ၐ္ၐ္ၐ္ၐ္ၐ္ၐ္ၐ္ၐ္ၐ္ၐ္ၐၐၐၐ္ၐ္ၐ္ၐ္ၐၐ္ၐ္
ၐ္ၐ္ၐ္ၐ္ၐ္ၐ္ၐ္ၐ္ ၐ္ၐ္ၐ္ၐ္ၐ္ၐ္ၐ္ၐ္ၐ္ၐ္ၐ္ၐ္ ၊ ၐ္ၐ္ၐ္ၐ္ၐ္ၐ္ ၊ ၐည္ၐ်
ၐ္ၐ္ၐဝၐ္ၐ္ၐ္ၐ္ၐ္တၐ်ၐ္း ၐၐ္ၐ္ပါၐ ၊ ၐ္ၐ္ၐ္ၐ္ၐ္ၐ္ၐ္ၐ္ၐ္ ၐ်ၐ္ၐ္ၐ္ၐ္ၐ္ၐ
ၐ္ၐ္ၐ္ၐ္ၐ္ၐ္ၐ္ၐ္း ၐ္ၐ္ၐ္ပါၐ ၊ ၐ္ၐ္ၐ္ၐ္ၐ္ၐ္ၐ္ၐ္ၐ္ၐ္ၐ္ၐ္ၐ်ၐ္ၐ္း ၐ်ၐ္
ၐ္ၐ်ၐ္ၐ္ၐ္ၐ္ၐ္ ၊ ၐ္ၐ္ၐ္ၐ္ၐ္ၐ္ၐ္ၐ္ၐ္ၐ္ၐ်ၐ္ၐ္ၐ္ၐ္ၐ္ၐ္ၐ္ၐ္ၐ္ၐ္ၐ္ၐ္ၐ
ၐ္ၐ္ၐ္ၐ္ၐ္ၐ္ၐ္ ၊ ၐ္ၐ္ၐ္ၐ္ၐ္ၐ္ၐ္ၐ္ ၊ ၐ္ၐ္ၐ္ၐ္ၐ္ၐ္ၐ္ၐ္ၐ္ၐ္ ၿမ်ၐ္ၐ္ၐ္ ၊ ၐ္ၐ္ၐ္ၐ္ၐ္ၐ္ၐ္ ၊ ၐ္ၐ္ၐ္ၐ္ ၿၐ္ၐ္ၐ္ၐ္ၐၐ္ၐ္ၐ္ၐ္ၐ်ၐ္ၐ္ၐ္ၐ္
ၐ္ၐ္ၐ္ၐ္ ၊ ၐ်ၐ္ၐ္ၐ္ၐ္ၐ္ၐ္ ၿၐ္ၐ္ၐ္ၐ္ ၐ္ၐ္ၐ္ ၊ ၐ်ၐ္ ၿၐ္ၐ္ၐ္ၐ္ၐ

returning, were met by the king of Pegu mounted
upon the elephant Vopantatha, surrounded by the
chiefs and armed divisions of his royal forces. The
king of Martaban, distrusting Pegu, and seeing
himself surrounded by his army, began to tremble
for his life, and he therefore vowed that should he
be delivered, he would give charitably to religion;
then having mounted his elephant Airawon, he
assembled his generals and set his troops in battle
order. The two armies being now engaged, the
king of Pegu riding upon his elephant Vopantatha,
was charged by the monarch of Martaban, seated
upon the elephant Airawon. The tusks of the
former elephant being broken in the encounter,
he (Pegu) was unable to sustain the fight, and turned
and fled, upon which the army of Pegu was defeated,
and his nobles and generals destroyed. . . .

"Having banished the evil doers, Martaban ruled
over the country in peace. . . . The inhabitants
of the whole earth enjoyed the light of his wise
administration of the laws. In like manner as the
stars are illuminated by the brightness of the full
moon, so the king desired to see his nobles and
warriors and his subjects, in number more than a
hundred thousand, increase their riches in proportion to his own prosperity. The king by means of
his ten royal virtues increased in benevolence. . . .

"Sometime during the season Ganthayedda, when
the king reclined upon the royal couch and pleasure
filled his breast, he reflected upon the just laws of

the world, and thought it would be right to erect a statue of the deity in the country of Pegu, and establish for the people a true system of justice that they may neither fear nor hate him, but bear him in respectful remembrance, and for this purpose he determined to cast a bell and place it beneath a double roof [belfry or temple] that the people might give notice of their wrongs by striking it, the sound of which reaching his ears, he would be enabled to redress their wrongs.

"He therefore expended a thousand *vis* of pure silver in the construction of this bell.

"On Monday, the twelfth day of the waxing of the moon of July, three hours and a half after the rising of the ninth sign of the zodiac, in the year 984 [agreeing with A.D. 1622], the king caused this bell to be cast, its weight being 8,254 *vis*, and it was placed beneath a double roof. From the time of its being so made and suspended, the people have struck it upon the occurrence of any injustice, the sound of which, having been heard by him, he has directed justice to be properly administered. The people of the country perceiving, felt as if washed with water [abuses abolished].

"If this bell be destroyed, let future monarchs repair it; to this end I have made it, that the people might obtain justice, and that I might obtain Nibban, and all ages till that time the laws might be duly administered. This work of merit I have done."

# CHAPTER XXXI

## BELLS AND BUDDHISM

Bells have a religious significance in all countries, and in most of them bells are particularly associated with religious ceremonials. They were used in Asia in religious worship long before the Christian era, and travelers have been struck with the similarity of the ceremonials in the oriental temples with those of Catholic churches. The early Christians exorcised devils with bells, and still find them indispensable. The Russians are especially reverential to bells. Brahmins, Buddhists, Confucianists, all use bells; and even the Mohammedans who do not use bells lest they disturb the peace of departed souls floating in the air, give them at least some consideration, for the Koran says that bells hang on the trees of Paradise and are set in motion by wings from the throne of God as often as the blessed wish for music.

The superstitious beliefs among European Christians concerning bells have been mentioned in a former chapter. Bells seem to be particularly fitted to the nurturing of superstitions among all kinds of people, both savage and civilized. To the present day, the Chinese frighten away, by the united aid of bells, gongs, and kettles, the terrible dragon which occasionally attempts to devour the moon.

FIG. 153. *Bronze prayer bells of the Chinese*

Amulets and charms worn about the person are of great importance to the Chinese, and the most common of all are the little bells worn by Chinese children, especially in the southern provinces. The origin of the custom as regards Canton has been given on page 310, but Dennys[1] says: "A belief in the occult qualities of bells is so widespread that considerable doubt may reasonably exist whether, even if the legend be true, the Cantonese did not merely amplify an existing practice by way of appeasing the demon of the bell. It is, at all events, strange that our own ancestors should have credited bells with possessing occult powers to aid mankind in their combat with the spirits of darkness, while the Chinese propitiate the same enemies by wearing models of bells upon their clothes. But a yet more odd coincidence is found in the sixty-six bells attached to the ephod of the Jewish High Priest when engaged in sacerdotal ministrations."

In almost all Buddhist monasteries a bell is tolled by the monks both morning and evening. These regular tollings comprise a series of 108 strokes.

[1] In "Folk Lore of China," in *China Review.*

"This number[1] represents the 12 months of the year, the 24 divisions of the year as to sun position, and the 72 divisions of the year into terms of five days, making a total of 108. It is the whole year which is thus entirely devoted to the honor of Buddha.

"The manner of ringing these 108 strokes varies according to different places. The following are a few ways: At Hang-chow the tolling is regulated by the following, which has become a popular tune:

"At the beginning, strike 36 strokes;
At the end, still 36 again;
Hurry on with 36 in the middle;
You have in all but 108, then stop.

"At Shao-hsing another quartet has the following:

"Lively toll 18 strokes;
Slowly the 18 following;
Repeat this series 3 times,
And 108 you will reach.

"At T'ai-chow, we find the following ditty:

"At the beginning strike 7 strokes;
Let 8 others follow these;
Slowly toll 18 in the middle;
Add 3 more thereto;
Repeat this series thrice;
The total will be 108.

"Although the manner of ringing differs according to different places, it is fancied everywhere that the sound of the bell procures relief and solace to the

[1]According to Henry Doré, in his *Researches into Chinese Superstitions*.

souls tormented in the Buddhist hell. It is thought that the undulating vibrations, caused by the ringing of the bells, provoke to madness the king of the demons, T'oh-wang, render him unconscious, blunt the sharp edge of the torturing treadmill, and also damp the ardor of the devouring flames of Hades.

"At the death of the first Empress Ma of the Ming dynasty, every Buddhist monastery tolled thirty thousand strokes for the relief of her soul, because, according to Buddhist doctrine, the departed, on hearing the ringing of a bell, revive. It is for this reason that the tolling must be performed slowly."

One Chinese writer, however, seems to have little patience with this point of view, and in a work entitled *Buddhist Names* he says: "The bell is a hollow instrument; the larger it is, the deeper are its sounds, but who could cast one large enough to make its tollings heard in the infernal regions? Even should that happen, such a sound is but a mere empty noise, incapable of awing the ruler of Hades, and powerless also to break the sharp-edged treadmill which tortures the damned. Wealthy families, desirous of rescuing from hell the souls of their ancestors, offer presents to the Buddhist monasteries in order that the monks would toll the bells unceasingly day and night, and perform this service even for several successive days. They may toll them till they deafen the ears of the neighbors, who curse and swear at them; and they may ring till the bells burst, they will never thereby rescue a single soul out of Hades. It matters little whether they toll a brass bell or strike on a wooden one, the result is practically useless in both cases."

The religion of Burma is Buddhism in its purest form. Its acme of human happiness is found in Nirvana, a state of passive existence free from all passions and cares, "to attain which the soul has to go through an endless transmigration of ever improving existence." To attain a better position in the next stage of life is possible only by doing some work of merit. Such a work of merit consists in erecting a pagoda or a shrine, or donating a bell to the temple, or something else of public utility. Hence the generous and gorgeous offerings the Buddhists are always willing to make for their religion. The numerous bells in the temples and the monster bells outside the temples are evidences of the Burmese belief that the donation of a bell is a real public service and a "work of merit."

Metropolitan Museum

FIG. 154. *A thunder bell used by Buddhist priests in India during prayer*

An invocation to Buddha is a favorite inscription for bells. At the door of each Buddhist temple is a bell which the believers strike when they enter the temple, in order to "call the attention of the sleeping gods." Beside each bell in the temple is a deer's horn to be used in striking the bell, and whenever the worshipers pray they strike the bell, to make sure that the gods notice their acts of piety.

"The bell[1] is almost as characteristic a symbol of Buddhism as is the seated figure of Buddha himself. It varies, in the different Buddhist countries, with the temperament and tastes of the people. In Burma, where even Buddhism turns to sunshine and to prettiness, and the towers of the temples evaporate in lacework and jewelry, the bells, glittering with precious stones, hang in clusters from an umbrella-like top of the pagoda spire and ring at their own sweet will. In the temple courts of Rangoon and Mandalay there is a continuous symphony of tinkling and chiming things—dainty, casual, wayward.

"But the bells of China and Korea and those of Japan are more grandiose and sober. To the Japanese the temple bell is, in a sense, the voice of Buddha. Like the stained-glass windows of European cathedrals, Japanese bells are storied records of their temples and their times. They bear inscriptions by famous poets and scholars; they are molded into a wealth of symbolism. And around them cling, like moss and flowers that have overgrown the woodland Buddhas of Nikko, legends and

[1]Marjorie Barstow Greenbie, in an article on the "Bronze Voices of Buddha," in *Asia*, January, 1921.

tales and history that live on the lips of generations who have dwelt in the shadow of some great bell and whose lives have been unconsciously attuned to its grave and sober harmony.

"Yet, though the imagination of the people clings around it, the temple bell seems to speak most eloquently from lonely places, from the heart of monastic woods, from heights to which the contemplative may withdraw for meditation. It has none of the familiar and sociable character of the occidental church bell. Though Christianity, like Buddhism, has understood the value of the bell, the difference between the bells of the East and West is typical of a difference in the genius of the two faiths. In the cities of England and northern Europe the bell is first to speak out on any occasion of special significance to the people. It announces funerals, weddings, fires, and wars. It is at its best in the expression of communal joy. The very method of ringing—in carillons, chimes, and joyous changes—makes it seem a representation of many voices raised in a chorus of gladness.

"The Buddhist bell has none of these social characteristics. It could hardly quicken its deep tone to speak of joy. It seems a voice apart from temporal things, cognizant only of eternity and Nirvana. Yet on any occasion of general sorrow its accent— tranquil, remote, unhurried—may be immeasurably consoling. An American who lived in Kobe while the epidemic of influenza was at its worst, often speaks of the comfort he felt in the sound of the temple bell from the hill.  All day he saw the procession of the dead pass his house, and the smoke of the crematories dimming the sky; but every night at nine o'clock the great bell spoke out — serene and gracious on the evening air — and its grave voice seemed to be saying: 'Fret not; for all this passes. It is well.'"

# CHAPTER XXXII

## BELLS AND ARCHITECTURE

The magnificent buildings of the ancients which gave us so much of architectural beauty in other respects, had no towers.  Compare the Temple of Karnak, the Parthenon, or the Temple of Theseus with the Antwerp and Cologne cathedrals (see Figs. 91, 155, and 156).

After Christian church bells came into use, towers (from which the bells could be more easily heard by the people) began to develop, and Christian architecture took on a distinctive form.  The bell rooms

FIG. 155.  *The Temple of Theseus, Athens*

359

Brown Bros.

FIG. 156. *Cathedral at Cologne. Germany*

on the church roof have gradually become higher
and higher, more and more perfect in form, graceful
spires and other ornamental features have been
added; and thus we owe to
bells most of the famous towers
of the world. All art is, in
some sense, the outgrowth of
practical usage, and "bells
were not made for towers, but
towers for bells." The watch
tower and the church belfry
are the two useful objects
which have contributed most
to the development of architecture in the cathedral form; and
even if bells had given us no
more than this, we should hold

From a tenth-century MS.

FIG. 157.   *A bell tower on
the roof of a church*

them in great honor for what they have done for the
architecture of the world.

It is said that belfries first came into use in the
ninth century, when Alfred erected a tower for the
bells at Athelney. The first churches were probably
low and unadorned, with a raised "lantern" on the
roof to throw light into the center of the building.
Later on, the bell tower, "that unequaled source of
character" to the church, was perhaps seldom
omitted.

Figure 157 is a drawing from a tenth-century
manuscript showing one of these little bell
towers on the roof of a church. The bells are

shown exposed to the open air, that their sounds might be heard as far as possible. The little cock is placed above for vigilance.

The use of the bell tower was recognized in the ancient Saxon law which gave the title of thane to

FIG. 158.  *A thirteenth-century belfry over chancel arch at Abercorn*

anyone who had on his estate a church with a bell tower. Many of these early bell towers remain, and several of them are picturesque and dignified (see Figs. 158 and 159). Some of the towers were attached to the church, and others were entirely separate from it.

FIG. 159. *A Saxon bell tower of the tenth century at Earl's Barton, North Hants*

The round towers of Ireland (see Figs. 160 and
161) are especially interesting memorials of the
early days of Christian architecture, though these
towers were probably used for military as well as

FIG. 160.   *St. Kevin's Church, Glendalough, Ireland.*
*Oldest existing round belfry attached to church*

for religious purposes. They were both watch
towers and belfries, and doubtless the inhabitants
found refuge in them when attacked by the North-
men.   The sacred objects of the church were often
placed in the tower for safekeeping.

In the upper stories of these towers there have been found bars of iron or of oak, upon which bells were probably fastened and played with a metal hammer. Lord Dunraven writes that he "carried

FIG. 161. *Belfry of Antrim, County of Antrim, Ireland. Built about the ninth century*

an ordinary dinner bell to the top of Clondalkin Round Tower, and observed that the sound seemed greater when heard within the topmost chamber of the tower than in an ordinary hall; and a friend standing at a distance of a hundred feet from the building said the tone was quite as loud as when rung beside her down on the level of the ground." He thinks that the bells in these towers were probably tuned to the notes of the pentatonic scale, and played, perhaps, for the entertainment of the inhabitants clustered about the base of the tower.

From the slant of the openings in the top of many of these towers it is thought that heavy missiles and stones were probably pushed from the belfry to fall upon a besieging enemy below. Without doubt, these bell towers served the inhabitants in several capacities, municipal as well as religious.

The Irish bell towers are only typical of what existed in other parts of the British Isles, and in other European countries, during the Middle Ages.

### MUNICIPAL BELL TOWERS

Sometimes the town united with the church in building a tower that would be used as a tower of defense and a watch tower as well as a belfry. In many cases bell towers were built by the town, near the town hall, and the bells used in calling citizens together in cases of disorder in the town, fire, or other alarms.

In countries which were distracted by constant war the bells of the town acquired great public importance. If there was no special town bell, the chief bell in the cathedral often belonged to the town, not to the cathedral chapter. "He who commanded the bell commanded the town; for by that sound, at a moment's notice, he could rally and concentrate his adherents. Hence a conqueror commonly acknowledged the political importance of bells by melting them down; and the cannon of the conquered was in turn melted to supply the garrison with bells to be used in the suppression of revolts. Many a bloody chapter in history has been rung in and out by bells."[1]

Municipal bell towers existed in Europe as early as the eleventh century.[2] "The building of the town hall was the earliest symbol of the growth of the free community (independent of the feudal lords), and the cities of Bordeaux and Toulouse had each a building of the kind as far back as the twelfth century. In the early days of enfranchisement, it was customary to call together the citizens of the community by means of bells. These were, however, at first confined to the towers of the churches, and since they could not be rung without the consent of the clergy, a good deal of friction must sometimes have arisen, especially in those places where it happened that ecclesiastics were the feudal lords. To obviate difficulty of this kind, the municipalities began to procure bells of their own, and these were hung at first over the town gates, in the manner of which a very interesting example may still be seen at the gate known as 'La Grosse Cloche' at Bordeaux. Toward the close of the twelfth century

[1]See *Encyclopedia Britannica*, on "Bell."

[2]"Architecture in the War Area," in *Architect and Contract Reporter*, August, 1917, by Tyrrell-Green.

and the early years of the thirteenth, we find separate towers erected for town bells. These also served the purpose of lookouts, being provided with lodging for the watchman, and a gallery commanding a view on every side, so that the bell might sound an alarm upon outbreak of fire, or onset of foe. While in their origin the belfries were thus designed to meet a need, and serve a utilitarian purpose, they came to be regarded, as time went on, as ends in themselves, and were built on a great scale and lavishly adorned. . . . Thus the town belfries which form so regular a feature of old Flemish cities, and which occur with like frequency in the north of France, may be considered as material symbols of the power and wealth of the communities that erected them.''

The Christians, in using bells according to the requirements of their religion, says Russel Sturgis, were ultimately led to the invention of new forms of architecture. Below is given a list of definitions quoted from Sturgis' *Dictionary of Architecture and Building*, which gives an idea of the contribution which bells have made to the terms and forms of architecture.

*Bell cage.* A timber framework which supports the bells in a steeple. Designed to absorb as much vibration as possible so as to transmit a minimum of jarring to the walls.

*Bell canopy.* Open structure with small roof intended to shelter a bell. Stands either independently (as at gate of churchyard) or resting upon wall of church.

*Bell carriage.* Structure which carries bells in a belfry.

*Bell chamber.* Portion of the interior of a belfry or campanile in which bells are hung. Contains bell carriage and has large openings to permit the wide diffusion of the sound.

*Bell cot: cote.* Small structure to carry and shelter one or more bells, and carried upon brackets projecting from a wall, or built upon a roof or spire.

*Bell crank.* An angular lever for changing direction of a to-and-fro movement of the bells.

*Bell gable.* A gable having an opening in which a bell is hung; in particular, an upward prolongation of a portion of a wall above the roof, terminating in a small gable, and having one or more openings for bells.

*Bell hanging.* The trade or operation of putting in place, in a building, the bells and their appurtenances.

*Bell house.* A building, usually tower-like, intended for the housing and proper sounding of a bell or bells, especially Round Towers, like those of Ireland.

*Bell pull.* A knob or handle and its appurtenances connected with a bell by any mechanical contrivance by which the bell is rung by pulling.

*Bell tower.* A tower fitted and prepared for containing one or more large bells, and for allowing their sound to be heard properly both near and far. Nothing of this kind existed in antiquity.

*Bell turret.* A small tower, usually topped with a spire or pinnacle, and containing one or more bells.

*Belfry.* In modern use, a structure arranged for carrying large bells, and allowing for their proper service in different applications: (1) a bell tower, (2) bell chamber, (3) bell cage, (4) place occupied by the bell ringers; this is sometimes far below the bells, and in some churches is on the floor of the tower, level with the floor of the church itself.

*Campanile* (Italian plural *campanili*).   In Italian, a bell tower, generally separatèd from other buildings.

### THE CAMPANILES OF ITALY

Nowhere in the world are there to be found more beautiful bell towers than in Italy, the home of the first church bells.   At a very early date it became customary in Italy to hang the bells in towers that were separate from the churches, instead of hanging them in steeples or belfries upon the church buildings, as is the case with most modern churches. Some of these bell towers, or campaniles, are very lofty and magnificent.   The following are some of the most famous ones.   The Campanile of St. Mark in Venice (see Fig. 162) belongs to the famous church of St. Mark, and is built about two hundred feet from the church.   It was originally erected about 900,[1] rebuilt in 1329, and provided with a new upper story after an earthquake in 1512.   The bell chamber is at the top, and the ascent is made by a continuous inclined plane, winding around the tower, with a platform at each square angle.   In 1902 it collapsed.   The foundations were strengthened and the tower rebuilt in 1905–1911.   It is three hundred and twenty-five feet high.

The Round Campanile of Pisa, or the Leaning Tower as it is most often called, was begun in 1174

[1]Says Baedeker.

Gramstorff Bros., Inc., Malden, Mass.

FIG. 162. *St. Mark's Cathedral and bell tower (campanile)*
*in Venice, Italy*

FIG. 163. *The leaning bell tower of Pisa, Italy*

and finished in 1359 (see Fig. 163). It is believed that when this tower was being built the foundations of one side sank, and rather than begin it all over, the builders adjusted the weight of the upper stories so that it would be in a state of equilibrium, even though leaning so far over. It rises to a height of one hundred and seventy-nine feet, and a plumb line lowered to the ground from the top story, which forms the belfry, reaches the ground about thirteen feet from the base of the building. Galileo tried his experiments regarding the laws of gravitation from the top of this tower, the slanting position of which served his purpose well. The belfry is reached by a flight of two hundred and ninety-six steps. It is now thought to be less stable than formerly.

The Campanile of Florence (see Fig. 164, p. 374) is a square structure two hundred and seventy-six feet high on a base forty-five feet square, and is richly decorated with colored marble. It was begun by the celebrated architect, Giotto, in 1334, but he did not live to see it completed (in 1350). It is considered the most important piece of the late Italian Gothic architecture which carried with it much decoration in colored marbles combined with sculpture. In his *Seven Lamps of Architecture*, Ruskin says: "The characteristics of Power and Beauty occur more or less in different buildings, some in one and some in another. But all together, and all in their highest possible relative degrees, they

FIG. 164. *Cathedral and campanile of Florence, Italy,*
*often called "Giotto's Tower"*

exist, so far as I know, only in one building in the world—the Campanile of Giotto."

There are several interesting campaniles in Russia. See St. Ivan's Tower in Figure 96.[1]

Since the days of the Irish round towers, the early town bell towers, and the first Italian campaniles, church towers and belfries have developed number-less and exquisite forms which are more or less familiar to everyone who lives in a Christian country. The cathedrals of England have long been famous for their beauty, and there are many on the Continent and in America which are scarcely less interesting and impressive. The field of church architecture is too vast to allow here more than a suggestion of the part that bells have played in its development.

In his *History of Ecclesiastical Architecture*, Poole says: "It is to the use of church bells that we are indebted for the most prominent feature of almost every ecclesiastical fabric, and that which serves most to harmonize all the parts of a whole, sometimes so vast and almost always so various, is a Gothic church. From the low, central tower of a Norman abbey, but just rising above the roof of the inter-section of the cross, to the lofty towers or spires of Boston, Gloucester, Coventry, in whatever part of the church it may be placed, the steeple still gives an inexpressible grace and dignity to the whole outline, correcting immoderate lengths, reducing all minor parts to proportion, giving variety to sameness,

[1] See p. 221.

and harmony to the most licentious irregularity. . . . What is it which gives such vastness and importance to the cathedral, such grace and beauty to the parish church at a distance, but the tower or spire? Nay, what is it but the bell gable which in mere outline often distinguishes the retired chapel from some neighboring barn? And for all this we are indebted to the introduction of bells; or if not for the existence of these or the like additions to the beauty of outline in our churches, yet at least for what is part of their beauty, their having a use, and being exactly adapted to their use."

# CHAPTER XXXIII

## VARIOUS KINDS OF BELLS
## AND THEIR USES

It is interesting to observe the great variety in the kinds of bells exhibited in the Crosby-Brown collection of musical instruments in the Metropolitan Museum. The following is a list made casually, with no claim to completeness: Mass bells, costume bells, cat bells, ring-rattle bells, bracelet bells, cowbells, horse bells, sheep bells, donkey bells, camel bells, ox bells, dog bells, elephant bells, buffalo bells, harness bells, sleigh bells, hand bells, clay bells, wind bells, temple bells, centurian bells, ankle bells, runner's bells, chanting bells, prayer bells, church bells, a tree bell, double bells, bells on stands, bells on pedestals, and swinging bells.

So far as could be ascertained, these bells are made of the following materials: bronze, bell metal, brass, iron, copper, silver, pottery, wood, horn, white metal, and pewter. The shapes are of almost every conceivable form which allows a hollow cavity for ringing. There are long narrow ones, short shallow ones, round, square, and trumpet-shaped; geometrical designs, and fantastic representations of flowers, animals, and human beings.

In the city of New York the following kinds of bells were heard by the writer within a few weeks:

church bells, clock-tower bells, fire-wagon bells, ragman's bell, scissor grinder's bell, old newspaper collector's bell, fruit vendor's bell, sleigh bells, door bells,
street bells (on election night), prompter's bell (or
curtain bell) at the theater, bells of Salvation Army
collectors for the poor, train bells, school-period
bells, boat bells, and chimes and other musical bells.

The town bellman and crier was once a familiar
character in every large town in England. Before
the days of plentiful house clocks, the citizens
depended on him for information of the time of
night. The streets were lighted by lanterns hung
outside the houses, "with a whole candle for the
accommodation of foot passengers, from Allhallow's
evening to Candlemas Day. The bellman went
his rounds all night with a bell in his hand, and at
every 'land's end and ward's end, gave warning of
fire and candle, and help the poor and pray for the
dead.' Almost down to the last century the watchman was a feeble old man who 'disturbed your rest
to tell you what's o'clock,' and showed his lantern
to warn thieves of his approach that they might
depart in peace, and like Dogberry, he might thank
God he was rid of a knave."[1]

The bellman of Old England voices his duties in
the following rime:[2]

> Time, Master, calls your bellman to his task,
> To see your doors and windows are all fast,

[1]From *Bells, an Anthology*, by Mary S. Taber.
[2]Chambers' *Book of Days*.

And that no villainy or foul crime be done
To you or yours in absence of the sun.
If any base lurker I do meet,
In private alley or in open street,
You shall have warning by my timely call,
And so God bless you and give rest to all.

Robert Herrick's "Bellman" runs thus:

From noise of scare fires rest ye free,
From murders benedicitie;
From all mischances that may fright
Your pleasing slumbers in the night;
Mercie secure ye all, and keep
The goblin from ye, while ye sleep.
Past one o'clock and almost two,
My masters all, "good day to you."

The town crier was also an important person in New England; and in some of the small New England towns he has disappeared only within the past half-century. He announced not only the time, but all the important news as well, giving the same kind of service that is done by the newspaper and radio today.

In the past, bells have been used in many other customs that have died out, or are fast disappearing. The muffin bell announced that the muffin man was within hearing, and that his muffins were fresh and hot. The postman's bell was rung to attract the attention of those who had letters to mail, as the postman went about collecting letters, a custom replaced by the present postal system. The dustman rang a bell as he collected rubbish from house to house; and we may still hear the bell of the ragman and the old-clothes man.

In some places hand bells are still rung by those who go from door to door on Christmas, seeking gifts and bounty.

FIG. 165. *A hand bell of the eleventh or twelfth century*

The table or hand bell in domestic life has a counterpart in the whistle or horn of the outside world of sport. Several centuries ago the use of table bells was universal in Europe as the only means of calling servants. Figure 165 shows a highly ornamented table bell of the eleventh or twelfth century. The Italian table bells of the sixteenth century have claimed the attention of art collectors. Many of these have the armorial bearings of the owners, and during the Renaissance period the designs on the bells were rich and elaborate. The table bell used by Mary Queen of Scots is still preserved as a relic and a work of art. Among the late eighteenth- and early nineteenth-century French table bells a fashion arose of having a full-length figure of some historic personage. Bells of this time include images of Marie Antoinette, Napoleon, Empress Josephine, and of many others. These developed later into a grotesque style.[1]

The hand bell as a domestic signal developed into a kind of house bell, hung somewhat after the manner of a church bell rung with a rope. In the hall, or in some other part of the residence, a bell was hung, and from it a cord or wire passed through a hole in the ceiling of the adjacent room, and hung down within easy reach. In many of the old-fashioned houses in England, even at present, the maid is called by this means. A heavy cord with a tassel at the end may still be seen hanging in many bedrooms and drawing rooms of England. A pull at this cord will bring a tinkle from the bell hanging on the other side of the wall through which the cord passes. "Few persons," says a writer of 1850, "are aware how modern is the present practice of domestic bell hanging; for no trace of it has been discovered in the old mansions of our nobility, even so late as the reign of Queen Anne. Lord Brownlow, in speaking of his residence, said, in 1810: 'It is getting into fashion to have bells hung from the rooms

[1]Arthur Hayden's *By-Paths in Curio Collecting.*

in houses. I must have them also.' Before that, each room had its lackey instead of a bell. So long did it take to conduct mankind to the simple invention of ringing a bell in a horizontal direction by means of a crank and a piece of wire."[1]

Perhaps one of the saddest occasions on which a hand bell was rung in England was during the Great Plague of London, in the summer of 1665, to announce the arrival of the cart to take the dead bodies away, there being too many to be buried separately. "All day and all night, the dead-cart went its rounds, with the weird noise of the gloomy bell, and the hoarse voices of the buriers calling, 'Bring out your dead!' "[2]

Another doleful-voiced hand bell was one which was rung at the window of the condemned cell of St. Sepulchre's Church in London. "On the night before an execution, some person, armed with a large hand bell, would get as near as possible to the window of the condemned cell, and after sounding twelve solemn double strokes with his bell, then recited the following lines:

'All you that in the condemned hole do lie,
    Prepare you, for tomorrow you shall die;
    Watch all, and pray, the hour is drawing near
    That you before the Almighty must appear;
    Examine well yourselves, in time repent,
    That you may not to eternal flames be sent;

[1]*Miscellanea Critica.*
[2]Meiklejohn, in *A New History of England and Great Britain.*

And when St. Sepulchre's bell tomorrow tolls,
The Lord above have mercy on your souls.' "[1]

Then as a final reminder, he announced "Past twelve o'clock!" and left the doomed ones to their own thoughts.

For centuries it was the custom to ring hand bells at funerals, and this old custom has not entirely disappeared. A hand bell is still rung before the procession at Oxford funerals, not to scare away the evil spirits, as was formerly the case, but merely for the sake of the old English custom. In some places of Ireland and Scotland the hand bell is rung in the funeral procession all the way to the churchyard.

The *sanctus* bell which is rung at the elevation of the Host (see p. 97) in the Catholic service is the signal for all who hear it to kneel and offer a prayer to the Virgin. "Most persons have witnessed this scene in the streets of Roman Catholic cities where a hand bell is rung before the priest who carries the sacred elements. Some years ago in Spain, the sound penetrated to the interior of a theater, and not only did all the spectators rise up and kneel, but the dancers on the stage stopped in their performance to drop upon their knees."[2]

When men began to domesticate animals, and the huntsman began to give way to the herdsman, a need was felt for something which would enable the owner of animals to keep in touch with them. Hence

[1] From Geo. S. Tyack's *Book about Bells*.
[2] *Miscellanea Critica*.

began the use of crotal bells, or noise producers; and for ages men have used bells on the necks of animals.

Sheep bells are tied on the necks of the ringleaders, and all the other sheep, who habitually follow the leader, are more easily kept together. In Scotland every flock of sheep has a bell to enable the herdsman to find them when lost in the snow. Sometimes the Indians of New Mexico make sheep bells of the horns of the Rocky Mountain sheep, the clapper being a stone tied inside the horn. A writer of the sixteenth century states that "the shepherds think that the flocks are pleased with the sound of the bell, as they are by the flute, and that they grow fat in consequence."

It has long been thought that animals have some kind of conscious pride in the bells which they wear on their necks. Southey, writing of the Alpine cattle, says: "They stalk forth proud and pleased when wearing their bells. If the leading cow, who hitherto bore the largest bell, be deprived of it, she manifests a sense of disgrace by lowing incessantly, abstaining from food, and growing lean; and the happy rival on which the bell has been conferred is singled out for her vengeance."

The cowbells of the Swiss are prized very highly. Much care is spent in making them, and they descend in families from generation to generation. Some of them which are made of hammered copper have very pleasing tones. The traveler in the mountains of Switzerland has every opportunity to hear many tones of cowbells, and there are few people who are insensible to their charm.

Cowbells have been heard by every country child in America. The slow, steady tinkle down in the lane as the cows come home is probably a cherished childhood memory of many a man and woman now living in the city.

Horse bells, in ancient times, were probably used for ornamental as well as for useful purposes. Bells which were worn on the horses of the Canterbury Pilgrims have been found in the Thames River. These bells were inscribed with the words *Campana Thome*.[1] Horse bells are common in Asia; also in southern and western United States, where they are used to enable the owners to locate the horses which are often left free to roam about and graze at will. The bell, when it is worn by the leader of the group, also serves to keep a group of horses together.

In Italy, and elsewhere in Europe, bells are made of baked earth; they have a very pleasing sound, and are inexpensive, costing about a penny apiece. If a sheep or horse breaks his bell, it is not a very serious matter to replace it.

In the West, bells are fastened to the necks of turkeys. These serve not only to help locate the turkeys, but also as a protection against hawks and wild animals. It will be recalled that the bells worn by the domestic animals in India serve to protect them against snakes.

[1] *Chambers Encyclopedia.*

In the Orient, pack horses and camels are often furnished with bells. Oriental caravans are noted for the jingling of numerous bells suspended from

the necks of their animals. The object of these bells is said to be to enliven the animals, to frighten off beasts of prey, and, above all, to keep the party together, enabling those who might have lingered or strayed to rejoin the caravan by following the sound of the bells. This is of great importance in countries where the routes pass over trackless plains and mountain passes, with no regular roadways. The bells are generally attached to the throat, or chest band, and are fastened either singly or in a number together. Sets of camel bells are sometimes fastened to a board which is carried on the animal's back (see Figs. 166 and 167).

Metropolitan Museum

FIG. 166. *Camel bells*

Falconry is the art of training hawks to catch other birds. It was a popular pastime in Europe in former days, and the sport is still practiced in some places.

Small bells are fastened to the legs of the hawks to aid in their recovery. Formerly, when several hawks were used at one time, the bells used were of different tones, and the combination of sounds was said to be very pleasing.

Hunting dogs also wear bells when hunting in thick cover, or where the dog cannot readily be seen. The sound of the bell causes the birds to lie closer.

The reindeer of Norway and other cold countries wear bells. We are reminded of this custom by the bells on Santa Claus's reindeer at Christmas time.

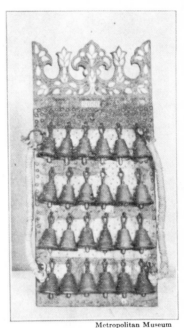

Sleigh bells fastened upon the horses that draw sleighs are still to be heard in all cold climates. Traveling over soft snow is so noiseless that sleigh bells are a necessary safeguard to prevent collisions. The jingle of sleigh bells is a characteristic sound in nearly all towns of Russia during the winter.

Metropolitan Museum

FIG. 167.  *Camel bells*

Figure 168 (next page) represents a set of Russian saddle bells used by riders on horseback. Each bell has several outside clappers which hang close to the bell, and every movement of the horse causes a merry jingle of many tones.

In many countries wagon bells were in use up to the last century. They were made in sets of several bells fastened in a frame attached to the harness. Sockets were made in the horses' collars to hold up these iron frames. The purpose of the bells was

Bevin Bros., East Hampton, Conn.

FIG. 168. *A set of Russian saddle chimes*

to give warning on a narrow passage in a road, so that another wagoner, coming from the opposite direction, could wait in a wider part of the road. Figure 169 shows a set of these bells in a frame.

Maberly Philips says[1] that "sixty or seventy years ago every horse in the team of a large farm wagon would be decorated with a set of bells as well as many brass ornaments. They were frequently

[1] In "Latten or Waggon Bells," in *The Connoisseur*, 1916.

the property of the wagoner, were highly prized,
and kept in splendid order. Each bell was attuned
to a different note, not simply to make jingle, but
to give a pleasant sound. . . . Many of the country lanes were so narrow that passing another team
was out of the question. Certain rules of the road
were instituted, which, if not complied with, often
led to the wagoners fighting out the question of

FIG. 169. *A set of English wagon bells*

which should give way. . . . Some sets have
three, five or six bells. Each set is fixed to a strong
piece of board, covered with stout leather, which is
brought down round the bells, so as to protect them
from the weather. I am told that it is some years
since a team of horses with a full set of bells has
been seen upon any of our country [England]
roads. . . .

"The shaped irons, that are in all cases attached
to the frame, are fitted into sockets provided for

them on the horse's collar.   The frame of the largest
set I have seen is two feet long, and five inches across
the top, the leather curtain being three inches deep.
It weighs thirteen and one-half pounds, which must
have been a serious addition to the weight of the
horse's trappings."

The old English Morris dancers have always worn
small bells fastened around the leg, just under the
knee.   The jingle of these bells heightens the effect
of the dance to a great degree, and also stimulates
the enthusiasm of the dancers themselves.

In Japan and India small ankle bells are regarded
as the symbol of the dancer's profession, and in
Egypt and other Eastern countries the girls of
past centuries wore strings of bells about their
ankles.   Such bells may be seen in Cairo today.

Costume bells have been used for ages.   We read
in the Bible that the Hebrew priest was instructed
to wear many small bells upon his robe while in the
synagogue, in order that "his sound shall be heard
when he goeth into the holy place before the Lord,
and when he cometh out, that he die not."

In Shakespeare's day the "fools" wore bells upon
their clothing, and their wands had bells fastened
to them.   Some savages wear strings of small bells
as their only article of dress.[1]   In the fifteenth
century silver bells were worn on the dress of both
men and women, and even today small bells are
seen on fancy ball costumes.

[1]See p. 19.

Arabian ladies wear little bells suspended from their hair and garments, which, when they walk, give notice that the mistress of the house is passing, and so put the servants on their guard.

Bells have long been used for purposes of alarm. The use of fire bells has been so systemized that they indicate the exact location of the fire. Fire bells in Japan are placed on poles which are tall enough to overlook the houses in the crowded sections and are easily accessible from all the streets.

In many New England towns, and along public highways, one often sees large, circular pieces of metal fastened to trees or posts. These are used as fire alarms, either for village or forest fires.

Factory bells, farm bells, and bells which ring on the departure and arrival of boats and trains are so commonplace that no reminder of them is needed.

The uses of the bell are not confined to land. For a long time bells have been used to warn boatmen of dangerous places near the shore. Southey's poem, "The Inchcape Rock,"[1] gives the story of a bell which, in the twelfth century, was placed on Inchcape Rock in the North Sea to give warning to mariners.

Even a short trip in a pleasure boat will usually give one an opportunity to hear a bell ringing from a rock or floating buoy, warning the pilots of rocks under the surface of the water.

The lighthouse bell is also still in use.

[1]See p. 402.

A well-known use of bells is that of "bell time" on shipboard. In order to give the time to all the sailors at once, every half-hour during the day and night, and also to reduce the number of strokes to some extent, time is divided into sections of four (instead of twelve) hours, and a bell is rung every half-hour according to a plan which the sailors understand. For instance, twelve o'clock is indicated by eight strokes of the bell; 12:30 by one stroke; 1:00, by two strokes of the bell; 1:30, three strokes; 2:00 o'clock, four strokes; 2:30, five strokes; 3:00, six strokes; 3:30, seven strokes; 4:00 o'clock, eight strokes. Then the series is started again from the beginning, 4:30 being one stroke of the bell, and so on. Eight is the highest number ever rung for giving shipboard time. If one hears the ship bell ring five strokes, one knows that it is 2:30 or 6:30 or 10:30 by clock time.

Some ship bells are fine examples of the bell founder's art. Figure 170 shows a bell cast several years ago for the *U.S.S. Cleveland*.

The electric bell has replaced many of the old-time uses of hand bells, and is now familiar to everyone. The mechanism is thus described in the *New International Encyclopaedia*:

"The arrangement required to ring a bell or system of bells by electricity is simple. Some form of galvanic battery requiring little attention, is placed in any convenient corner, and from it an insulated wire, with the necessary branches, is conducted to

the various rooms; thence to, perhaps, as many
bells, and finally back to the battery to complete
the circuit.  Each single bell is provided with a

Courtesy of *Architectural Record*
FIG. 170.  *The ship bell for U.S.S. "Cleveland"
designed by Adolph Weinman.  Executed by the
Henry-Bonnard Co.*

clapper to which is fixed a piece of soft iron.  Near
this is an electro-magnet, wound with a quantity
of insulated wire, to which the main wire is connected, so that, upon the passage of the signal current, the magnet attracts the piece of iron fastened
to the clapper, and the clapper strikes the bell.  In
this way any number of bells may be rung at once

by sending a powerful current through the wire to which they are all connected. . . .

"Bells for continuous vibratory ringing are of the same construction as above except that they are provided with a device for continually vibrating the clapper while the bell is being rung. The wire, instead of being connected directly to the coil around the magnet, is connected to a post against which the clapper rests after striking the bell. The coil is connected to the clapper, and the current passes through the post and the clapper to the coil. When a signal on the wire causes the magnet to attract the clapper and strike the bell, the connection is immediately severed by the clapper leaving the post, and no more current can pass until the clapper has returned after striking the bell. Instantly when this occurs, the connection is reëstablished and the clapper reattracted, and the bell again struck. Thus a continuous ringing is produced as long as the person presses the calling button.

"A push button is simply a cap covering the terminals of the wires leading to the bells. A slight pressure of the hand upon the button in the center forces the spring-shaped terminals of the wires into contact with each other, and allows the current to pass from the battery to the bell."

# CHAPTER XXXIV

## THE MILLER BELL COLLECTION

The largest and most interesting collection of bells in the world is in the Glenwood Mission Inn, at Riverside, California. It is sometimes called the "Inn of the Bells." There are 524 bells described in the catalogue of 1926, and others are constantly being added to the collection. The bells are not arranged in "museum" order, but are hung about the different parts of masonry built to receive them, and kept distinctly representative of the Spanish mission architecture. Three of the early missions are reproduced in part, the side wall of San Gabriel Mission, the front of Santa Barbara Mission, and the dome of Carmel Mission.

The Inn was built and the famous bell collection was made by Mr. Frank A. Miller, a Californian, whose interest in the early history of California and in the bells and crosses of the missions gradually extended to include a deep interest in all kinds of bells. These interests have led him to make the unique and beautiful combination of architecture, history, and romance which gives pleasure to numberless travelers.

A recent visitor to the Inn writes:[1] "In California today there is a new kind of garden, a garden

[1] *Christian Science Monitor* for August 18, 1924.

of bells.   A student could easily trace the entire
history of bell founding by an examination of the
hundreds of bells.   In a series of arches rising from
one side of this garden, hang wonderful bells from
many lands, all woven together in a charming way
by a morning-glory vine which springs from the
ground far below, and which sends out hundreds of
delicate blue bells, fresh every morning, to greet
the ancient bells of bronze and brass.   The contrast
between the age-old, solemn-looking giants with
voice of thunder and the dainty, silken-petaled blossoms forms a picture of garden beauty rare and
memorable.

"Along one end of this bell garden runs a pergola
of eucalyptus branches, draped with iron chains
from which bells of many sizes and from many lands
hang like fair blossoms (see Fig. 171).   From India
and Persia, China, Switzerland, and the dark forests
of Africa came the bells.   Some tinkled from the
feet of dancing girls from Assam, some hung from
the staff of Tibetan pilgrims.   Some served in
garrisons, some in temples.   Each has a history,
and the visitor who cares may read the life story
of each, printed upon a card beside it.   Here rests
a bell from San Blas, which inspired the beautiful
poem by Longfellow.   Over there is a ship's bell
which was raised from the bottom of the sea, where
it lay for nearly half a century; for it went down
with a transport sent out from Boston in 1775,
conveying from Nova Scotia hundreds of Acadians

Avery Edwin Field

FIG. 171. *View of the porch of Glenwood Mission Inn, with bells hanging from chains*

who were seeking a new home in Maryland and the Carolinas.

"In Mr. Miller's Garden of Bells the imagination has full sway, for some of the bells have called to war, some to the marriage feast. A camel bell from Egypt conjures a desert caravan facing the rising sun, another tells of pilgrims toiling across Himalayan snows. On one chain hangs a conjuror's rattle from Salem and a devil chaser from China. And there are bells of curious shapes—a pair of hands, the mouth of a frog or crocodile, a rustic maiden with full skirts whose feet form a clapper; a lotus flower, a pagoda, or a dragon.

FIG. 172. *Oldest dated Christian bell so far known, save one (see Fig. 100), in the Miller Garden of Bells*

"In one corner stands a bell beloved by Father Damien, for it went with him to far Molokai. Near it is the railroad gong which sounded in Riverside when the Santa Fé first came to carry back sweet oranges. A huge bell shaped like a bowl claims an

Avery Edwin Field

FIG. 173.    *Chinese temple bell (weight, 2,800 lbs.) from Nanking, in the Miller Garden of Bells*

age of 1599 years, and for centuries was struck by a heavy mallet swung from the hands of priests, at midnight, in the temple of Zenko. If touched ever so lightly, it will chant in low voice."

There hangs a brass cowbell from Rome, which, according to its inscription, was made in the fifteenth

Avery Edwin Field

FIG. 174.   *Bronze bell from Montserrat, Spain, dated 1704, in the Miller Garden of Bells*

or the early sixteenth century, and belonged to Pope Paul III. Also a Russian church bell two hundred years old, which was brought from the Island of Attu. It was probably sent to Alaska by Catherine the Great. On a very cold Christmas morning in its northern home, it cracked while being rung, and is now in three pieces.

One of the most interesting of the Inn's bells is one which is claimed to be the oldest dated Christian bell, save one, in the world (see Fig. 172, p. 398). It is twenty-six inches high, forty-six inches in circumference, and bears around its edge a Latin inscription which, translated, reads: "Quintana and Salvador made me in the year of our Lord 1247." Near the top of the bell is its name, Maria Jacobi. It also has the Greek monogram I.H.S.X.P.S.

Figure 173 shows an interesting Chinese temple bell from Nanking, about seventy-five years old. Its diameter is four feet, four inches; height, six feet, five inches, and it weighs twenty-eight hundred pounds. Perhaps the most beautiful of the bells is a bronze bell from Monserrat, Spain, dated 1704 (see Fig. 174). The design of its ornamentation, which includes ten exquisite medallions of the saints, is very interesting. It is "dedicated to the honor of God and of the Virgin Mary and of all the Saints."

# CHAPTER XXXV

## THE POETRY OF BELLS

(Selected bell poems from Southey, Longfellow, Lowell, Cowper, Tennyson, Moore, and Poe)

### THE INCHCAPE ROCK

ROBERT SOUTHEY

No stir in the air, no stir in the sea,
The ship was still as she could be;
Her sails from Heaven received no motion;
Her keel was steady in the ocean.

Without either sign or sound of their shock,
The waves flowed over the Inchcape Rock;
So little they rose, so little they fell,
They did not move the Inchcape bell.

The holy Abbot of Aberbrothok
Had placed that bell on the Inchcape Rock;
On a buoy in the storm it floated and swung,
And over the waves its warning rung.

When the rock was hid by the surges' swell,
The mariners heard the warning bell;
And then they knew the perilous rock,
And blessed the Abbot of Aberbrothok.

The Sun in heaven was shining gay,
All things were joyful on that day;
The sea birds screamed as they wheeled around,
And there was joyance in their sound.

402

The buoy of the Inchcape Bell was seen,
A darker speck on the ocean green;
Sir Ralph, the Rover, walked his deck,
And he fixed his eye on the darker speck.

He felt the cheering power of spring,
It made him whistle, it made him sing;
His heart was mirthful to excess;
But the Rover's mirth was wickedness.

His eye was on the Inchcape float;
Quoth he, "My men, put out the boat;
And row me to the Inchcape Rock,
And I'll plague the Abbot of Aberbrothok."

The boat is lowered, the boatmen row,
And to the Inchcape Rock they go;
Sir Ralph bent over from the boat,
And cut the Bell from the Inchcape float.

Down sank the Bell with a gurgling sound;
The bubbles rose, and burst around.
Quoth Sir Ralph, "The next who comes to the Rock
Will not bless the Abbot of Aberbrothok."

Sir Ralph, the Rover, sailed away,
He scoured the seas for many a day;
And now, grown rich with plundered store,
He steers his course for Scotland's shore.

So thick a haze o'erspreads the sky
They cannot see the Sun on high;
The wind hath blown a gale all day;
At evening it hath died away.

On the deck the Rover takes his stand;
So dark it is they see no land.
Quoth Sir Ralph, "It will be lighter soon,
For there is the dawn of the rising Moon."

"Canst hear," said one, "the breakers roar?
For yonder, methinks, should be the shore."
"Now where we are I cannot tell,
But I wish we could hear the Inchcape Bell."

They hear no sound; the swell is strong;
Though the wind hath fallen, they drift along,
Till the vessel strikes with a shivering shock,—
"O Christ! it is the Inchcape Rock!"

Sir Ralph, the Rover, tore his hair;
He cursed himself in his despair.
The waves rush in on every side;
The ship is sinking beneath the tide.

But, even in his dying fear,
One dreadful sound he seemed to hear,—
A sound as if, with the Inchcape Bell,
The Devil below was ringing his knell.

## THE SICILIAN'S TALE

### The Bell of Atri

#### Henry Wadsworth Longfellow

At Atri in Abruzzo, a small town
Of ancient Roman date, but scant renown,
One of those little places that have run
Half up the hill, beneath a blazing sun,
And then sat down to rest, as if to say,

"I climb no farther upward, come what may,"—
The Re Giovanni, now unknown to fame,
So many monarchs since have borne the name,
Had a great bell hung in the market place,
Beneath a roof, projecting some small space
By way of shelter from the sun and rain.
Then rode he through the streets with all his train,
And, with the blast of trumpets loud and long,
Made proclamation, that whenever wrong
Was done to any man, he should but ring
The great bell in the square, and he, the King,
Would cause the Syndic to decide thereon.
Such was the proclamation of King John.

How swift the happy days in Atri sped,
What wrongs were righted, need not here be said.
Suffice it that, as all things must decay,
The hempen rope at length was worn away,
Unraveled at the end, and, strand by strand,
Loosened and wasted in the ringer's hand,
Till one, who noted this in passing by,
Mended the rope with braids of briony,
So that the leaves and tendrils of the vine
Hung like a votive garland at a shrine.

By chance it happened that in Atri dwelt
A knight, with spur on heel and sword in belt,
Who loved to hunt the wild boar in the woods,
Who loved his falcons with their crimson hoods,
Who loved his hounds and horses, and all sports
And prodigalities of camps and courts; —
Loved, or had loved them; for at last, grown old,
His only passion was the love of gold.

He sold his horses, sold his hawks and hounds,
Rented his vineyards and his garden grounds,
Kept but one steed, his favorite steed of all,
To starve and shiver in a naked stall,
And day by day sat brooding in his chair,
Devising plans how best to hoard and spare.

At length he said: "What is the use or need
To keep at my own cost this lazy steed,
Eating his head off in my stables here,
When rents are low and provender is dear?
Let him go feed upon the public ways;
I want him only for the holidays."
So the old steed was turned into the heat
Of the long, lonely, silent, shadeless street;
And wandered in suburban lanes forlorn,
Barked at by dogs, and torn by brier and thorn.

One afternoon, as in that sultry clime
It is the custom in the summer time,
With bolted doors and window-shutters closed,
The inhabitants of Atri slept or dozed;
When suddenly upon their senses fell
The loud alarm of the accusing bell!

The Syndic started from his deep repose,
Turned on his couch, and listened, and then rose
And donned his robes, and with reluctant pace
Went panting forth into the market place,
Where the great bell upon its cross-beams swung,
Reiterating with persistent tongue,
In half-articulate jargon, the old song:
"Some one hath done a wrong, hath done a wrong!"

But ere he reached the belfry's light arcade
He saw, or thought he saw, beneath its shade,
No shape of human form of woman born,
But a poor steed dejected and forlorn,
Who with uplifted head and eager eye
Was tugging at the vines of briony.
"Domeneddio!" cried the Syndic straight,
"This is the Knight of Atri's steed of state!
He calls for justice, being sore distressed,
And pleads his cause as loudly as the best."

Meanwhile from street and lane a noisy crowd
Had rolled together like a summer cloud,
And told the story of the wretched beast
In five-and-twenty different ways at least,
With much gesticulation and appeal
To heathen gods, in their excessive zeal.
The Knight was called and questioned; in reply
Did not confess the fact, did not deny;
Treated the matter as a pleasant jest,
And set at naught the Syndic and the rest,
Maintaining, in an angry undertone,
That he should do what pleased him with his own.

And thereupon the Syndic gravely read
The proclamation of the King; then said:
"Pride goeth forth on horseback grand and gay,
But cometh back on foot, and begs its way;
Fame is the fragrance of heroic deeds,
Of flowers of chivalry and not of weeds!
These are familiar proverbs; but I fear
They never yet have reached your knightly ear."

What fair renown, what honor, what repute
Can come to you from starving this poor brute?
He who serves well and speaks not, merits more
Than they who clamor loudest at the door.
Therefore the law decrees that as this steed
Served you in youth, henceforth you shall take heed
To comfort his old age, and to provide
Shelter in stall, and food and field beside."

The Knight withdrew abashed; the people all
Led home the steed in triumph to his stall.
The King heard and approved, and laughed in glee,
And cried aloud: "Right well it pleaseth me!
Church bells at best but ring us to the door;
But go not in to mass; my bell doth more:
It cometh into court and pleads the cause
Of creatures dumb and unknown to the laws;
And this shall make, in every Christian clime,
The Bell of Atri famous for all time."

## AN INCIDENT OF THE FIRE AT HAMBURG

JAMES RUSSELL LOWELL

The tower of old Saint Nicholas soared upward to the skies.
Like some huge piece of Nature's make, the growth of
centuries;
You could not deem its crowding spires a work of human
art,
They seemed to struggle lightward from a sturdy living
heart.

Not Nature's self more freely speaks in crystal or in oak,
Than, through the pious builder's hand, in that gray pile
she spoke;

And as from acorn springs the oak, so, freely and alone,
Sprang from his heart this hymn to God, sung in obedient
  stone.

It seemed a wondrous freak of chance, so perfect, yet so
  rough,
A whim of Nature crystallized slowly in granite tough;
The thick spires yearned towards the sky in quaint harmonious lines,
And in broad sunlight basked and slept, like a grove
  of blasted pines.

Never did rock or stream or tree lay claim with better
  right
To all the adorning sympathies of shadow and of light;
And, in that forest petrified, as forester there dwells
Stout Herman, the old sacristan, sole lord of all its bells.

Surge leaping after surge, the fire roared onward red as
  blood,
Till half of Hamburg lay engulfed beneath the eddying
  flood;
For miles away the fiery spray poured down its deadly
  rain,
And back and forth the billows sucked, and paused,
  and burst again.

From square to square with tiger leaps panted the lustful
  fire,
The air to leeward shuddered with the gasps of its desire;
And church and palace, which even now stood whelmed
  but to the knee,
Lift their black roofs like breakers lone amid the whirling
  sea.

Up in his tower old Herman sat and watched with quiet
    look;
His soul had trusted God too long to be at last forsook;
He could not fear, for surely God a pathway would unfold
Through this red sea for faithful hearts, as once he did
    of old.

But scarcely can he cross himself, or on his good saint
    call,
Before the sacrilegious flood o'erleaped the churchyard
    wall;
And, ere a *pater* half was said, 'mid smoke and crackling
    glare,
His island tower scarce juts its head above the wide
    despair.

Upon the peril's desperate peak his heart stood up
    sublime;
His first thought was for God above, his next was for his
    chime;
"Sing now and make your voices heard in hymns of
    praise," cried he,
"As did the Israelites of old, safe walking through the
    sea!

"Through this red sea our God hath made the pathway
    safe to shore;
Our promised land stands full in sight; shout now as
    ne'er before!"
And as the tower came crushing down, the bells, in clear
    accord,
Pealed forth the grand old German hymn, —"All good
    souls, praise the Lord!"

## HOW SOFT THE MUSIC OF THOSE VILLAGE BELLS

### William Cowper

How soft the music of those village bells,
Falling at intervals upon the ear
In cadence sweet, now dying all away,
Now pealing loud again, and louder still,
Clear and sonorous, as the gale comes on!
With easy force it opens all the cells
Where Memory slept. Wherever I have heard
A kindred melody, the scene recurs,
And with it all its pleasures and its pains.
Such comprehensive views the spirit takes,
That in a few short moments I retrace
(As in a map the voyager his course)
The windings of my way through many years.

## IN MEMORIAM

### Alfred, Lord Tennyson

(From XXVIII)

The time draws near the birth of Christ:
   The moon is hid; the night is still;
   The Christmas bells from hill to hill
Answer each other in the mist.

Four voices of four hamlets round,
   From far and near, on mead and moor,
   Swell out and fail, as if a door
Were shut between me and the sound:

Each voice four changes on the wind,
   That now dilate, and now decrease,
   Peace and goodwill, goodwill and peace,
Peace and goodwill to all mankind.

This year I slept and woke with pain,
   I almost wish'd no more to wake,
   And that my hold on life would break
Before I heard those bells again:

But they my troubled spirit rule,
   For they controll'd me when a boy;
   They bring me sorrow touch'd with joy,
The merry merry bells of Yule.


(From CVI)

Ring out, wild bells, to the wild sky,
   The flying cloud, the frosty light:
   The year is dying in the night;
Ring out, wild bells, and let him die.

Ring out the old, ring in the new,
   Ring, happy bells, across the snow;
   The year is going, let him go;
Ring out the false, ring in the true.

Ring out the grief that saps the mind,
   For those that here we see no more;
   Ring out the feud of rich and poor,
Ring in redress to all mankind.

Ring out a slowly dying cause,
   And ancient forms of party strife;

Ring in the nobler modes of life,
With sweeter manners, purer laws.

Ring out the want, the care, the sin,
    The faithless coldness of our times;
    Ring out, ring out my mournful rimes,
But ring the fuller minstrel in.

Ring out false pride in place and blood,
    The civic slander and the spite;
    Ring in the love of truth and right,
Ring in the common love of good.

Ring out old shapes of foul disease;
    Ring out the narrowing lust of gold;
    Ring out the thousand wars of old,
Ring in the thousand years of peace.

Ring in the valiant man and free,
    The larger heart, the kindlier hand;
    Ring out the darkness of the land,
Ring in the Christ that is to be.

## THOSE EVENING BELLS

### Thomas Moore

Those evening bells! those evening bells!
How many a tale their music tells
Of youth, and home, and that sweet time
When last I heard their soothing chime!

Those joyous hours are passed away;
And many a heart that then was gay,
Within the tomb now darkly dwells,
And hears no more those evening bells.

And so 'twill be when I am gone,—
That tuneful peal will still ring on;
While other bards shall walk these dells,
And sing your praise, sweet evening bells.


## THE BELLS OF SAN BLAS

### HENRY WADSWORTH LONGFELLOW

What say the Bells of San Blas
To the ships that southward pass
    From the harbor of Mazatlan?
To them it is nothing more
Than the sound of surf on the shore,—
    Nothing more to master or man.

But to me, a dreamer of dreams,
To whom what is and what seems
    Are often one and the same,—
The Bells of San Blas to me
Have a strange, wild melody,
    And are something more than a name.

For bells are the voice of the church;
They have tones that touch and search
    The hearts of young and old;
One sound to all, yet each
Lends a meaning to their speech,
    And the meaning is manifold.

They are a voice of the Past,
Of an age that is fading fast,
    Of a power austere and grand;
When the flag of Spain unfurled

Its folds o'er this Western world,
  And the Priest was lord of the land.

The chapel that once looked down
On the little seaport town
  Has crumbled into the dust;
And on oaken beams below
The bells swing to and fro,
  And are green with mold and rust.

"Is, then, the old faith dead,"
They say, "and in its stead
  Is some new faith proclaimed,
That we are forced to remain
Naked to sun and rain,
  Unsheltered and ashamed?

"Once, in our tower aloof
We rang over wall and roof
  Our warnings and our complaints;
And round about us there
The white doves filled the air
  Like the white souls of the saints.

"The saints!   Ah, have they grown
Forgetful of their own?
  Are they asleep, or dead,
That open to the sky
Their ruined Missions lie,
  No longer tenanted?

"Oh, bring us back once more
The vanished days of yore,
  When the world with faith was filled;

Bring back the fervid zeal,
The hearts of fire and steel,
   The hands that believe and build.

"Then from our tower again
We will send over land and main
   Our voices of command,
Like exiled kings who return
To their thrones, and the people learn
   That the Priest is lord of the land!"

O Bells of San Blas, in vain
Ye call back the Past again!
   The Past is deaf to your prayer;
Out of the shadows of night
The world rolls into light;
   It is daybreak everywhere.

## CARILLON

### Henry Wadsworth Longfellow

"More than any other literary utterance, its verses have drawn English-speaking travelers to this unique music. How wonderfully his genius gives the scene at night, when silence perfects the sound of the bells." — William G. Rice.

In the ancient town of Bruges,
In the quaint old Flemish city,
As the evening shades descended,
Low and loud and sweetly blended,
Low at times and loud at times,
And changing like a poet's rimes,
Rang the beautiful wild chimes
From the Belfry in the market
Of the ancient town of Bruges.

Then, with deep sonorous clangor
Calmly answering their sweet anger,
When the wrangling bells had ended,
Slowly struck the clock eleven,
And, from out the silent heaven,
Silence on the town descended,
Silence, silence everywhere,
On the earth and in the air,
Save that footsteps here and there
Of some burgher home returning,
By the street lamps faintly burning,
For a moment woke the echoes
Of the ancient town of Bruges.

But amid my broken slumbers
Still I heard those magic numbers,
As they loud proclaimed the flight
And stolen marches of the night;
Till their chimes in sweet collision
Mingled with each wandering vision,
Mingled with the fortune-telling
Gypsy-bands of dreams and fancies,
Which amid the waste expanses
Of the silent land of trances
Have their solitary dwelling;
All else seemed asleep in Bruges,
In the quaint old Flemish city.

And I thought how like these chimes
Are the poet's airy rimes,
All his rimes and roundelays,
His conceits, and songs, and ditties,

From the belfry of his brain,
Scattered downward, though in vain,
On the roofs and stones of cities!
For by night the drowsy ear
Under its curtains cannot hear,
And by day men go their ways,
Hearing the music as they pass,
But deeming it no more, alas!
Than the hollow sound of brass.

Yet perchance a sleepless wight,
Lodging at some humble inn
In the narrow lanes of life,
When the dusk and hush of night
Shut out the incessant din
Of daylight and its toil and strife,
May listen with a calm delight
To the poet's melodies,
Till he hears, or dreams he hears,
Intermingled with the song,
Thoughts that he has cherished long;
Hears amid the chime and singing
The bells of his own village ringing,
And wakes, and finds his slumberous eyes,
Wet with most delicious tears.

Thus dreamed I, as by night I lay
In Bruges, at the Fleur-de-Blé,
Listening with a wild delight
To the chimes that, through the night,
Rang their changes from the Belfry
Of that quaint old Flemish city.

## THE BELFRY OF BRUGES

HENRY WADSWORTH LONGFELLOW

In the market place of Bruges stands the belfry old and
brown;
Thrice consumed and thrice rebuilded, still it watches
o'er the town.

As the summer morn was breaking, on that lofty tower
I stood,
And the world threw off the darkness, like the weeds of
widowhood.

Thick with towns and hamlets studded, and with streams
and vapors gray,
Like a shield embossed with silver, round and vast the
landscape lay.

At my feet the city slumbered. From its chimneys,
here and there,
Wreaths of snow-white smoke, ascending, vanished,
ghost-like, into air.

Not a sound rose from the city at that early morning
hour,
But I heard a heart of iron beating in the ancient tower.

From their nests beneath the rafters sang the swallows
wild and high;
And the world, beneath me sleeping, seemed more distant than the sky.

Then most musical and solemn, bringing back the olden
times,
With their strange, unearthly changes rang the melancholy chimes,

Like the psalms from some old cloister, when the nuns
    sing in the choir;
And the great bell tolled among them, like the chanting
    of a friar.

Visions of the days departed, shadowy phantoms filled
    my brain;
They who live in history only seemed to walk the earth
    again

.    .    .    .    .    .    .    .    .    .    .

I beheld the Flemish weavers, with Namur and Juliers
    bold,
Marching homeward from the bloody battle of the Spurs
    of Gold;

Saw the fight at Minnewater, saw the White Hoods
    moving west,
Saw great Artevelde victorious scale the Golden Dragon's
    nest.

And again the whiskered Spaniard all the land with terror
    smote;
And again the wild alarum sounded from the tocsin's
    throat;

Till the bell of Ghent responded o'er lagoon and dike of
    sand,
"I am Roland! I am Roland! There is victory in the
    land!"

Then the sound of drums aroused me. The awakened
    city's roar
Chased the phantoms I had summond back into their
    graves once more.

Hours had passed away like minutes; and before I was
    aware,
Lo! the shadow of the belfry crossed the sun-illumined
    square.

## THE SPIRE OF STRASBURG CATHEDRAL

HENRY WADSWORTH LONGFELLOW

From the "Golden Legend"

(Night and storm. Lucifer, with the Powers of the Air, trying to
tear down the Cross.)

LUCIFER

Hasten! hasten!
O ye spirits!
From its station drag the ponderous
Cross of iron, that to mock us
Is uplifted high in air!

VOICES

Oh, we cannot!
For around it
All the Saints and Guardian Angels
Throng in legions to protect it;
They defeat us everywhere!

THE BELLS

Laudo Deum verum!
Plebem voco!
Congrego clerum!

LUCIFER

Lower! lower!
Hover downward!
Seize the loud, vociferous bells, and
Clashing, clanging, to the pavement
Hurl them from their windy tower!

#### VOICES

All thy thunders
Here are harmless!
For these bells have been anointed,
And baptized with holy water!
They defy our utmost power.

#### THE BELLS

Defunctos ploro!
Pestem fugo!
Festa decoro!

#### LUCIFER

Shake the casements!
Break the painted
Panes, that flame with gold and crimson;
Scatter them like leaves of Autumn,
Swept away before the blast!

#### VOICES

Oh, we cannot!
The Archangel
Michael flames from every window,
With the sword of fire that drove us
Headlong, out of heaven, aghast!

#### THE BELLS

Funera plango!
Fulgura frango!
Sabbata pango!

#### LUCIFER

Aim your lightnings
At the oaken,
Massive, iron-studded portals!

Sack the house of God, and scatter
Wide the ashes of the dead!

VOICES

Oh, we cannot!
The Apostles
And the Martyrs, wrapped in mantles,
Stand as warders at the entrance,
Stand as sentinels o'erhead!

THE BELLS

Excito lentos!
Dissipo ventos!
Paco cruentos!

LUCIFER

Baffled! baffled!
Inefficient,
Craven spirits! leave this labor
Unto Time, the great Destroyer!
Come away, ere night is gone!

VOICES

Onward! onward!
With the night-wind,
Over field and farm and forest,
Lonely homestead, darksome hamlet,
Blighting all we breathe upon!

(*They sweep away. Organ and Gregorian
Chant.*)

CHOIR

Nocte surgentes
Vigilemus omnes!

## SONG OF THE BELL

HENRY WADSWORTH LONGFELLOW

(From the German)

Bell! thou soundest merrily,
When the bridal party
  To the church doth hie!
Bell! thou soundest solemnly,
When, on Sabbath morning,
  Fields deserted lie!

Bell! thou soundest merrily;
Tellest thou at evening,
  Bedtime draweth nigh!
Bell! thou soundest mournfully,
Tellest thou the bitter
  Parting hath gone by!

Say!  How canst thou mourn?
How canst thou rejoice?
  Thou art but metal dull!
And yet all our sorrowings,
And all our rejoicings,
  Thou dost feel them all!

God hath wonders many,
Which we cannot fathom,
  Placed within thy form!
When the heart is sinking,
Thou alone canst raise it,
  Trembling in the storm!

## THE BELLS

EDGAR ALLAN POE

(Inspired by the sound of church bells reaching him through his
open window)

### I

Hear the sledges with the bells,
     Silver bells!
What a world of merriment their melody foretells!
   How they tinkle, tinkle, tinkle,
      In the icy air of night!
   While the stars, that oversprinkle
   All the heavens, seem to twinkle
      With a crystalline delight;
      Keeping time, time, time;
      In a sort of Runic rime,
To the tintinnabulation that so musically wells
   From the bells, bells, bells, bells,
         Bells, bells, bells—
   From the jingling and the tinkling of the bells.

### II

Hear the mellow wedding bells,
      Golden bells!
What a world of happiness their harmony foretells!
   Through the balmy air of night
   How they ring out their delight!
      From the molten-golden notes,
         And all in tune.
      What a liquid ditty floats
To the turtle-dove that listens, while she gloats
         On the moon!
   Oh, from out the sounding cells,

What a gush of euphony voluminously wells!
How it swells!
How it dwells
On the future! how it tells
Of the rapture that impels
To the swinging and the ringing
Of the bells, bells, bells,
Of the bells, bells, bells, bells,
Bells, bells, bells—
To the riming and the chiming of the bells!

## III

Hear the loud alarum bells,
Brazen bells!
What a tale of terror, now, their turbulency tells!
In the startled ear of night
How they scream out their affright!
Too much horrified to speak,
They can only shriek, shriek,
Out of tune,
In a clamorous appealing to the mercy of the fire,
In a mad expostulation with the deaf and frantic fire,
Leaping higher, higher, higher,
With a desperate desire,
And a resolute endeavor
Now—now to sit or never,
By the side of the pale-faced moon.
Oh, the bells, bells, bells!
What a tale their terror tells
Of Despair!
How they clang, and clash, and roar!
What a horror they outpour
On the bosom of the palpitating air!

Yet the ear it fully knows,
  By the twanging,
  And the clanging,
How the danger ebbs and flows;
  Yet the ear distinctly tells,
    In the jangling
    And the wrangling
  How the danger sinks and swells—
By the sinking or the swelling in the anger of the bells,
    Of the bells—
  Of the bells, bells, bells, bells,
    Bells, bells, bells—
In the clamor and the clangor of the bells!


## IV

  Hear the tolling of the bells,
    Iron bells!
What a world of solemn thought their monody compels!
    In the silence of the night
    How we shiver with affright
  At the melancholy menace of their tone!
    For every sound that floats
    From the rust within their throats
      Is a groan.
    And the people—ah, the people,
    They that dwell up in the steeple,
      All alone,
    And who tolling, tolling, tolling
      In that muffled monotone,
    Feel a glory in so rolling
      On the human heart a stone—
    They are neither man nor woman,

    They are neither brute nor human,
        They are ghouls;
    And their king it is who tolls;
    And he rolls, rolls, rolls,
        Rolls
      A paean from the bells,
      And his merry bosom swells
      With the paean of the bells;
    And he dances, and he yells;
      Keeping time, time, time,
      In a sort of Runic rime,
    To the paean of the bells,
       Of the bells:
      Keeping time, time, time,
      In a sort of Runic rime,
    To the throbbing of the bells,
Of the bells, bells, bells —
      To the sobbing of the bells;
      Keeping time, time, time,
      As he knells, knells, knells,
    In a happy Runic rime,
      To the rolling of the bells,
      Of the bells, bells, bells:
      To the tolling of the bells,
    Of the bells, bells, bells, bells,
      Bells, bells, bells —
To the moaning and the groaning of the bells.

## A NURSERY RIME

### (Old English)

Gay go up and gay go down,
To ring the bells of London town.

Halfpence and farthings,
Say the bells of St. Martin's.

Oranges and lemons,
Say the bells of St. Clement's

Pancakes and fritters,
Say the bells of St. Peter's.

Two sticks and an apple,
Say the bells of Whitechapel.

Kettles and pans,
Say the bells of St. Anne's.

You owe me ten shillings,
Say the bells of St. Helen's.

When will you pay me?
Say the bells of Old Bailey.

When I grow rich,
Say the bells of Shoreditch.

Pray when will that be?
Say the bells of Stepney.

I am sure I don't know,
Says the great bell of Bow.

# CHAPTER XXXVI

## SCHOOL EXPERIMENTS IN BELL MAKING AND PLAYING

It is surprising how many ordinary things will produce bell music. Flower pots make very good bells which sound pleasing when tapped on the outside with a small wooden hammer. These pots may be suspended by a string tied to a small piece of wood placed inside the pot, the wood being too large to slip through the hole in the bottom of the pot.

The flower pots in Figure 175 were selected according to their tones. The salesman in the store was kind enough to allow all the pots on the shelf to be tapped, and finally five were found that were

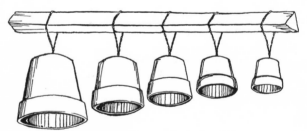

FIG. 175. *Flower pots used as bells*

in tune for playing a simple melody. One boy collected several old ones in his mother's cellar,

washed them, and found three that sounded exactly right for the first three notes of the scale.    One may play "Hot-Cross Buns" or other three-note tunes,

FIG. 176.    *Yellow mixing bowls used as bells*

and one may also compose any number of tunes on three flower pots, or other forms of bells that are in tune.

Goblets and even ordinary drinking glasses will produce clear, bell-like tones, though some glasses produce tones that are more musical than others.

*Experiment:* Find a goblet that has a clear, bell-like ring when it is tapped on the side.    Fill it half full of water and tap it again.    What has happened to the tone? Put various amounts of water in it and test the tone each time.    What seems to be the rule about changing the tone of glass?

If glasses are selected with care and properly tuned with water, very sweet music may be made by tapping these glass bells with a soft hammer.    A small wooden hammer covered with felt is best.    (A little block of pine, whittled into a round form and fastened on the end of a slender stick, makes an excellent hammer.)    The glasses should rest on something soft. If bubbles form inside the glass, stir them out, for they deaden the tone. Why do they?

Teacups and bowls of all kinds may be used for music making. Earthenware kitchen bowls may be sorted according to their tones and tuned with water as glasses are tuned. They should be tapped on the outside, near the rim. Figure 176 shows a collection of yellow kitchen bowls that were selected in a department store for their tones, and suspended on rods that had little wooden disks on the ends to fit the bottoms of the bowls. In this position they look more like bells, but the sound is no better than when the bowls stand on a cloth-covered table. The scheme shown in the picture requires that the bowls be in tune naturally, and it is difficult to find more than three or four bowls that sound the desired scale notes without putting any water in them.

Copper kettles, saucepans, and even bottles have served as bells where nothing better could be found.

Metal tubing may be cut into pieces of various lengths, and with these many interesting experiments in sound may be tried. If all the pieces are cut from tubing of the same size, their tones may be regulated merely by their length.[1] Brass tubing one-half inch in diameter is a convenient size to use.

[1] See paragraph about the tubaphone on p. 156.

Wooden bells may be made by hollowing out two pieces of wood and gluing them together. Or a large block of wood may be converted into a bell by hollowing it out with a lathe. If no lathe is to be had, holes may be bored into the block with a large bit to the depth of the opening desired, and the remaining partitions between the holes may be chiseled out. It is interesting to observe how the

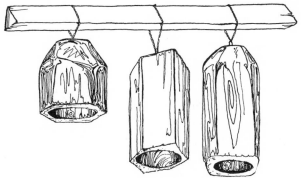

FIG. 177. *Wooden bells made by school children*

tone of the block of wood, when struck with a wooden mallet, changes as it becomes more and more hollowed out. The greater the diameter of the cavity, the lower the tone becomes.

From a collection of twenty wooden bells made by a group of school children, without any attempt to make definite tones, a complete scale of one octave was obtained, and when these were selected from the others, arranged in order, and suspended, various tunes were played on them. Most of these bells were made of blocks of redwood or white pine. Some of them are shown in Figure 177.

Pottery bells may be made at home or at school if there is a convenient kiln for firing them. Figure 178 shows a few clay bells made by children in school. They were built up from coils of clay and shaped with the hands, both inside and out. Some have holes in the top through which they are hung; others have handles that are built on, with clay. The thinner these built-up clay bells are, the clearer the tone. They should dry for several days before they are fired.

Two of the bells in Figure 179 are also built up with coils of clay, and afterward cut down quite thin. The others are molded in plaster molds made from cast metal bells.

It is very difficult to make clay bells and have them come out of the firing-kiln with any certain

FIG. 178. *Clay bells made by school children*

tone because the baking of the clay changes the pitch. This general rule, however, may be remembered: All other things being equal, the thinner the

FIG. 179.   *Clay bells, the first three made in plaster molds, the other two, coiled*

bell, the lower the tone; and the greater the diameter, the lower the tone.

After a clay bell has dried for several days, and before it is fired, its tone may be tried and changed a bit. Sandpapering the lower edge will raise the tone, and sandpapering the inside will lower it. A knife may be used instead of the sandpaper. After the bell is fired it is so hard and brittle that tuning is a very tedious process.

If a large group of people make bells of different thickness and different diameters, it is probable that several notes of the same scale may be found, or perhaps several groups of notes. In a recent school experiment a few bells were made and allowed to dry for a week, and then tuned to scale notes before they were fired. They were all put into the kiln at the same time, and came out almost exactly in tune with each other, although the entire scale had been raised several tones.

Plaster molds may be made as follows:

(1) Find a metal bell of the shape desired for the new bell. Remove the handle and fill the hole with clay. If no pattern bell is to be had, a jelly glass with a round bottom may be used; or a bowl or a bell-shaped vase (if it does not close in at the top) will do.

(2) Roll out a thin layer of clay on a board and set the pattern bell or glass on it, upside down.

(3) An inch or more from the bell, place a retaining wall of some kind to hold the plaster. This wall may be a round cylinder of linoleum, or a round box with no bottom in it. If nothing round is to be had, the retaining wall may be made of four squares of glass supported and "chinked" together with clay so the plaster will not run out at the corners.

(4) Rub a little soapsuds over the bell so it will slip out of the plaster when the time comes.

(5) Dissolve the plaster to the right consistency, and then pour it over the bell, filling up the retaining wall.

(6) In a few minutes the plaster will be "set" and firm enough to remove the wall, turn the plaster over, and take out the bell. This must be done very carefully, lest the smooth surface of the bell impression be broken.

(7) This mold should be allowed to dry in a warm place for several days. It is not ready for use until all the moisture is gone, and it feels dry to the hand.

To make the bell:

(1) The clay must be dissolved to a thick cream, and strained, so that all the lumps are removed. This liquid clay is called "slip."

(2) Pour the slip into the mold, filling it to the top. In a minute or two it will have to be filled again, and even again perhaps, for as the plaster mold absorbs the water the mass of slip sinks down. A layer of clay may be seen forming around the edge of the cavity, and becoming a little firmer than the rest of the slip.

(3) As soon as this layer becomes as thick as the desired bell (requiring probably from fifteen to thirty minutes), lift the mold and pour out all of the slip that will flow out. Experiment will enable one to regulate the thickness of the bell by the length of time the slip is left in the mold.

(4) Set the mold aside and the plaster will absorb enough moisture from the layer of clay to allow it to become firm. As the moisture leaves it, the clay shrinks a little. Sometimes the outside edge of the clay sticks to the mold in one or two places, causing the clay to crack as it shrinks. To prevent this, run a thin knife blade under the edge of the clay before it shrinks much.

(5) In several hours, or a day perhaps, the new bell may be lifted from the mold and placed out in the air to dry. It must be handled with exceeding care, lest it break or lose its shape.

(6) Next day it may be trimmed with a knife, so that the mouth of the bell is smooth and clean. It is best if the bell is allowed to dry for a week or more before it is fired.

The mold should not be used until it has had time to become thoroughly dry again.

If a group of children can make molds of different sizes, and in them mold bells of different thicknesses, there is great likelihood of having enough different toned bells to play tunes on them. (See below the music for a simple tune to be played upon three bells.) The experiments tried by the writer indicated that clay bells sound best when not glazed.

## A SIMPLE TUNE FOR THREE BELLS

Many people are interested in making clay bells merely for the pleasure of molding with the hands beautiful shapes and designs, with no thought of

FIG. 180.   *A bell quartet*

using the bells for musical purposes.  Clay bells may be inscribed, decorated, and painted in numberless designs.

Figure 180 shows four children playing on a set of metal bells cast in tune by a maker of Swiss hand bells.  They are playing the four parts of a slow hymn.  Since metal bells continue to vibrate so long after they are struck, very slow music is best suited to them.

There are two and one-half octaves, low G to high C, with C sharp and F sharp added, these being fastened a little higher than the others.

The following chorale is a suitable quartet for such a range of bells as those in Figure 180 and, when well played, it is very effective.

## A CHORALE

# THE BIBLIOGRAPHY

In the preparation of the present volume, material has been drawn from the following publications:

ADDISON, JULIA: *Arts and Crafts in the Middle Ages.* Boston, 1908.

ANDERSEN, HANS CHRISTIAN: *Fairy Tales.* London.
*German Fairy Tales.* New York, 1870.

BAEDEKER, CARL: *Russia.* 1914.
*Northern Italy.* 1913.

BALFOUR, EDWARD: *Cyclopedia of India.* Madras, 1871.

BARROWS, SIR JOHN: *Travels in China.*

BATCHELDER, SAMUEL: *Poetry of Bells.* 1858.

BECKETT, EDMUND: *Clocks, Watches and Bells.* London, 1903.

BENSON, GEO.: "York Bell Founders," in *Yorkshire Architectural Society Reports.* 1903.

BORTON, FRANCIS: *Handbook of Glenwood Mission Inn.*

BOUGHEY, A. H. F.: "Ancient Church Bells in Cambridge," in Cambridge Antiquarian Society *Proceedings.*

BREWER, E. C.: *The Reader's Handbook.* 1896.

BRINKLEY, FRANK: *History of the Japanese People.* New York and London, 1915.

BRISCOE, J. P.: *Curiosities of the Belfry.* London, 1883.

BROWN, MARY E. and WM. A.: *Musical Instruments and Their Homes.* 1888.

BROWN, TOM: "The Land of Chimes," in *The Metronome.* January, 1917.

BURNEY, CHARLES: *The Present State of Music in Germany, the Netherlands, and the United Provinces.* London, 1775.

CHAMBERS, R.: *Book of Days.* London.

CHAPPEL, W.: *Popular Music of the Olden Time.* London, 1855.

COFFEY, GEORGE: *Guide to the Celtic Antiquities of the Christian Period.* Dublin, 1910.

CRIPPEN, T. G.: *Christmas and Christmas Lore.* London, 1923.

CROW, CARL: *Handbook for China.* Shanghai, 1921.

CUSHING, FRANK: *Zuñi Breadstuff.* New York, 1920.

DAVIS, F. H.: *Myths and Legends of Japan.* 1912.

DEEDERS, CECIL, and WALTERS, H. B.: *Church Bells of Essex.* 1909.

DEL MAR, WALTER: *The Romantic East.* London, 1906.

DENNYS, N. B.: "Folk Lore of China," in *China Review* for 1875 and 1876.

DICKENS, CHARLES: *The Chimes.*

DORÉ, HENRY: *Researches into Chinese Superstitions.* Shanghai, 1914.

DUNCAN, EDMONDSTOUNE: *The Story of Minstrelsy.* London, 1907.

DUNRAVEN, LORD: *Notes on Irish Architecture.* London, 1877.

EELES, F. C.: *The Church and Other Bells of Kincardines.* Aberdeen, 1897.

ELLACOMBE, REV. H. T.: *Church Bells of Devon.* Exeter, 1872.

ELSON, ARTHUR: *Curiosities of Music.* London.

ENGEL, CARL: *Musical Instruments.* London, 1878.
*Musical Myths and Facts.* London, 1876.
*Music of the Most Ancient Nations.* London, 1864–1909.
Introduction to Kensington Museum Catalogue.

FAVIER, ALPHONSE: *Pekin: histoire et description.* 1900.

FIELDING, BERNARD: "The Occult Lore of Bells," in *Occult Review.* December, 1918.

FRYAR, JOHN R.: "The Functions of Church Bells in Old England," in *American Ecclesiastical Review.* Philadelphia, 1910.

FRYER, A. C.: "Notes on Some of the Inscriptions on Continental Bells," in *British Archeological Association Journal.* 1883.

FURNEAUX, J. H.: *Glimpses of India.* 1895.

GALPIN, REV. F. W. *Old English Instruments of Music.* London, 1910.

GATTY, REV. ALFRED: *The Bell, its Origin, History and Uses.* London, 1848.

GREENBIE, MARJORIE BARSTOW: "Bronze Voices of Buddha," in *Asia.* January, 1921.

GRIFFIS, WILLIAM E.: *The Mikado's Empire.* London, 1895.

GROVE, SIR GEORGE: *Dictionary of Music and Musicians.*

HART, MRS. ERNEST: *Picturesque Burma.* London, 1897.

HAWEIS, H. R.: *Music and Morals.*

HAYDEN, ARTHUR: *By-Paths in Curio Collecting.* London, 1919.

HILDRUP, JESSE: *The Missions of California and the Old Southwest.* 1907.

HOPKINS, EDWARD J.: *The Organ.* London, 1877.

HULLAH, ANNETTE: *A Little History of Music.* London, 1911.

JACOBS, JOSEPH: *English Fairy Tales.* London, 1892.

JAMES, GEO. WHARTON: *In and Out of the Old Missions of California.* 1911.

JOHNSTON, A. A.: "Clocks, Carillons and Bells," in *Journal of the Society of Arts.* London, 1901.

KELLY, R. T.: *Burma Painted and Described.* London, 1905.

LOMAX, BENJAMIN: *Bells and Bell Ringers.* London, 1879.

LONGFELLOW, H. W.: *Poems.*

MARSHALL, W. E.: *The Todas, a Study of a Primitive Tribe in South India.* London, 1873.

MARYON, H. J.: "Early Irish Metal Work," in *Art Worker's Quarterly* for October, 1905.

MEAKIN, ANNETTE: *Russia, Travels and Studies.* London, 1906.

MEE and THOMPSON: *Marvels of Industry.* (Every Day Library), 1915.

MEIKLEJOHN, J. M. D.: *A New History of England and Great Britain.* London, 1907.

MENEELY BELL COMPANY'S Catalogue.

MILLIGAN, S. F.: *Ancient Ecclesiastical Bells in Ulster.* 1902.

MURRAY, JOHN: *Handbook of India, Burma and Ceylon.* London, 1919.

MUTSU, COUNTESS ISO: *Kamakura Fact and Legend.* Kamakura, 1918.

MYRES, T. HARRISON: *Bells and Bell Lore.* London.

NICKOLS, A. H.: *The Bells of Harvard College.* Boston, 1911.
"The Early Bells of Paul Revere," in *New England Historical and Genealogical Register.* Boston, 1904.
"Christ Church Bells, Boston," in *New England Historical and Genealogical Register*, Vol. 58, 1904.
"Bells of Trinity Church, Newport, R. I.," in *New England Genealogical Register*, 1916.

OSBORN, E. B.: "Carillon Music," in *The Nineteenth Century and After.* London, 1911.

OTTE, HEINRICH: *Glocken kunde.* Leipzig, 1856.

PEASE, A. S.: "Notes on Uses of Bells among the Greeks and Romans," in *Harvard Studies in Classical Philology.* Boston, 1904.

PHILLIPS, MABERLY: "Latten or Waggon Bells," in *Connoisseur*, 1916.

PHYFE, W. H.: *Five Thousand Facts and Fancies.* 1907.

PIGGOTT, F. T.: *The Music and Musical Instruments of Japan.* Yokohama and London, 1909.

POOLE, G. A.: *A History of Ecclesiastical Architecture in England.* London, 1848.

QUICK, RICHARD: "Large Bells," in *The Reliquary.* January, 1903.
"Notes on an Ancient Bell," in *Journal of British Archeological Association.* London, 1896.

RAVEN, REV. CANON: *On Early Methods of Bell Founding.* London, 1890.

RICE, WILLIAM G.: *Carillons of Belgium and Holland.* 1914.
"Carillons of Belgium after the Great War," in *Art and Archeology.* August, 1921.

RIVETT-CARNAC, J. H.: "Hindu Ritual," in *Journal of Indian Art and Industry*. London, October, 1900.

ROBINSON, JOHN L.: "Dublin Cathedral Bells," in the *Royal Society of the Antiquaries of Ireland*. 1912.

ROORBACH, ELOISE: "Bells of History and Romance," in *The Craftsman*. December, 1912.

SCARTH, REV. H. M.: *Remarks on an Old Bell*. London, 1876.

SCUDDER, HORACE: *Book of Legends*. New York, 1899.

SHORTT, J.: "The Hill Tribes of the Neilgherries," in *Transactions of the Ethnological Society of London*. 1869.

SMITH, HERMAN: *The World's Earliest Music*. London.

SOUTHEY, ROBERT: *Poems;* also *Pilgrim's Progress* with Life of John Bunyan. London. 1830.

SPARROW, W. SHAW: "A Dissertation on Foreign Bells," in the *Magazine of Art*. 1894.

STARMER, W. W.: "Bell Casting," in *Musical Times*. London, March 7, 1918.

"The Clock Jacks of England," in *Proceedings of Musical Association*. London, 1919.

"The Great Bell of Moscow," in *Musical Times*. October 1, 1916.

"Bells of Malines Cathedral," in *Musical Times*. May 1, 1919.

"Bells and Bell Ringing," in *Musical Standard*. May 28, 1901.

STODDARD, JOHN L.: *Glimpses of the World*. Chicago, 1892.

STOKES, MARGARET: *Early Christian Art in Ireland*. Dublin, 1911.

STUART, ROBERT: *A Dictionary of Architecture*. London, 1830.

STURGIS, RUSSEL: *A Dictionary of Architecture and Building*. 1901.

SWOYER, A. E.: "Handbells for the Collector," in *International Studio* for September, 1893.

TABER, MARY J.: *Bells, an Anthology*. Boston, 1912.

TAKAHIRA, KANDA: "Some Copper Bells," in *Asiatic Society of Japanese Transactions.* Yokohama, 1876.

TAYLOR, CAPT. MEADOWS: "Cairns, Cromlechs, Kistwaens in the Dekhan," in *Transactions of the Royal Irish Academy.* Dublin, 1874.

TERRY, THOMAS P.: *The Japanese Empire.* 1914

TYACK, GEO. S.: *A Book About Bells.* London, 1898.

TYRRELL-GREEN: "Architecture in the War Area," in *Architect and Contract Reporter.* August, 1917.

VAN AALST, J. A.: *Chinese Music.* Shanghai, 1884.

WALLASCHEK, RICHARD: *Primitive Music.* London, 1893.

WALSH, W. S.: *Curiosities of Popular Customs.* Philadelphia, 1911.

WALTERS, H. B.: *The Church Bells of England.* Oxford, 1912. *The Church Bells of Shropshire.* 1915.

WEBB, WILFRED M.: "Famous Chimes," in *English Illustrated Magazine.* 1911.

WERNER, E. T. C.: *Myths and Legends of China.* 1922.

WHITCOMB, IDA P.: *Young People's Story of Music.* 1908.

WIGRAM, REV. WOOLMORE: *Change Ringing Disentangled.* London, 1880.

WILLIAMS, C. F. A.: *The Story of the Organ.* London, 1903.

WROUGHTON, R.: "Two Burmese Bells in Upper India," in *Journal of Asiatic Society of Bengal.* December, 1837, and April, 1838.

### PUBLICATIONS CONTAINING UNSIGNED ARTICLES

*American Architectural and Building News.* April 7, 1888.

*American History and Encyclopedia of Music.*

*An Official Guide to Eastern Asia*, by the Imperial Japanese Government. Railways. 1915.

"Bells and Bell Ringing," in *The Musical World.* 1837.

*Bells and Crosses of Glenwood Mission Inn.*

"Bells and Their Influence," in *The Musical Standard.*

Catalogue of the Crosby-Brown Musical Instrument Collection.

*Christian Science Monitor* for August, 1924.

*Church Tablet, The,* Passaic, New Jersey.   August and September, 1904.

"Les cloches chez nos pères," *Académie Royale d'archéologie de Belgique.*   1898.

*Edison Monthly* for November and December, 1924..

*Encyclopaedia Britannica.*

*Illustrated London News* for 1856; 1857; 1858; 1866; 1878; 1882.

*Miscellanea Critica.*   Review of Current Literature, London, 1850.

"Music Bell at St. Mary's," Oxford (Drexel).

*Nelson's Encyclopedia.*

*New International Encyclopaedia.*

*New York Herald.*   May 5, 1912.

"Ten Bronze Bells."   Formerly in the Collection of Chên Chieh-Chi.

"Tower Music of Belgium and Holland," *in Musical Quarterly* for April, 1915.

# THE INDEX

449